DREAMS AND PROFESSIONAL PERSONHOOD

SUNY Series in Dream Studies
Robert L. Van de Castle, Editor

DREAMS AND PROFESSIONAL ____
_____ PERSONHOOD

The Contexts of Dream Telling and Dream Interpretation among American Psychotherapists

MARY-T. B. DOMBECK

State University of New York Press

Published by
State University of New York Press, Albany

©1991 State University of New York

For information, address State University of New York Press,
State University Plaza, Albany, N.Y., 12246

Production by Marilyn Semerad
Marketing by Theresa A. Swierzowski

Library of Congress Cataloging-in-Publication Data

Dombeck, Mary.
    Dreams and professional personhood : the contexts of dream telling
and dream interpretation among American psychotherapists / by Mary-
T.B. Dombeck.
        p. cm.—(SUNY series in dream studies)
    Includes bibliographical references and index.
    ISBN 0-7914-0588-5—ISBN 0-7914-0589-3 (pbk.)
    1. Dreams.   2. Psychotherapists.   3. Ethnology.   I. Title.
II. Series.
    RC499.D7D66   1991
    154.6'34'0973—dc20   90–9780
                                                                CIP

10   9   8   7   6   5   4   3   2   1

CONTENTS

Contents   vii

LIST OF TABLES

LIST OF FIGURES

PREFACE

I have chosen three dreams that I had while working on this research to introduce these preliminary remarks. The dreams expressed for me the understanding I was gaining about the process of my work.

1. I am traveling. I am told by a lady from the embassy that I ought to go through customs and have it stamped on my passport. As I go through customs, the words *Back to the Future* appear on one of the monitors.
   I am now on a campus. It seems like a large urban center. I am listening to a man who has come especially to speak with me. He has come to meet me at a crowded bus stop with another man who has brought him.

2. An enclosed area. I see a native woman who is wearing a black dress. She lives in a valley where there is oil underground. I know this woman. I live with her part of the time. The rest of the time I live with another woman who tells me all about this native woman.

3. I am in my home. My family is there. Everything is as usual. I notice a native woman in a dark dress. She has come to visit me. She wants to stay until the afternoon. I make something to eat.

These dreams spanned the dates of the research. I had the first one in the early stages, while I was making arrangements for field work. The second dream came to me several months after I had begun the field work. The third did not come until most of the writing was done. I look upon these dreams as a series that tells the story of the transformation that occurs in the anthropologist during the ethnographic process.

In ethnographic research the perspectives of the outsider and the insider are both crucial. The anthropologist is a traveler, an outsider in the land of her sojourn. Learning about the people's customs is not enough. She must "go through customs." In this process she is asked to declare what she brings with her from her source to her destination. Thus, past and future are related to each other and to the present work.

Moreover, she cannot just remain a traveler. She must become more than a tourist. She must speak with the natives and get to know them well. She must live with them for part of the time. The rest of the time she must listen, understand, interpret, and articulate what she has learned.

By the end of the study, she allows the native woman in her own house and makes a meal. It is a sign of her own transformation. It is not enough to go into the field with curiosity, a point of view, and a methodology. One must humbly modify one's methods and constructs when they do not fit native concepts and understandings. This process is represented symbolically in the last dream in which the native woman wants to stay for a prolonged visit. The dream ends with preparing a meal. One starts the research process as a gatherer and somehow one emerges transformed into a cook. An anthropologist is not simply an objective collector of cultural artifacts.

During this process the boundaries between ethnographer and native remain. For it is in the relationship *across boundaries* that understandings develop and new connections are made. Native concepts and observer constructs need to be articulated as clearly as possible and must be kept as distinct as possible. The ethnographer's constructs are developed not only in her training but also in her life experiences. She brings to her work her professional personhood as it is interpreted in herself.

When, as a young woman in my early twenties I came to the United States from the Middle East, I was quite used to participant observation. My education in social anthropology some twenty years later was a delightful and integrating experience. It was like discovering that I had been talking prose all my life without knowing it. It was also a stimulating and challenging analysis of my own process, as well as of the methods of my mentors and other ethnographers.

I had been trilingual since I was six, and I remember the occasional discomforting experience of not understanding what was being said to me. I also remember being able to translate what was being said by some members of my social network to others. When your mother, your grandmother, the milkman, and the teacher at school all speak in different languages you learn to translate. You also learn about miscommunication, multivocality, social personhood, and personal idiosyncracy. Some things cannot be accurately translated, not only because words fail, but also because contexts are either unknown, unclear, or inappropriate. Interpretation is not a one-sided explanation, but a relationship of different contexts amid and across boundaries. The interpreter is both an insider and an outsider and, therefore, is personally engaged as a participant. It is remarkable and notable that the experiences of a bewildered child trying to choose a word from three different languages is not qualitatively different from that of an anthropologist trying to locate a meaning when the same word is used in three different contexts.

The topic of dreams, dream telling, and dream interpretation have interested me since early childhood. I remember relatives and acquaintances telling dreams to one of my aunts who was adept at dream interpretation. I recall some of the dreams brought to her and the dialogue between her and the dreamers about the dreams. Most important in my memory is the assurance with which she asserted to some of her nieces that they also could learn about dreams. I have never lost my interest in dreams and dream telling. Dream telling engages imaginal and thematic aspects of human communication. In this way it facilitates personal storytelling at different levels. Even when the dream is alleged to be insignificant and unrelated to oneself, when it it told to another it becomes a contextually communicated personal story.

My interest in psychotherapy developed serendipitously. It was not a profession I specifically chose; it seems to have chosen me. With credentials in nursing and pastoral ministry, I found it natural to listen to people, and strange that I now lived in a country where one could

earn a living by doing so. It was stranger still that in my training prac-
ticums my teachers, supervisors, and clients thought I was equal to the
task, and that I, myself, had more than a passing fascination with it. I
have been a psychotherapist for ten years.

As an outsider to the United States and to the practice of
psychotherapy, I find the practice quite odd. Persons come to talk
about themselves to a total stranger who is designated for the purpose
by a comprehensive system of specific skills and a wide array of
credentialing procedures. The ritual around the work itself involves a
somewhat inflexible arrangement with regard to space, time, and process.

As an insider to the practice of psychotherapy, I see the practice
as a unique and invaluable opportunity for a person to tell and hear
one's own personal story. The therapist is asked to hear someone's
story and to share someone's perspective for a while. In the presence of
this invited stranger the teller can get a new vantage point from which a
new space, time, and outlook can be created. In psychotherapy as in
anthropology, boundaries are important. The therapist can neither ignore the person's tale nor be completely assimilated into it without losing therapeutic perspective and usefulness. The process occurs amid
and across boundaries that remain, although it is hoped that both participants will have changed by the end of the relationship.

My education in psychotherapy is rooted in the discipline and
profession of nursing, which I began to learn before coming to the
United States. Although the practice of nursing is diverse and adap-
table to different eras and settings, I found remarkable consistency and
consonance in the practice of nursing on both continents. Whether sitting with, doing with, doing for, or doing on behalf of another, the
nurse has an opportunity and a responsibility to foster health and provide a caring presence in contexts of human vulnerability and suffering.

It may be that the dream of the native woman in the black dress
who lives in the valley also represented for me a person in a context of
suffering. Another person's experience is usually approached from the
outside as if it were a foreign country full of rich potential. It can be
entered respectfully, shared temporarily, and contemplated carefully
and attentively by another. But it must not be invaded, occupied, or
even developed by another. It is the natives' responsibility to use the
rich oil if they want to do so. In nursing, as in psychotherapy and an-

thropology, boundaries are important. Native and observer participate in each other's lives within contexts involving social roles, relationships, rules for action, and personal meaning and idiosyncracy. Social rules and personal responses are intertwined in every thought and action. Certainly in every dream that is told.

From the emic point of view, the distinction I make in this book between the *person* and the *self* is experientially nonexistent. The person *is* the self and the self *is* the person. Having said that, I hasten to add that the analytic distinction between *person* and *self* is extremely useful in a study of "natives" of Western complex societies. That is because of the tendency of the Western "native" to understand both the person and the self in terms of the psychological ego. This is reinforced in the United States by a high valuation on individualism. Moreover, this tendency to fuse the person and the self, subsuming them within an individualistic psychologistic ego has found its way into psychological, sociological, and anthropological theories. It is difficult for the Western "native" to contemplate issues of personhood without, on the one hand, confusing them with issues of the self or, on the other hand, relegating them to notions of social persona or social role. Having a dream is an experience of the self with implicit manifestations of personhood, but telling a dream is an action of the person with implicit expressions of the self. This research is about dream telling, so I have focused on the *person*.

I have lived in the United States for many years. I have symbolically "gone through customs" and "had it stamped on my passport." Like my dream self I know the "native" well. However, the outsider's sense of quizzical curiosity about those customs and persons is still there. It becomes aroused when I hear Americans tell their dreams to one another and to me. Hence this study.

I am profoundly grateful to my family, especially to James, who has supported my efforts through different study programs.

My friends Linda Carter-Jessop and Joe Gibino have listened to my musings, and my friends in the Dream Group have listened to my dreams about this research. It is impossible to create without musing and dreaming. I am thankful they were there to listen and affirm.

I am especially indebted to Alfred Harris, my mentor and advisor. He has taught me to be patient and persistent with my own process by being patient and persistent with me. He has taught me to think analytically and critically and continues to sharpen my insights by challenging me to greater clarity. He suggested and guided, but never intruded. He is a model mentor. I am thankful to Walter Sangree for being interested in this research, and to Grace Harris for her ongoing clarification of the concept of *person*.

My mentor and colleague Madeline Schmitt has set an example of excellence for many years. I am grateful that she combines high standards with generous support and guidance. She understands the creative process and it is appropriate that she attend the birth of this project.

Barbara Tedlock, Benjamin Kilborne, and Gilbert Herdt have been kind enough to read this manuscript and have offered valuable suggestions. It is fair to say that their own excellent work involving dream telling in other societies have both inspired and instructed me. I am indebted to them.

I am thankful to the Alumni Seed Fund of the University of Rochester School of Nursing for an award which helped defray the costs of the early parts of this project.

I am profoundly grateful to Judy Begandy for her competence in transcribing, typing, and word processing. But she did more than that. She became an enthusiastic and loyal partner, coaxing computer disc and meeting deadlines for this project. I could not have done it without her.

This research would have been impossible without the therapists and staff of the two community mental health centers. They were generous with their thoughts and words as well as with their time. They taught me about dream telling, psychotherapy, and personhood. I am grateful to them.

Mary-Thérèse Behar Dombeck

I

Introduction: Background and Foreground

When I first came to this country more than two decades ago, one thing that intrigued me was the way Americans introduced any conversation about dreams: "This is going to sound crazy, but I dreamed that . . ." "Let me tell you this dream; it's sort of bizarre!" "I had this weird dream last night, you'll probably think it's one for the shrink." The topic came up not infrequently in casual social gatherings: the dream was introduced as a conversation starter, usually with an apologetic phrase related to its odd or inexplicable elements; the dream was then acknowledged by exclamations of interest and general laughter; and either the topic of dreams was dropped or another "crazy dream" was introduced by someone else. The settings of these conversations have been parties, student lounges in colleges, staff lounges at work, or neighborly kitchens and living rooms. It was also noteworthy to me that the word *dream* had different disparate connotations in common language. To be said to "live in a dream" is not a compliment. A person who lives in a dream is oblivious to practical concerns and not likely to succeed in "real life." On the other hand, an ardently desired goal or purpose is also called a *dream*. A neighbor of mine at the time kept referring to a house she had purchased as "the house of her dreams" and "her dream house" because it had everything she had wanted in a house. Similarly a female fellow student, while talking to me privately, referred to a male acquaintance as a "dreamboat," the embodiment of her desires.

Although the dream is a biological and psychological phenomenon, the telling of a dream is a social event. Cherished learned ways of knowing, thinking, feeling about dreams are reflected in what people say about dreams, to whom they talk about them, and how they talk about them. Their cultural ideas shape, guide, facilitate or restrict their words and actions relative to dream telling.

In this investigation I explore dream telling in the context of psychotherapy in the setting of two community mental health centers. Community mental health centers[1] were chosen because they represent an expansion in the accessibility of the mental health resources and employ a variety of therapists.[2] Because of the reference to telling "shrinks,"[3] I have been curious about whether the topic of dreams comes up in psychotherapy, whether therapists are regarded as expert dream interpreters, whether they regard listening to dreams as part of their role, and, if none of the above were true, how to explain the ambiguous references connecting dream telling to psychotherapy.

In this research cultural ideas are seen as symbolizing and expressing social relations. The settings provided an opportunity to observe and ask how different therapists understood their professional functions in relation to their patients, their peers, their supervisors, and also in relation to an institution for which the provision of psychotherapy and other mental health services are essential aims. The two community mental health centers provided services for two of the four catchment areas of the city. Both centers employed psychiatrists, psychologists, nurses, and social workers who provided psychotherapy as well as support staff employees like secretaries, receptionists, intake coordinators, and financial case managers.

Dream telling in any society is best studied in the context of native theories of the dream experience as well as the contextual discourse frames in that society (Tedlock 1987). Therefore, for the purposes of this research on dream telling in the context of psychotherapy in American institutions, it will be necessary to include a brief review of studies in the psychological and clinical, as well as the anthropological, disciplines. Because of the extensiveness of the literature (Parsifal-Charles 1986) only summaries will be presented here with a focus on the seminal and significant studies.

In dream research, the relationship across disciplines has had an impact, positive and negative. For example, the significance of research studies has been reduced when, on the one hand, one discipline conducts research as though the findings of other disciplines do not exist or, on the other hand, when analytical concepts, measurement tools, and techniques from one discipline are inappropriately applied to data from another discipline. Unfortunately examples of the former are plentiful in psychological and clinical dream research, and examples of the latter are plentiful in anthropological dream research. There are also studies that have used advances in other disciplines so that the study of dreams has been illuminated for both disciplines. Salient examples of interdisciplinary dialogue among researchers will be presented.

RESEARCH IN THE PHYSIOLOGY OF DREAMING AND DREAM PSYCHOLOGY

The study of dreaming and dream psychology has been rooted in the field of the physiology of sleep. Kleitman, the father of modern experimental research on dreaming, saw his first paper on the effects of prolonged sleeplessness published in 1923 (Kleitman 1923), and although he remained primarily interested in the physiology of sleep, his students Aserinsky and Dement concentrated their research on dreaming. A critical step in the development of dream psychology was electronic sleep monitoring. Electroencephalograms (EEG) were used to measure brain waves during different stages of sleep. Extra circuits were used to show eye muscle movements (EOG) and to measure muscle tone (EMG). During a study of the cyclic variations of sleep in infants, Aserinsky observed rapid eye movements (REM) that were concomitant with other physical changes during the sleep cycle (Aserinsky and Kleitman 1953). More experiments followed with infants and different adult populations. Dement and Kleitman discovered a predictable relationship between eye movements during sleep and dream activity (Dement and Kleitman 1957). Snyder called the REM portion of the sleep cycle "dreaming sleep" (Snyder 1963). Goodenough investigated dream reports following gradual and abrupt awakenings from different stages of sleep and confirmed his hypothesis regarding differences between REM and other stages of sleep. Non-REM reports of dreams by subjects were more thoughtlike, less visual, and lacked the characteristics of fantasy (Goodenough et al. 1965).

The scientific community continued to explore dreams in the context of the field of the physiology of sleep (Wolpert 1960; Foulkes 1966; Oswald 1966; Hartman 1967; Witkins and Lewis 1965; Kramer 1969). Topics of interest were the phenomenon of narcolepsy (Vogel

1960; Rechtschaffen et al. 1963) and the effects of hunger and thirst on sleep and dreaming (Dement and Wolpert 1958; Bokert 1967), dream recall (Goodenough 1967, 1978; Cohen and Wolfe 1973; Cohen 1974; Belicki and Bowers 1982; Belicki 1987), and dream deprivation (Dement and Fisher 1963; Sampson 1965). The approach of these experiments was generally speaking to investigate the physiological and psychophysiological correlates of dreaming.

Kleitman's research in the physiology of dreaming and modern sleep monitoring procedures sparked an interest in studying the content of dreams. Hall's research represents the first attempt to analyze the dream content itself quantitatively (Hall 1953). Later he and Van de Castle (1966) analyzed the content of 10,000 dreams under designated categories; for example, settings and objectives, characters, success, failure, emotions, and castration. They developed several empirical and theoretical scales to assist in the quantitative content analysis process. They also explored many of the problems concerned with the reliability of dream content measurements (Van de Castle 1969). These and other scales were used in subsequent studies in the content analysis of dreams by other researchers.

The approach of these studies, generally speaking, was to gather psychological data from the dreamer before or after gathering the dream report, which was obtained by waking the subject at a specific point in the sleep cycle. Dream content was related to such variables as age (phase in the life cycle), gender, socioeconomic status, race, and personality (Lott 1963; Hall and Domhoff 1963; Brennies 1970; Elkan 1969; Weiss 1969). The effects of drugs and the laboratory situation on dream content was explored in numerous studies (Whitman et al. 1960, 1961, 1969; Dement, Kahn, and Roffwarg 1965; Domhoff and Kamiya 1964; Hall 1967; Kramer et al. 1968; Domhoff 1969; Carroll, Lewis, and Oswald 1969; Weisz and Foulkes 1970). Winget and Kramer (1979) have described and commented on the methodological features of 132 dream content scales and rating systems. They have also presented a thorough tabular summary of dream content studies. The content analysis method has been useful in quantifying elements such as characters, outcomes, and social interactions in dream reports and has helped assess which elements occur over time and which changes seem to be associated with each other. The quantifiers of dreams have been careful in their statements of what conclusions one could draw from the quantifications. Lind has suggested that inter-pretations of the results may be based on the idea of frequency as an expression of concern or preoccupation in regard to scored events. For example, the frequent occurrence of a particular character or interaction suggests the dreamer's concern with it in waking life. Thus the relationship between the dream and waking activity can be explored (Hall and Lind 1970; Lind 1987).

The content analysis of dreams has also provided a way to examine trends and patterns of change over time. Foulkes's longitudinal studies of children's dreams are good examples of this use of content analysis (1982). The investigation of each age group included dream reports in a dream laboratory. He provided a summary of the content analysis by age groups and concluded that the dreams portrayed cognitive-symbolic processes capable of revealing how we think about ourselves.

Foulkes's later work represents a change in the emphasis in dream research from the psychophysiological concomitant of dreaming and dream content to the cognitive psychological analysis of those mental processes that become active in dreaming. The primary concern is with "*how* we are thinking when we are dreaming rather than *what* we are thinking" (Foulkes 1985: 13). Foulkes suggests that, whereas the dream can give us clues about the nature of the human mind, the dream itself is not making a particular statement; and whereas dreaming represents a cognitive model activated by a person's memory, planning, and conscious organization, the dream itself does not contain a coded meaning or a translatable message. Foulkes's perspective on dreaming calls into question any clinical approaches that focus on the interpretation of dream content. Although he does not say that the dream has no purpose and asserts that the dream can give us rich clues about the sources of dream imagery, it is unclear how the cognitive science of dreaming can be utilized clinically.

To summarize, research in dream psychology has attempted to respond to the problem of how dreams are constructed and what is the relationship of dreaming to the body, especially the brain. This has led researchers to conduct an abundance of research projects in the psychophysiology of dreaming, dream content analysis, and cognitive psychological analysis of dreaming. The advantages of these studies have been to discover more exact and quantifiable information about the processes and products of the brain. This research has been stimulating; however, the basic questions related to the cause, nature, and function of dreams remain unanswered. The limitations of psychophysiological research have become apparent when experiments are conducted in a reductionist manner by focusing on physiology, biology, and psychophysiology as though phenomenological, experiential, interactional, social, and cultural variables did not exist (Fiss 1979; Dennett 1981; Davidson 1981; McCarley 1981; Rechtschaffen 1983).[4] Moffitt and Hoffman (1987) comment on a pertinent and lucid critique of the "single-mindedness and isolation of dream psychophysiology." It is their opinion that it represents the influence of the ideas about and beliefs in the mind-body dualism that are ubiquitous in Western societies, even in research communities. We show in this study that the ethos of mind-body dualism informed therapists and staff at community mental health centers in their understanding of dream telling and dream interpretation and the therapeutic encounter.

CLINICAL OBSERVATION AND RESEARCH IN DREAMS

Not all psychological and cognitive dream research has been single-minded and isolated. Clinicians have approached dreams from three directions; namely, observation of existing ideas and theories of dreams in the clinical arena, the application of various research methods to explain perennial human experiences and to solve persistent human problems, and the popularization of research and clinical modalities related to dreams.

Clinical Observations of Existing Ideas and Theories of Dreams

Ideas and theories of dreams are numerous and ambiguous in societies with Judeo-Christian and Hellenic influences in their histories. The historical literature on dreams in Western societies is very extensive. My purpose here is only to mention summarily a few salient contributions to the development of cultural ideas and beliefs that were relevant in Freud's background.

Ancient Near Eastern texts dealt extensively with the subject of dreams. In ancient Mesopotamia "message" and omen dreams were considered important; however, simple everyday dreams were regarded with caution, were sometimes considered evil and put in the same category as demon possession (Oppenheim 1966). This ambivalent attitude is reflected in talmudic and biblical texts, which have abundant references to dreams with rules and stories about interpreting them and receiving guidance from them, as well as rules and cautions for avoiding them. These opposite attitudes reappear throughout church history. Modern religious studies endorsing attention to dreams for the purpose of gaining religious insight and spiritual growth read as scholarly apologies for the Judeo-Christian tradition of dream interpretation in biblical and church history texts (Kelsey 1968; Savary, Berne, and Williams 1985).

The Greek classical tradition acknowledged the importance of message and oracular dreams and augmented this importance by the practice of dream incubation for healing. There was also an open attitude toward ordinary daily dreams. Freud commented on the work of Artemidorus of Daldis because of his suggestion that the interpreter should ascertain the dreamer's age, sex, occupation, and other socially relevant facts before interpreting the dream, rather than always resorting to fixed interpretations in dream books (Freud 1965 [1900]).

The Hellenic ethos of free inquiry into all things was reflected in the humanistic post-Cartesian world of Freud. Descartes, whose ideas emerged from lucid dream experiences and who nevertheless relegated them to the realm of accidental irrational events secondary in importance to rational waking thought, had left his mark on the eighteenth and nineteenth centuries. In reaction to Descartes, and therefore in acknowledgement of his influence, came the Romantic, naturalistic, phenomenological, and nationalistic philosophies of Freud's time. Reason seemed to be succeeded by the violence of revolutions. This is the historical context of Freud's landmark book on dreams (1900), which was one of his earlier works and which provided the "royal road" to the rest of his theories.

For Freud the dream is a disguised fulfillment of a repressed wish. Dreams are a product of the mind, a form of thinking in which we appear not to *think* but to *experience*, that is to say we attach complete belief to the hallucinations (Freud 1965 [1900]: 50). This is a compromise structure. One of its functions is to *guard sleep* from forbidden guilty disturbances and, at the same time, to *allow repressed instinctual impulses to be known* in some way by the conscious mind. This is done in symbolic linguistic images that have a particular meaning for each dreamer. Therefore, the interpretation of dreams is "the royal road to a knowledge of the unconscious activities of the mind" (Freud 1965 [1900]: 608).

It is not possible to overestimate the impact of Freud on the twentieth century in Western societies. His influence is felt in the arts, sciences, and in many domains of human endeavor. He is variously understood and misunderstood, quoted and misquoted, accepted and rejected. Most of the dream theorists who followed him have constructed their own theories by testing his. Most of the research on the use of dreams in psychotherapy is descriptive and anecdotal, taking the form of case studies and life histories. Freud himself had taken such an approach.

Jung 1965 ([1961], 1964, 1966, 1974) saw the dream as a creative, purposeful expression of the unconscious. He rejected Freud's theory of *disguised fulfillment* and *displaced symbolism*. The purpose of the dream was not to fulfill repressed wishes but to help achieve and point to psychological balance. Although, like Freud, he related each dream symbol to the person who dreamed it by asking for the dreamer's associations, he also derived interpretations for dream symbols from parallels in mythological stories.

For Adler (1931, 1954) who was also a younger contemporary of Freud's, as for Freud, the ingredients for dreams come from the *day's residues*, which were emotionally laden thought processes and memories of the day of the dream. However, the purpose of the dream was not to fulfill repressed wishes, but it was a way of expressing problems not resolved in waking life. The purpose of the dream was to move the dreamer to the fulfillment of life goals, and thus reinforce the dreamer's life-style.

For Lowy (1942) the primary function of dreaming was to evoke emotion and to regulate the psyche. A dream connected past experiences with present emotions. Although it was helpful to interpret dreams, only a few dreams were remembered, and the process of dreaming fully accomplished its purposes outside of waking life. Moreover, it was not always helpful to *analyze a dream* because the dream should be considered in its totality and has an idiom of its own having more to do with the process of dreaming than with the interpretation of dreams.

Erikson (1954) advocated a method of analyzing the *manifest content* not only as a disguise for the *latent thoughts* but also as valuable in itself in reflecting the dreamer's life-style and stage of development. In it dreams *not only fulfill repressed wishes*, they also reflect the gains of the synthesizing ego in resolving developmental crises. Erikson constructed his theory of dreams by adding significantly to Freud's theory rather than by rejecting it.

French and Fromm (1964), also psychoanalysts, believed that dream interpretation had a problem-solving function. The dream was organized around a central focal conflict in interpersonal relations. The analyst approached the dream *not only intuitively and analytically*, but also logically by understanding its cognitive structure and systematically checking his intuitions against it. They believed the dream had a logic of its own different from the logic of waking thought but related to it.

Fritz Perls (1969), who was also trained as a psychoanalyst, rejected Freud most radically. *Instead of analyzing* a dream, Perls wanted to integrate the dream symbols with each other as though they were fragmented parts of the personality. The dream was *not to be interpreted* but to be experienced as an existential message.

Boss (1958) was a student of both Freud and Jung. He thought the dream should not be analyzed, synthesized, or explored scientifically. The dream was only for experiencing. Boss (1977) provided numerous case studies documenting the value of allowing normal adults and patients with psychiatric diagnoses to experience his phenomenological approach to dreams.

For Piaget (1962) dreams could be either compensatory or adaptive. He took issue with Freud's concept of the *censoring functions of consciousness*. In his view symbolic nonrational thought was a way of assimilating affective schemas focused on the subject pole of person-world interactions. However, this assimilation was an important part of cognition and provided a complex balance for the functions of accommodation that focused on the object pole of person-world interaction. Therefore, if dreams had the capacity to *fulfill wishes*, they could do so unconsciously as well as consciously. It is *not simply a process of disguise*, but a way of achieving awareness (Piaget 1962: 211–212).

These are only a few of the many dream theorists who have been affected by Freudian ideas and have observed or refuted them in their own clinical practices. Their theories have generated different methods and schools of psychotherapy that have continued to test Freud's and their own theories of dreams.[5]

The Applications of Research Methods to Clinical Problems

The dilemmas faced by dream researchers in Western societies are analogous to the dilemmas faced by Western medical and health-oriented traditions in general. The capacity to dream derives from a human individual's anatomical and biochemical structure. Certain neuroanatomical and neurophysiological aspects of dreaming can be quantified, measured, and analyzed. However, although the capacity to dream is universal, the experience of dreaming, the understanding and languaging of the dream, the telling of a dream to another, the interpretation of the dream are all sociocultural and personal. Integers become quantifiable only by ignoring their uniqueness. The dilemma has been, on the one hand, to push mathematical measurements beyond the limits of usefulness or, on the other hand, to assume that nothing can be counted or analyzed objectively because every individual context is different and unique. Clinical research is often caught on the horns of this dilemma, unwilling to give up objectivity and numbers while faced constantly with the problem of analyzing the troublesome exceptions, and the exceptional single cases.

Fiss (1979, 1983), in reviewing dream research literature appeals to experimental dream scientists and clinical psychotherapists to not ignore each other's findings. He deplores the fact that, on the one hand, prolific research is derived from the study of "brains" and not from the study of "dreamers" and, on the other hand, that most clinical notions of dreaming are derived from untested theories "as if REMs had never been discovered."[6]

Most of the studies on clinical problems are attempts to compare the dream reports of specialized groups or subjects with troublesome conditions or diagnoses with the dream reports of normal subjects, to gain insight into the conditions or personality of the dream reporter. These include studies on nightmares (Van Bork 1982; Hartman 1984; Belicki 1985, 1987), insomnia (Bertelson and Walsh 1987), patients with duodenal ulcer (Armstrong et al. 1965), chronic asthmatic patients (Weiss 1969), enuretic boys (Pierce 1963), patients with postwar anxiety (Greenberg, Pearlman, and Gampel 1972), heavy smokers (Kales et al. 1970), patients with schizophrenia (Arey 1971; Freedman, Grand, and Karacan 1966; Kramer et al. 1969), and depression (Beck and Ward 1961; Kramer 1966; Kramer at al. 1966, 1968; Van de Castle and Holloway 1971).

The clinical studies most relevant to this research have been the ones that have shed light on the clinical setting, the clinical process, and the context of dream telling. Whitman, Kramer, and Baldridge (1963) discovered interesting differences in dreams told by the same patient to the experimenter in the laboratory and later to the psychiatrist: dreams that the dreamer anticipated might bring a negative response by the psychiatrist were not told and maybe not recalled. In a later commentary on this study Kramer explains that the selective reporting "had to do with the psychology of the interpersonal situation between the dream reporter and the dream listener which illuminated the therapeutic or reporting relationship" (Kramer 1986). Winget and Kapp (1972) conducted a study of pregnant women. They discovered that those who had the most anxious dreams of labor and childbirth had the least prolonged labor, while those who had least childbirth dreams had the most prolonged labor. Findings supported the value of dreams for assimilating anxiety in the clinical situation. Another study on the adaptive value of dreams was done by Fiss and Litchman (1976) on psychiatric inpatients. They discovered that REM dream enhancement was associated with symptom relief. Cartwright, Tipton, and Wicklund (1980) investigated the relationship of dream work and the dropout rate in psychotherapy. Patients were given a two-week program of accessibility to their dreams in the dream laboratory by being awakened during REM sleep periods. Each morning the dreams of the night before were discussed with the experimenter, who was not a therapist. Those subjects who recalled and discussed dreams stayed in psychotherapy at a significantly higher rate than those who did not. Relating dream research to clinical practice remains problematic because most researchers are committed to empirical accuracy and most clinicians are committed to experiential and interactional validity. Some collections of essays and research have attempted to address this difficult integration (Madow and Snow 1970; Wolman 1979; Natterson 1980).

One of these studies is worthy of mention here. Snyder (1970) analyzed the contents of over 600 REM reports collected in a sleep laboratory from 250 subjects. He discovered that most dream speech was recalled by the dreamers, that it was ordinary and undistorted, and that the dreams showed cognitive reflection. He concluded that there was general congruity and continuity between dream life and waking life. If the experience of dreaming life corresponds to the experience of waking life, then it is difficult to accept the relevance of the findings of the purely cognitive approaches of dream psychology. Snyder's experimental phenomenological study is still taken seriously by contemporary researchers in dream psychophysiology (Moffitt and Hoffman 1987: 168) and cognitive psychology of dreams (Hunt 1987: 260).

Fiss (1983) presents us with assumptions and three investigative paradigms for clinical research on dreams. The assumptions are that clinical research *can* be scientifically sound *as well as* clinically relevant and that it is to be focused on dreamers and not on brains. The three laboratory paradigms for investigations are *dream interpretation*, in which REM time is interrupted thus increasing the dreamer's motivation to continue dreaming in order to concentrate attention on problem solving; *dream enhancement*, in which dreams are highlighted by focusing the dreamer's attention on them, especially with REM dreams, which are therapeutically more beneficial; and *dream incorporation*, in which dream content is influenced by specific presleep stimuli, and the effects of these stimuli are studied after the dream. Although none of these methods is new, Fiss calls attention to them as being especially useful to the traditional research-oriented clinician.

The Popularization of Research and Clinical Modalities Related To Dreams

In the past fifteen years there has been a trend toward popularization of the clinical research and clinical modalities, as well as the exploration of common human experiences related to dreams that do not cause problems; for example, lucid dreaming, dream recall, and dream telepathy. These experiences have been studied by professionals and also focused on by the general public.

In selected cases the professionals have made an effort to popularize their work. Faraday's books (1972, 1974) read as self-help guides for intelligent lay readers. She elucidated many dream theories, particularly the Gestalt approach. Garfield (1974) gave suggestions for improving dream recall, lucid dreaming, and for "redreaming" (1984);

and Delaney (1979) advocated a dream incubation method. All these books were very popular and have sold extremely well. Other popular books on dreams have advocated new methods of working with dreams (Williams 1980; Mindrel 1982; Taylor 1983; Savary et al. 1985; Gendlin 1986; Siegel 1986). These do not represent the first or the only popular books on dreams (Weiss 1944; Zolar 1984). They do, however, represent an effort by professionals to deprofessionalize the study of dreams and blend popular ideas, clinical experiences, and dream psychology. The Association for the Study of Dreams is the first American professional association open to anyone, lay or professional, seriously interested in studying dreams.

The trend toward deprofessionalizing and popularization of dream work has had an effect on the research community, noteworthy to the social analyst. On the one hand, it has brought to the general public an interest and some understanding of dream research and, on the other hand, it has provided the research community the interest to do research on topics not previously considered important or research-able. It also has pointed to the importance of the setting and the atmosphere in which research is done.

Ullman, a psychoanalyst whose work on dream telepathy received mixed reviews and who calls his current dream work with groups a technique for deprofessionalizing dream work (Ullman 1987a), has some very important comments on the importance of the context and setting on dream work and on dream research: "What comes into our dreams are social products. We can't dream about images that don't exist somewhere in society. We can put them together, we can mold them and so on, but they had to come from out there. And since they come from out there, they very often speak as much to the unsolved problems of society as they do to the unsolved problem of the individual" (Ullman 1987a: 5). He deplores the fact that the general public is afraid of dreams and that the only socially sanctioned arrangement for doing dream work is psychotherapy (Ullman 1987b: 1, 4).

Lucid dreaming is the experience of knowing that one is dreaming while the dream is going on and the capacity, which can be learned, to retain that awareness and control the nature of one's dreams (Green 1968; LaBerge et al. 1981a, 1981b; LaBerge 1985). The lucid dreamer while dreaming makes an intentional sequence of eye movements, which is determined beforehand with the experimenter, thus communicating intentionally with the experimenter while asleep. These experiments have been hailed as "LaBerge's proof" that lucid dreaming can be demonstrated in the laboratory (Moffitt and Hoffman 1987: 153).

Lucid dreaming is a very important topic for the scientist as well as for the general public because it represents one of the methods of working with dreams that is supposed to increase creativity and mental health. Domhoff (1985) considers lucid dreaming an aspect of the "new mystique of dreams" in America, along with Senoi Dream Theory, in which dream material is discussed, reenacted, and transformed in waking life. This approach is supposed to promote peacefulness, cooperation, and creativity. Domhoff discussed the controversial work of Kilton Stewart (1946, 1954, 1969) and especially the enthusiastic adoption of it in American society in the 1960s. He uses the work of Robert Dentan's ethnography (1968) to cast doubt on the authenticity of Stewart's work. Domhoff links the appeal of Stewart's ideas in the 1960s to an ethos of utopian idealism expressed through the human potential movement. His book has caused a reaction from Senoi dream enthusiasts, on the one hand, who say that the theory "works whatever its origins," and, on the other hand, from critics and reviewers like Faraday who thought Stewart was fraudulent (Faraday and Wren-Lewis 1984) and who wonders why anthropologists did not contradict Stewart earlier (1988). Domhoff's later communication about his book is that the mystique of dreams presents an allegory "about the perennial search for authenticity and self-improvement that is deeply rooted in American values" (Domhoff 1988: 1).

Thus, research on dreams in America has had three important influences that are still powerful today; namely, the availability of electronic sleep monitoring that has made it possible to conduct experiments, the influence of Freud on clinical practice, and the popularization of dream work.

ANTHROPOLOGICAL RESEARCH IN DREAMS AND DREAM TELLING

The subject of dreams has rarely been the principal focus of ethnographies, although there is much information about dreams and dream telling in ethnographies that focus on related subjects: for example, religion (Rattray 1927; Boas 1930; Spier 1933; Firth 1934; Speck 1935); divination (Bastide 1968; Tedlock 1978); spirit possession, trance, or other altered states of consciousness (Bourgignon 1954, 1965, 1972); witchcraft (Pitt-Rivers 1970); medicine and healing (Forde 1931; Wallace 1958; Vogel 1982); and cross-cultural personality studies (Eggan 1961; Honnigmann 1961). These studies use a variety of methodologies and approaches.

Most of the reviewers of anthropological studies of dreams acknowledge the influence of Freud and psychoanalysis on dream research. Also, a few studies, extremely important for this research, deal with the social functions of dream telling. Studies on the influence of Freud and studies on the social functions of dream telling will be reviewed separately in this section.

The Influence of the Psychoanalytic Framework in the Study of Dreams in Non-Western Societies: Five Examples

The most obvious evidence of Freud's influence was an increased interest in the study of dreams as Freudian theories became known in the second and third decades of the twentieth century (Lincoln 1935; D'Andrade 1961; Eggan 1961; Barnouw 1985 [1963]; Textor 1967; Bourgignon 1972; O'Nell 1976; Kennedy and Langness 1981; Dentan 1987a).

Before Freud the interest in dreams was related to an intellectualist interest in the study of "primitives" and "primitive mentality." Taylor (1958 [1871]) discussed the significance of dreams in a variety of societies. He thought that primitives made little distinction between dream images and waking reality. Levy-Bruhl (1923) postulated that primitives were indifferent to the laws of contradiction because they accepted their dreams as true. Freud himself encouraged an interest in anthropology among his entourage. In 1909 he wrote a letter to Oppenheim, a classical scholar, to invite collaboration on the subject of dreams in mythology and folklore. This resulted in a coauthored essay that was published posthumously (Freud and Oppenheim 1958). Their conclusion was that "Thus on this occasion we have been able to establish the fact that folklore interprets dream symbols in the same way as psychoanalysis, and that, contrary to loudly proclaimed popular opinion, it derives a group of dreams from needs and wishes which have become immediate" (p. 65).

It is significant that both Seligman and Rivers, who were physicians interested in developing anthropological fieldwork
methodologies, were also both greatly influenced by Freud, *and* were
interested in dreams. Rivers wrote two seminal works on dreams. In
the first one he concluded that the dream experiences in primitive
cultures supported most of Freud's theories (Rivers 1918). In the second one he departed from Freud's concept of wish fulfillment, stating
that dreams were attempts to solve in sleep conflicts that were disturbing in waking life (Rivers 1923). Seligman was interested in examining
the universality of dream themes in various cultures to discover
whether the psychology of the unconscious could provide a useful approach to basic anthropological problems. In his introduction to Lincoln's pioneering book on dreams, Seligman expressed dissatisfaction
with the rigidity of interpretation in both the Freudian and Jungian approaches (Lincoln 1935: xi). Lincoln's book represents the first inten-
sive use of psychoanalytic theory to analyze cultures, as well as the first
and most extensive anthropological comparative research on dreams
and dream telling. Lincoln saw the dream as a transitional process from
which originate cultural patterns. He emphasized the distinction between culture pattern dreams and individual dreams that had been
made by classical scholars and scholars of the ancient Near East
(Dodds 1951; Oppenheim 1966). This distinction has been retained
and researched in many studies.[7]

The literature on dreams and dream telling is so extensive that it
is impossible to review it all. Yet in no topic is the close and, at times,
uneasy relationship between psychoanalysis and anthropology more
evident than in the study of dreams and dream-related behavior.
Therefore, my purpose here is to (1) select only five different examples
of the relationship between anthropological studies and Freudian
theory and (2) address the social functions of dream telling as they appear in selected anthropological studies on dreams and dream-related
topics.

The first illustration is from the work of Geza Roheim, who
was a psychoanalyst, a friend of Freud's, and the first ethnologist to ad-
vocate and utilize a psychoanalytic approach to interpret culture. He
was encouraged by Freud and subsidized by one of Freud's followers,
Princess Marie Bonaparte, to make psychoanalytic-anthropological
studies of Australian tribes (Roheim 1945). Roheim applied Freudian

theory as a code to interpret cultures. For example, he viewed the immortality myths of Australian aborigines as a denial of separation anxiety. He found the Oedipus complex and castration anxiety in the manifest dreams of his informants and applied his analysis of the latent thoughts to his analysis of the culture. He also presented an investigative methodology for the anthropologist in the field (Roheim 1947).

In the next few years ethnographic studies of dreams and related subjects became part of a subfield called *culture and personality*, in which the Freudian idiom was used freely and Freudian concepts were applied, albeit a little more cautiously (Wilbur and Muensterberger 1951).

The second example is presented in one of the contributors to the essays in honor of Geza Roheim: George Devereux (1951). Devereux's contribution to psychoanalysis and anthropology is unique. He called his method *ethnopsychiatry*. He described a psychoanalytic treatment with projective tests, at least thirty interviews, and dream interpretations using the Freudian theory in a way that adapted it to his patient's culture. He criticized anthropologists who refused to modify Freud as well as those who felt compelled to "throw out the baby with the bath water" (Devereux 1951: 191). Therefore, in interpreting dreams he took into consideration not only personal associations but also cultural evaluations of dream symbols. In studying the cultural phenomenon of dream learning among the Mohave Indians (Devereux 1957), he considered individual shaman's different versions of a dreamed myth and proposed that both the manifest content and the latent thoughts were important. This method of achieving personal empathic communication in the context of cultural understanding is also described by Kracke (1981) and Kilborne (1978).

The third case is represented in the work of Bronislaw Malinowski (1927), who took Freud's work seriously enough to challenge it. In fact, he seemed to use Freud's theory of dream interpretation as a springboard for his own theory. His famous controversy with Ernest Jones led him to propose the substitution of the matrilinineal family complex for the Freudian Oedipus complex (Malinowski 1927: 135–147). He postulated a functional analysis of dreams, for the two different types of dreams: the official dream and the individual dream. The "official dream" was a dream by one individual for the whole community; for example, a dream about a good spot for a fishing expedition. The function of the "individual dream" or "free dream" was to evoke feeling and motivation for action: "for these natives, remarkably enough, reverse the Freudian theory of dreams, for to them the dream is the *cause* of the wish" (Malinowski 1927: 94). In his process of interviewing and questioning informants, Malinowski was as masterful, persistent, and sensitive an interviewer as Freud looking for the latent information under the manifest dream symbols through the dreamer's associations.

The fourth example is found in the work of Dorothy Eggan (1952, 1961, 1966) and researchers who did content analyses on the manifest content of the dreams of their informants (Schneider and Lauriston 1969; Lee 1970; LeVine 1966; O'Nell and O'Nell 1963; Gregor 1981). Eggan suggested that content analysis studies were useful for analyzing cultural and personal as well as universal symbols (Eggan 1952). She maintained that there was an interaction between the manifest dream and the belief and value systems of society of the dreamer, therefore she postulated culture-bound interpretations in which Freudian concepts unilaterally imposed on non-Western societies were of limited value.[8]

The fifth illustration is in Benjamin Kilborne's work (1978, 1981a). He studied dream interpretation in Morocco, always placing the dream report in the particular social situations in which they functioned as communications. The questions that he posed for himself in his research are, Who tells the dream? To whom is it told? What is the role and status of the dreamer and the dream interpreter? What is the nature of their interaction? What is the function of dream telling, interpretation, and evaluation in Morocco? Is there a relationship between the dreams people have and their social values and cultural patterns? He reviewed traditional Islamic Moroccan concepts of dream interpretation, described the functions of the interpreter, and provided traditional interpretations for each dream *as well as* a Freudian interpretation. His method demonstrated that no single theory of dream interpretation is suitable for dream interpretation without taking into consideration the social context in which dreams are told and the native interpretation of the dreams.

Tedlock (1987) in her critique of dream researchers, confirms that the social context in which the dream is reported to others may be as important as the dream itself. The dream itself provides only an analysis of the imagery. This is not enough without the interpretation of the circumstances, social status, events, and reaction to the imagery that the dreamer provides (Tedlock 1981: 314).

Issues of the Social Functions of Dream Telling as per Selected Anthropological Studies

Kilborne made the point that anthropological studies of dreams and dream interpretation have suffered seriously from a failure to distinguish between the dream as experienced and the dream as reported (Kilborne 1981a: 295). The dream as a reconstructed report is inseparable from the particular social context. In the following studies the researcher commented on issues of social functions of the dream, on the role and status of the dreamer and the dream interpreter, on the relationship between dreams and social values, cultural patterns and myths, and on the dream telling interaction.

Most ethnographers noted that dreamers and especially interpreters had to have *special roles and statuses* to be entitled to tell and hear dreams. Among the Mohave Indians (Devereux 1957) young aspiring dream interpreters presented their dreams for interpretation and shamans or seasoned interpreters told the shamanic lore while they modeled for the novices their new social role. The Quiche Maya (Tedlock 1978) taught the young novices to interpret their dreams through direct discussions of sensations in their hands and legs and by sharing the sensation in their own bodies as they heard the dream before the initiation. Dream interpreters called *day keepers* also practiced as diviners and curers *whose services were sought* even beyond regions of Quiche communities. Among the Mae Enga of New Guinea (Meggitt 1962) and the Walbiri of Australia (Meggitt 1965), the dreams of young men while they were in seclusion in the clan lodge were valued by all. During these times a young man might acquire *the status and reputation of a specialized dreamer*. Meggitt told an anecdote of a man who dreamed, told, and interpreted his dreams so that external events proved him correct. However, no one regarded his dream as significant. They dismissed the dream and its interpretation as a lucky guess because the man was not regarded as a special teller and interpreter of dreams (Meggitt 1962: 221). The telling of dreams seemed to *confer social power* for the Yuma of the Gila River (Spier 1933). Nobody but a dead chief's son could dream the necessary powers to succeed his father.

Charsley tells us of an African church in western Uganda where dreams were shared regularly in the context of the church service. The dreams were about church and church members, and the telling of dreams resulted in confessions (Charsley 1973). Because of the importance placed on the paradigm of dream interpretation as a channel of communication with God in that particular church community, dream telling became a way to contribute valuably to the group life. Charsley discovered that, although all members were allowed to tell dreams in church, in practice the tellers of dreams were active members. In fact, they were active members of a special kind: young men and women who held less powerful positions told dreams less often than older males who were active members of the church. As for dream interpretation, it was regarded as *a special gift from God and was restricted to a few recognized leaders*. These were in practice almost always the senior office holders. Charsley's social analysis shows that, for that church, dream telling became "a channel through which members could bid for status within the group by attempting to contribute valuably to its life" (Charsley 1973: 252).

Among the Saulteaux of North America (Hallowell 1942), the ability to conjure was acquired as a dream blessing, and a quest or call was seen in a vision. It was from the vision that a person received power to carry out the calling. Further examples of how dream telling was used for *socialization* can be seen from the Hopi (Eggan 1966). Dream telling was used to educate the younger members of the community about tribal history and tradition (pp. 262–263). Similarly among the Mohave Indians (Devereux 1957) the myth was dreamed and sung ritually to receive the power to heal. Among the Negritos of the Philippines (Stewart 1954), the function of dream telling was also *to socialize and educate*. Dreamers were told that they have dreams for the sake of the community and admonished to bring something of value from their dreams to the community.

In Kilborne's study (1978), the Moroccan dream interpreters were Koranic schoolmasters who saw themselves in the role of reassuring parents, thus encouraging the dreamers to assume the role of "good" responsible children. Dreamer and dream interpreters relied on shared fantasies about the situation in the dream and drew on the

cultural belief in saints and *djinn*.⁹ Thus, *the normative ideals* of obe-
dient, responsible, and moral citizenship *were upheld*.

These few ethnographic examples suggest that dream telling
and dream interpretation are inextricably connected to issues of
social role, status, social power, and socialization into the particular
society in which they occur. The ability to tell dreams and interpret
dreams is related to the attributes and capacities that comprise a social
person.

This review of the literature on dream research demonstrates the
validity of Tedlock's critique that, *in general*, anthropological researchers have ignored the fact that dream communication in non-Western
cultures is partially dependent on native theories about the dream experience and *in general*, psychological researchers have ignored that
their subject's communication of dreams were socially and contextually
determined (Tedlock 1987).

This research is an ethnographic study of dreams and dream telling in American society, a subject virtually ignored by ethnographers
(Collins 1984). The dearth of ethnographic dream research studies in
America is juxtaposed with the prodigious amounts of psychological
research on dreams in America since the advent of sleep monitoring,
the recent popularization of dream work, and publication of articles
about research on dreams in the popular press. The influence of Freud
and psychoanalysis is as strong in studies of clinical practice as it is in
anthropological research. In spite of these patterns, Western
ethnographers have been more likely to study dream telling in non-
Western societies than Western societies. The popular press
demonstrates ambivalent beliefs relative to dreams. There are articles
on both the meaninglessness and meaningfulness of dreams.¹⁰ It is
clear that in American society dreams and dream telling lack the important official functions they have in societies where dreams guide
ritual and individual behavior. Seligman, however, in Lincoln's classical
book on dreams, suggests that dreams are so important in many
societies that "the possible importance of them should not be overlooked in other societies where the dream does not play an overt part
in the culture" (Lincoln 1935: xi).

It is important to state explicitly, although I implied it earlier, that
most of the clinical theories and research in dream psychology have
become a part of the constellation of ideas and beliefs about dreams

and dream telling in the local settings described in this research. In America dream telling is a private activity that has not been accorded public importance. Psychotherapy is one of the private settings in which dream telling is designated to customarily occur.

FIELD WORK: ISSUES OF TIME

The research project was conducted in two Community Mental Health Centers in a city with a population of 240,000 (approx.). The CMHCs serve two of the four catchment areas of two counties with a population of approximately 758,000. The first center is connected with, and situated within a hospital that I shall call *Riverpool* and the other, which I shall call *Newell*, has three community sites located in different parts of the county within the catchment area.

I negotiated with administrators at each site for permission to interview therapists, staff, and patients. Both administrators indicated on the telephone that it would be complicated to obtain permission to interview patients because of confidentiality and suggested that I limit my interviews to therapists. The administrator at Newell CMHC said that although interviewing outpatients who came for treatment was conceivably possible, it would "take a *long* time" to get permission to do so. I got the impression that pressing the issue would jeopardize entry into the systems so I decided to settle for permission to interview therapists. I was also allowed to sit in the staff lounge as well as general waiting rooms in between appointments. This gave me an opportunity, particularly at two of the Newell sites, to hear patients' interactions in the waiting room and to have conversations with the staff in the staff lounge, which was used by both the support staff and the psychotherapy staff. I introduced myself as a student of anthropology and only told the topic of my study if I was asked. Within the first two weeks I would be greeted by the staff with a comment about dreams. The comments were ambivalent like "Don't ask me about my dreams, they are too crazy" or "Let me tell you this dream." During several lunch hours in the lounge, dreams and dreaming became the topic of conversation along with dieting, recreation, food, and the weather. The topic of dreams seemed to be introduced for my benefit. Dreams were told to one another and to me, and several women among the support staff requested permission to be interviewed. My request to interview members of the clerical staff who were not therapists was granted, and the staff of the day treatment center, the partial hospitalization program, and the support staff were added to my list of potential interviews.

In each center, I attended a staff meeting at which I was introduced as a student of anthropology and asked about my research. The questions were related to how anthropologists study dreams.[11] There were allusions to the popular books with dreams as a reference point. At one of the Newell sites there were questions about my accent; questions about how long I had been in this country, and how long I had been a student. At the Riverpool Center I was invited to attend one of the case presentations in the interdisciplinary setting of the team meeting. At that meeting and at other meetings I was a silent observer.

Many of the therapists and support staff at both centers who were not at these meetings and had not been there when I was formally introduced assumed I was a doctoral student of psychology. Whenever this happened I would restate my discipline and field of study. This would occasionally result in puzzled looks, and I was asked again, "but how does an anthropologist study dreams here?" "I'm looking for your opinions and ideas about dreams and for the customs related to dream telling here." One resident psychiatrist said, "Gotcha! We're your tribe." However, a few of the therapists and nontherapists did not seem to make the distinction between the fields of psychology and anthropology when it came to studying dreams, even after clarification. I was also told that I *should* have studied psychology because "there is much more about dreams in the field of psychology."

The interviews were done at both centers within the span of eight months from December 1986 to July 1987. By the third month there seemed to be a rumor among the clerical staff and some of the day treatment therapists at one of the Newell sites that I was an expert in dream interpretation. One of the social workers was disappointed when I did not interpret her dream of cats. "I always dream of these cats, I was wishing you could tell me what that means. We had such a short time to talk maybe we can talk again. I have so many strange dreams." In our subsequent talks she continued to talk as though I was a dream interpreter.

In both centers I found a familiarity and openness to research. They seemed to have participated in research before. The clinical psychology students who were trainees alluded to their own research and wished me good luck. They were glad to advance the cause of a fellow graduate student. One of them wanted to read my proposal so that she could get some ideas for her own research. When I reminded her that we were in different disciplines she claimed it would, nevertheless, be helpful. Most people seemed to have an established and familiar idea regarding the protocols for participating in research. When I would start my interviews in an open-ended manner, I would be asked whether it was time to answer the questions on the questionnaire. (I had mentioned a short questionnaire in my letter inviting their participation.) The idea of research seemed to be connected more with questionnaires than with having conversations. For the same reason there was, in general, no objection to my tape recorder. The one exception to that came from a young woman psychologist who was uncomfortable about having one of her client's dreams audiotaped. She was concerned about violating confidentiality. She said, "this woman (her client) has such an issue with trust that she would never trust me or anyone else again if she knew I had told this dream to anyone, or if she saw it in print anywhere." I assured her that I would not print the dream, and that nobody would know who she was, just as I did not know who her client was. The dream seemed to be the symbol of her client's most private information.

People tried to be helpful in supplying me with reading material. The suggestions ranged from professional books about psychotherapy techniques to a dream numbers book which could be used to win lotteries. Other suggestions were that I should talk to a psychoanalyst, a hairdresser with psychic abilities, a "professional" psychic, and a minister. These were persons who had demonstrated an interest and expertise in dream interpretation, and who they thought could be more helpful to me than nonexperts like themselves.

At Riverpool seven of the nurses knew of my association with the nursing profession. They knew I was a nurse who was studying anthropology. (Only two of the seven knew of my interest in dreams.) This was an important alliance which encouraged them to trust me. Yet, in at least two of the interviews the knowledge that they assumed we shared about the nursing profession became a deterrent of explicit clarifications. During one interview when I asked for specific clarification about some of the statements the interviewee made, she sounded impatient. "Well, I'll tell you, *as though you didn't know*, that the status of nurses in this particular institution is quite good because we have faculty positions; outside of here it's not too terrific, I think people outside think that nurses clean up, take care of doctors, say 'yes sir,' do what they're told; that they're like glorified servants. *I'm not telling you something you don't know!*"

Issues of time are important in field work. The investigator needs to understand and participate in the customs and arrangements about time as they arise in the field. The fifty-minute hour is an institution of psychotherapy. This time unit dominated my own day. Interviews with me had to be sandwiched between interviews with patients. So I generally got fifty minutes, too. Therapists seemed to be very comfortable and relaxed with the fifty-minute interviews. But when fifty minutes had passed there was always uncomfortable fidgeting, glances at the clock, and even comments about having to stop. I also discovered that if I needed to call therepists to schedule appointments, I was more likely to reach them within the 10-minute transition before the next hour. When therapists wanted to talk more they sometimes scheduled another fifty-minute appointment, usually on another day. The other alternative was to talk faster, to grow more restless, to transgress briefly into the next hour with increasing discomfort, or to stop abruptly. Those were all different styles of ending the interview.

The fifty-minute hour affected the clerical staff as well as the therapists. Secretaries were free to interview me when the therapists were counseling with patients in a fifty-minute unit of time. At times our interview would be interrupted by a phone call. Secretaries had more phone calls a few minutes to the hour. Other clerical staff persons who were not secretaries spoke to me during their lunch hour.

Time constraints were apparent at both centers. People seemed to hurry in and out of appointments. I found the pace faster and more hectic at Riverpool than at Newell. Yet many of the therapists at the Newell centers spoke of having to complete a specific amount of therapy hours during a week. This seemed to be a quota of income-producing therapy hours that was expected of them. There was also pressure to see a large number of patients for short-term therapy. One of the social workers who had been a therapist for more than ten years commented on the time constraints. "There's more and more pressure to treat people within a short time span. It's rather sad because some things never happen that fast. It takes time to make changes within the individual instead of just their circumstances."

It was remarkable that therapists with these time constraints wanted to talk to me at all. I found people generous with their time. I did not pay them for participating in the study. People seemed to enjoy talking about dreams and dream telling. The seven nurses who knew I was a nurse and four psychology doctoral students may have made an effort because of their loyalty to a fellow nurse or fellow student. But others did not have this reason for wanting to participate. It occurred to me that they enjoyed talking and being heard. One of the psychiatrists relaxed back in her chair, cradled her head in her hands and started her story like this: "I will go back to childhood and tell you something about dreams as useful before I was trained." Then she proceeded to give me a history of dreams and dream telling in her life. Of course, we were not finished at the end of the fifty-minute time. She stopped abruptly and asked me to return at the same time on the next week.

When I made comments about their generosity with time I received comments about the importance of research, or about my "interesting" topic. Two of the administrators told me that, because they had encouraged their staff to participate in the research, the least they could do was participate themselves. Approximately 62 percent of the therapists who received invitations to participate in the research accepted. Most of the ones who declined told me they had no time to speak with me. Only five out of the eighty people who received letters declined without giving me an explanation.

Forty-nine therapists agreed to set time aside to speak with me. Nine were physicians (two women and seven men), ten were nurses (all women), fifteen were psychologists (seven women and eight men), and fifteen were social workers (eleven women and four men). Members of the suport staff were recruited by posting invitation to participate in the staff lounges. Nine women responded at the Newell Center sites. No one on the support staff at Riverpool responded. My understanding of this is that they did not see the notice, which was less an issue of time than of space.

THE SETTINGS: ISSUES OF SPACE
Riverpool

The Department of Psychiatry at the Riverpool Hospital was founded in 1946. Although outpatient services had been offered from the outset, there has been a rapid expansion of these services since the opening and annexation of the Community Mental Health Center in 1969. The services include a child and adolescent psychiatric clinic, an older adult clinic for aged patients, an adult clinic, an extended care program for the chronically mentally ill, a family and marriage clinic, a day treatment center, and programs for chemical abuse. The administrator gave me only the names of the therapists who worked at the adult clinics, thirty names in all.

I had been associated with the inpatient units of the hospital in 1977 as a graduate student nurse, but I had no knowledge of the outpatient department and ambulatory services. When I asked one of the administrators where the Community Mental Health Center was located, she said, "we're not really in a 'where'; technically there is a separate wing on the ground floor, but that does not really contain all of it or describe all of us. We're sprawled all over the place. Some of the psychologists are on the second floor and some of the psychiatric residents are in the basement, and then there are intake offices on the main wing of the ground floor."

I became aware of many institutions that had grown organically around each other and into each other. Some had spread out like vines and others had remained and grown around whatever was there, making for an interesting social ecology. For example, although the offices of therapists in the CMHC were to be found on three different floors, a few of the offices on the official CMHC wing did not belong to CMHC personnel. There was one particular person in an office next to the nurses' counseling offices who was not a therapist, but no one seemed to know who she was. The woman's name was on the door and I saw her briefly at times. When I looked up her name in the directory, I discovered that she was a nonmedical instructor of medical students. It seemed strange to me that people were assigned to offices next to people of different departments or programs and stranger still that they did not go out of their way to communicate with each other. The outpatient department, the specialty clinics, and the CMHC had grown gradually in all directions to accommodate new programs. The growth was concomitant with the growth of the medical school, the service and training of psychologists within the Department of Psychiatry, the expansion of the School of Nursing, and the Department of Social Work. Psychologists and social workers with seniority and experience received faculty positions in the School of Medicine. Nurse psychotherapists had faculty positions in the School of Nursing. Most of the therapists I interviewed who were not trainees had faculty positions as well as hospital titles.

I found it hard to situate myself in suitable places for participant observation. The atmosphere was more like a busy airport than a marketplace. In a marketplace people seek each other out to buy and sell, in an airport people are hurriedly and worriedly headed to particular destinations and closing doors behind them; there is little time or inclination for conversation. There were access windows for information and different waiting areas around clusters of offices. When I stopped to ask for the location of Dr. A., I was asked if I had an appointment with him and told to wait until he came to collect me. I found out that this was a necessary arrangement because resident psychiatrists who shared an office could not always hold private interviews in their own office. Thus patients did not see their psychiatrists in the same room every time they came. I asked one of the psychiatrists whether this arrangement was satisfactory. His response was: "They're so *spaced-out* [my emphasis] anyway—it doesn't seem to matter." (He had not noticed the pun.)

Although people were pleasant and cordial when they were asked for directions, I found the place rather inhospitable and decided to ask what people thought about, and felt about, the space where they were working. I asked about office space, and where people met formally and informally. I was told that formal meetings were held by appointment in special meeting rooms, which were reserved for the purpose. These were not staff lounges for informal gatherings.

My question about staff lounges was met with knowing and cynical smiles from nurses and social workers. They told me that physicians had a reading room to which only they had the key. The exclusive room was a gift donated to the psychiatric residents. "They sometimes work seventy hours a week," said one of the nurses. "Maybe they need a place to relax in the evenings." Another nurse conceding the same point added, "but they took *our* space! that was originally a kitchen that we *all* used. That's a very *sore spot* [my emphasis] with people here." (She did not seem to notice the pun.)

Within the next two weeks I was invited to an interview with one of the psychiatric residents in the exclusive reading room. The reason he gave me for using that space was "because my office in the basement is not very comfortable, and you [meaning me] would be more comfortable here."

The room was located in a central corridor of the ground floor community mental health wing. It was attractively decorated. There were books and periodicals in bookcases along two walls. The third wall had large portrait photographs of distinguished-looking psychiatrists (nine men and one woman). There was a couch, a small refrigerator, a telephone, and a television. The room could not really be called a private area because several psychiatric residents, men and women, shared it and used it sporadically when they were "on call," and on the rare occasion when they took time to relax. I was told that nineteen residents used the room. These included the psychiatric residents who covered medical inpatient units, psychiatric inpatient units, and specialty services, as well as psychiatrists of the CMHC.

Our interview was interrupted twice. One time the door opened to admit a young woman who asked, "Is this supervision?" My interviewee's answer was unceremonious and cryptic, "No! This is interviewing!" She said, "Excuse me!" and left. She did not appear to need further explanation. Another time when the telephone rang he became restless and then declared his decision not to answer it. I got a feeling for the barrage of demands that continually bombarded the psychiatric residents. In that environment communication is economical and, at times, abrupt.

At the end of that interview, to which he gave his full attention and which he seemed to thoroughly enjoy, he got up swiftly, wished me good luck, and walked to the door ahead of me. Before leaving he said: "Remember to take all your equipment with you; if you forget something in this room you'll never get it back." He left and the door lock clicked. I never got a chance to ask if he meant that I would have a hard time procuring a key to reenter the room or if equipment left in the room had been borrowed, misappropriated, or stolen. I remained in the room to browse alone, write a few field notes, and gather my materials. While I was there a woman walked in and looked surprised by my presence. She did not ask me any questions, and I did not explain. It occurred to me that explanations were not volunteered in this place among the staff. There did not seem to be time to explain things.

If people needed to find out things, they asked. If they did not ask, it was assumed that they knew; and if they did not know and did not ask, they did not wish to be burdened with irrelevant information, so verbal communication was sparse and reserved for essentials.

My next goal was to see how "uncomfortable" the basement offices were. But a trip to the area of the psychiatric residents' offices alone did not tell me much. There were dark corridors and closed doors. It was not until I had interviews scheduled in the basement that I saw the stark offices with metal desks and metal chairs that two psychiatric residents shared. The office had not been decorated to look comfortable. There were very few personal memorabilia. The only personal item in that room was a photograph of his wife and baby to which he frequently referred. I was told that these basement offices felt unsafe to some of the psychiatric residents. At a team meeting a woman resident requested a place other than the basement to interview a patient who had a history of criminal behavior and chemical abuse.

The issue of the exclusive reading room had upset the staff enough to cause the director of ambulatory services, a psychiatrist, to designate a room on the ground floor as a lounge for the nonmedical staff. It was allegedly used by the nurses, social workers, and secretaries. One of the social workers told me during an interview that whereas the physicians' reading room was coed, the staff lounge was for women only; the logic of this statement became clear when she also volunteered the information that there was only one male social worker, and he "does not come around here too much." The staff lounge was also locked and, one day when I was attempting to post a notice in it, inviting the support staff to participate in my study, it took several inquiries to locate a key. The notice was finally posted but there were no responses to my invitation. My guess is that the lounge is seldom used by anyone. This was substantiated when I asked one of the nurses where she meets informally with her colleagues. She said, "I like to hang out with people in the hall, there's also the staff lounge; we only use it in bits and pieces" (I think she meant seldom and sporadically).

The psychologist trainees shared rooms on the second floor that were as stark and institutional as the rooms in the basement. But the halls on the second floor were brighter and more pleasant.

The offices on the ground floor CMHC wing assigned to therapists who were not trainees looked warmer and more comfortable because of the personal memorabilia on the walls, desks, and floors. Still, the decor was simple and somewhat spartan. One of the young social workers who had been there for less than a year broke the tradition by decorating her room very colorfully. This caused her to feel like a nonconformist. She said, "I did some different things to this room. When I first brought this bear (referring to a large stuffed bear on one of her chairs) to be used therapeutically, I got the feeling that it was a strange thing to do; that people were wondering: well, what *do* you do in here?" Although the rules about how to furnish and decorate office therapy rooms were not explicit, there was pressure to follow implicit shared understandings about what was considered a professional environment.

Thus, the Community Mental Health Center at Riverpool was housed within a special wing of the Department of Psychiatry of the Medical Center. However, all of the center's activities were not contained in that wing, nor were all the offices of the wing related exclusively to the CMHC. This made for an atmosphere of disconnected isolation. Neither the exclusive reading room for psychiatric residents nor the staff lounge for nonmedical staff served as an informal gathering place. Because this was a site for training therapists of different disciplines, there was a general concern for efficiency and competence, that is, individual therapists were concerned about their own efficiency; it was difficult to perceive any concern about the efficiency of the whole system. There was little frivolous or "unnecessary" conversation. Communication was economical and succinct, and occasionally insufficient and abrupt.

At Riverpool I interviewed twenty-one therapists. Four were psychiatric residents, two were attending psychiatrists who were also instructors, seven were clinical nurse specialists, three were clinical psychology trainees, two were psychologists, and three were social workers. All of the nurses and social workers were women; four of the physicians were men and two were women. One of the psychologists was a man and four were women.

Newell

The Newell Mental Health Center was established in 1979. The center operates out of three community sites serving three different parts of the catchment area. The first and largest is situated on a busy road in a large sprawling suburb, very close to large shopping malls and other businesses. The second is in a newly reconstructed train station warehouse in a low-income urban area, and the furthest one is in a small college town with access to a few rural communities at the edge of the county. This one also was housed in a reconstructed warehouse. Moreover, the administrative offices coordinating the whole effort were housed in yet another office building close to the suburban site.

The center was to make mental health services available to the community. The services included ambulatory mental health treatment, continuing treatment programs for the chronically mentally ill, a day treatment program to provide acute care, counseling, and social and vocational skills for adults. There were also a youth outreach and education program, a social recreational and prevocational program for adult clients and former clients, a program designed to support and educate single parents, and other educational programs.

Early in the field work I intended to go to only one site at one time so that I could get a good sense of the ethos of the place and an accurate account of the facts about it, before moving on to another one. However, I found that after six weeks at the suburban site I was learning much about the other two sites as well. The sites were interactionally connected at all levels. There were regular meetings of the administrators from the three sites. A few of the staff (particularly consultants and supervisors) worked out of two sites. Moreover, the support staff occasionally relieved each other at different sites. There were frequent telephone conversations between staff members at different sites. There was also a gossip and rumor network. The staff often talked about the other sites in complimentary or critical ways, in the same way that members of large extended families know and talk about each other. For example, there were comments about the relocation of the urban center that happened just before I visited them: "I'm glad they're finally moving out of that old building; I don't know how they could work under those conditions." There was also a rumor at the suburban site about an alleged architectural error or incompleteness in the design of the bathrooms in the new buildings at the urban site: apparently some of the toilets had not been provided with room dividers. This story was passed on with amusement and prankish references to the "community bathrooms."

In my field work, I was referred to people across sites: "have you talked to X at urban? He's a good man, knows a lot about dreams; you should talk to him." One day there was confusion about where I was to meet a psychiatrist who consulted at both sites. I waited for him at the suburban office, but he did not come. The secretary who knew his schedule assured me that he would not come because, "he *never* comes here on Monday!" She assured me that the confusion was probably not caused by my error but by his. She explained that "he works in so many places he sometimes forgets what day it is."

The Newell Center had three sites and although each site was in a different part of the catchment area and had a distinct ethos, the agency functioned as one institution. There seemed to be frequent communication and both formal and informal networks between the sites. There were connections at all levels of the institutional hierarchy.

Newell: Suburban Site

The suburban center was located in a modern one-story office building on a main road with many businesses, retail stores, and restaurants, where the traffic was constant and noisy. The building had a large waiting room, large meeting rooms, a large patient lounge equipped with stove, refrigerator, blackboard, and round tables where much of the group work was done. There were also areas for accounting and record keeping, a business office, and a staff lounge, which was the hub of social interaction for the staff.

The staff lounge was equipped with a large table that could accommodate ten for lunch, a stove, refrigerator, storage cabinets, a large notice board, and a copying machine. The room was in constant use, for coffee breaks, for lunch, for copying, for gossip and for informal meetings. "I'll meet you in the staff room in an hour." There were meetings to wait for a late member of a luncheon excursion to restaurants. "If you're here, would you please tell her we went to the restaurant across the street!"

I could spend a whole day in the staff lounge waiting for two fifty-minute appointments (one in the morning, one in the afternoon) and not spend more than 10 minutes alone! Therapists came in between patient appointments for coffee and snacks: people were making, heating, or eating their lunch in small groups. The janitorial staff came in at midmorning, when everyone else was working; and the clerical staff occasionally came for short breaks at midafternoon. Both therapists and support staff members came in to use the copying machine, and administrators came in to post notices on the notice board.

People talked to one another in the lounge and, therefore, they also talked to me. Conversation was general. There was some discussion about dreams. The most enthusiastic dream tellers were the staff of the day treatment program who had not been on the original list of therapists to interview. The day treatment staff members were young and had bachelor's degrees in psychology, social work, or nursing, but no advanced training, degrees, or licenses to do primary psychotherapy. They provided support, leadership, and group psychotherapy for the patients in the day treatment program. I discovered that this group had a tradition of sharing their dreams with each other frequently, especially in the morning. They worked closely together and as co-group leaders and had developed a feeling of being a team. It was a close-knit group.

I did not notice any other close-knit groups. Some of the therapists talked with each other across disciplines and there were staff meetings (I was only invited to one staff meeting in each of the Newell sites). There were supervision meetings and consultation meetings, which are usually multidisciplinary. Therapists in the same discipline did not gather together regularly. When people went out to lunch together, occasionally they went in mixed groups of therapists and clerical staff. But many times the secretaries, without therapists, went to lunch together. Each secretary knew the schedules of the therapists for whom they provided clerical support. They were very loyal to each other and to "their" therapists; therefore, they were very helpful to me: "You can catch her better at three o'clock; she's really exhausted, I don't think she'll want to talk to you today." As I talked with people at the suburban site of the Newell Center, one theme came up repeatedly from different points of view: changes in the center—some recent change and impending change.

Several of the therapists told me that the "agency" had changed greatly in a very short time span. It had grown within a few years from a few small storefront clinics to a mental health center that served a quarter of the county. I discovered that the growth had necessitated several new levels of administrative leadership and that soon the suburban center would move to the campus of a large area hospital. Meanwhile the services and the staff had expanded.

Those changes were alluded to in different ways by different people. One of the administrators said that the suburban center was feeling the "growth" more than the other sites and "growth is taxing on the staff." Some of the therapists spoke of "low morale" among the staff members. One of the social workers put it this way: "There's a lot of pressure to see a lot of clients because of the realities of financing, so the perspective of the place has changed. Because of our schedules we're all alone in our own little offices, uninvolved with others; we try to get out for lunch together but we're always in a hurry."

Another social worker told me that in spite of the interchange between the clerical staff and the clinical staff, they had some "differences" with each other. "Clerical staff feel that although the clinical staff are more educated they don't know the *real world*; clinical staff feel like the clerical staff are naive and don't know the complexities of people or themselves."

The "stress" at the suburban office was rumored at urban; when I asked why there was stress, there was always reference to the changes caused by the rapid growth of the agency, which was affecting the suburban site more directly than the other two sites.

Newell: Urban Site

By the time I went to the urban site, I knew some things about the people who worked there. I had heard about the place, and at least some of the staff had heard about me. I had been asked to postpone my visits until the move was completed.

The reconstructed warehouse was large and able to combine the outpatient clinic with the continuing treatment program. The therapy offices and meeting rooms were on the ground floor of one side of the building, and the continuing treatment section was on two levels at the other side. The large patient community room was on the first floor, and the continuing care offices were on the second floor. The staff lounge was a very large room, with, as yet, little furniture in it. It was not used frequently. I had an interview in the open staff lounge, and there was only one interruption.

I became aware of a sense of pride in the staff of the urban site. Their pride was communicated through their opinions of their working environment. There were many comments about the unsavory neighbors of the old building they had just vacated. They told me these things in the tone of people who tell their history and their war stories.

There was a sense of idealism in serving the poor and "bringing mental health to the disadvantaged." One of the social workers who had been there for many years put it this way: "You know, the building really doesn't matter as much as what happens when someone comes into it. We had a very good reputation in the community even in the old building. People aren't fooled by a fancy building. They come where they get help. Now the people who come here feel respected because we have provided this lovely building for them."

Another therapist, also a social worker, said that Newell Community Mental Health Center was founded by people who were interested in giving high-quality care and that, until recently, the whole center had retained the homelike quality of a private group practice. She wished that the agency would not become more rigid and formal as levels of leadership were added. A psychologist described the urban staff as having a "unique spirit, necessary to run the show."

My own observation of the urban staff was that people knew and trusted each other. Things were less regimented with regard to time, and space boundaries were less rigid. In the offices of the continuing treatment section, office doors were left open, and people were frequently in and out of each other's offices. Even the therapy offices seemed to be left open when not in session. People were accessible to each other. They seemed to be close to each other, and although they were not inhospitable to me, they did not seem as eager as the staff in the suburban office to engage me in conversation. They seemed to accept that I was there without needing to entertain me or to be entertained.

When I asked whether they were experiencing "stressful changes," they denied it. The move had not been stressful; it had been a relief. One of the case workers said: "Any difficulties we have are from a challenging job, not from anything else." Others said specifically that it was better to work at the urban site than the suburban one, but could not elaborate except to add that "it is a pleasure to work in a place where people are primarily pleasant."

Newell: Small Town-Rural Site

The small town site of the Newell Mental Health Center was situated in a reconstructed warehouse at the edge of the county in the vicinity of several rural communities. The site had no special programs or outreach efforts as the other two sites did, but was used as a clinic for mental health services and provided individual therapy, group therapy, and family therapy.

The building was not large, but the counseling rooms were spacious. Offices contained more personal belongings than the offices at the suburban and urban offices. One of the offices looked like a personal study area, and others also looked like they had been occupied and lived in for a long time. The atmosphere was relaxed, and boundaries of space and time were flexible and permeable. For example, I interviewed one of the secretaries in one of the therapist's offices with his permission while he was busy in another room. The secretaries in other sites did not have this kind of access to the therapists' offices.

It was the only site where people did not adhere to the fifty-minute units of time for speaking with me. In fact, when I approached one of the therapists who had been referred to me because of his interest in dreams and asked him for an appointment, he said, "Well, actually I happen to be free right now!" I had never interviewed someone without a prearranged appointment before coming to this site.

At the staff meeting, boundaries seemed to be fluid also. Chairs were brought in from a different room as a small room was rearranged to accommodate the group. Although business was conducted, food was offered and shared. At the meeting people spoke deliberately and unhurriedly with humor. There was a sense of group cohesiveness. Yet, it seemed as though the group "took me on" together. I was asked many questions with interest and curiosity, as well as caution. The whole group was interviewing me!

Several of the therapists and one of the secretaries had been there for more than five years. They knew the history of the whole center, not only the small town site. A therapist referred to himself as one of the founding fathers of Newell; another told me stories of the early days of the Newell Center.

The theme that recurred frequently in the interviews was one of "therapeutic freedom." It was perceived that the therapists in the urban and rural offices had retained some of the autonomy that characterized the early history of the center. "Therapy was a more creative sort of process in the earlier days of the agency than it is now. So if dreams are mentioned, the therapist feels less repressed; he is free to pursue them with the client." When I asked what was inhibiting the freedom and creativity, I was told the constraints of having to constantly increase financial productivity (this was referred to as *assembly-line mentality*) made the administration change the direction of the therapy itself. Again, I was told that the suburban office was feeling this kind of pressure more acutely than the other two sites. I was also told that staff members of the office were feeling some of the changes and were responding to them in their own way: "Decisions are being made up there in autocratic style now about what's happening down here so people here are more *protective of their own space!*"

In summary, although the three Newell sites functioned as one agency, the staff in each site had distinct perceptions of their own site, which was congruent with the opinions of the staffs of the other two sites.

The suburban site was perceived as growing fast in numbers, programs, and charges. There was anticipation of moving soon onto the campus of the large hospital that became a symbol of those changes. The anticipated loss of the old familiar building was a symbol of the loss of the old familiar little "agency" that was growing into a major provider of mental health in the county. Space and time boundaries were rigid, but the staff lounge provided a central meeting place.

The staff at the urban site, which had just effected a move from an old unsuitable building to a small, clean, newly reconstructed building, felt invigorated and retained the idealism to which they were accustomed. They would continue to serve the poor and bring mental health to the disadvantaged in the new building. Space and time boundaries were less rigid and more open. The lounge with no door and the bathroom with no walls were symbols of this openness that some of the therapists understood to be short lived.

The staff at the small town–rural site retained their own place and had no prospects of moving, but they were very cognizant of what was going on at the other two sites. They had a sense of history and compared present times with the good old days of "therapeutic freedom." Space and time boundaries were more fluid among the staff. The group was cohesive and they encountered me, a stranger, cautiously by interviewing me together as a team. They were indeed "protective of their space."

At the Newell sites I interviewed thirty-seven people: three were physicians (all men); ten were psychologists (seven men and three women); three were nurses (all women); twelve were social workers (four men and eight women), and nine women were on the support staff.

Two Dreams

In comparing the Riverpool Center with the Newell Center we see a different sort of idealism in each one. At Riverpool, the idealism was related to learning and excellence, to competency and efficiency, but these concerns were evident in each therapist individually. There did not seem to be a concern for the efficiency of the whole system. The staff did not feel a sense of community. There was an atmosphere of disconnected isolation.

At Newell there was a sense of community and teamwork, but there was also a fear of losing the old idealism of outreach and preventive mental health. Members of the staff at the suburban site were feeling the discomfort of the projected changes most acutely. However, there was a sense in the three Newell sites of losing the comfortable familiar agency and moving on to become a major mental health provider for the county.

In my interviews I asked people to tell me their theory of dreams, their ideas and experiences in dream telling and psychotherapy. They told me their dreams, their client's dreams, and their interpretations of both; they told me what they thought of their work and the place where they worked. At times I received a glimpse of what they thought of themselves and how they experienced themselves.

A major assumption of this study is that dreams are not just private fantasies but they also represent shared symbolic structures of the local and large social environment. To illustrate this assumption I will, at this point, include two dreams: one told by a postdoctoral clinical psychologist at the Riverpool Center and one told by an administrator of the Newell Center. The dreams, and the dreamer's thoughts and feelings about them, reflected each dreamer's concerns as well as structures of the local social environment of each center.

The dream from the Riverpool psychologist was told to me by the first respondent to my study. He was very eager to be part of the study.

The dream report: "The dream is not very clear. It is hard to remember all the details. I know I'm dreaming of this difficult client, but I don't remember all the details. I'm being boxed into a corner or something like that. This has something to do with my supervisor. I have to give a presentation of the case at Grand Rounds, and I'm being criticized for what is happening."

His comments on the dream: "Working with this kind of client has always been very stressful for me. She is very manipulative with her suicidal gesturing. At times I feel put on the spot. So when she starts to do that I dream of her, and I forget the details (laughing). A good example of repression don't you think?"

The dream told by the Newell administrator related to a client, too. The dream is about trying to get his client into the hospital.

The dream report: "I dream about going through the work; working with the family to get him in."

His comments about the dream: "I see the dream as some emotional attachment for me, both with the patient and with the site, where I had done some work before. Maybe it refers to struggles I engage in, in terms of whether it's easy or hard to get people hospitalized, or hard to get them out once you get them in. Maybe the dream is just a replaying of what's currently important. There is a kind of ending experience for me and a getting ready to move on."

Each dreamer's comments on the dream related the dream to his own *personal* symbolism about his work, his client, and himself. However, each dream also described images that were derived from and reflective of the *local social situation* at the respective center.

The Riverpool dream reflected the isolation, the concern with learning and being evaluated, as well as the difficulty with remembering all the details of a very taxing environment.

The Newell dream was concerned with the preparation for hospitalization at a time when one large part of the center was in the process of preparing to literally move onto the campus of the hospital. The dreamer also said he understood the dream to illustrate the concerns with the effect of hospitalization; he introduced the theme of ending at a time when the staff were worried about the move and concerned about losing the old ideals.

ANALYTIC CONCEPTS AND RESEARCH QUESTIONS

Each dreamer shared with his dream his experience of being a *self*. The dreams contained and evoked thoughts, feelings, and motivations. Each dreamer began examining his own awareness of his dream and himself with a critical eye. The first dreamer judged himself to be repressing details; the second evaluated himself to have emotional attachments that might prove troublesome in his professional role. There was an element of conscience along with reflexive consciousness.

However, the dream also contains information about each one as a social *person*: about his professional roles and relationships and rules related to those. There were expectations that each act in a certain way as a morally responsible adult who was also a therapist. One dream portrayed the rigors of being supervised and criticized; the other reenacted the whole gamut of difficult ethical dilemmas related to mental health hospitalization. Moreover, reflective self awareness was also an expectation that each took for granted.

It is not uncommon for people in Western societies to speak of *person* and *self* as synonyms. Westerners are also prone to describe themselves subjectively as individuals and psychological entities rather than as members of society. For this reason I want to distinguish the *person* as a member of society, invested with social capacities and responsibilities, to be the author of actions considered to have a reason (Mauss 1938; Beck 1965; Fortes 1973; Harris 1989) from the *self* as a product of social experience, symbolically able to take the role of the other, to look into oneself as in a looking glass; a self capable of reflective self-regard (Cooley 1964 [1902]; Mead 1934 [1913]; Goffman 1959).

At points of intersection, the dream connects the study of humans as biological entities, as selves, and as persons. When studying dreaming in humans as *biological entities*, scientists assume biological givens such as a normally functioning brain, the capacity for language and speech, and the capacity for remembering and telling. The research in dream psychology, the research in content analysis, and cognitive studies all assume these capacities.

When studying dreams and dream interpretation in humans as *experiencing selves*, the dream is seen as an experienced phenomenon evoking feelings and motivations that allows symbolic dialogue between parts of the self; it is a stage in which the dreamer is creator, actor, director, and producer. There are different schools of clinical thought that look at dreams in this way. Clinical research has the burden of attempting to do research while regarding each *self* as unique. Clinical case studies, life histories, a few cross-cultural studies, and phenomenological research on dreams are attempts to study unique subjects. It is this kind of research the therapists I interviewed were most familiar with, although many had read studies on dream psychology.

When studying dreams, dream telling, and dream interpretation in humans as *social persons*, a dream report is seen as a social communication that is part of the constellation of ideas and beliefs and a part of the customary patterns of behavior. Dream telling is seen as having a specific social function and inseparable from the particular social situation. The dream is told by persons with specific social roles and capacities to other persons with specific roles and capacities. Most of the dream studies that have been done in humans as social persons have been done on dreamers of non-Western societies.

In this research I use the analytic concept of *person* to study dreams, dream telling, and dream interpretation among the therapists and staff members in two community mental health centers. I show that there is a local and traditional "mythology" of dream telling and dream interpretation. I show that psychotherapists have certain capacities related to dream telling, including the capacity and responsibility to engage in self-reflection. I describe and analyze the cluster of capacities and entitlements that are symbolically related to the social functions of different psychotherapists in the two community mental health centers; namely, psychiatrists, psychologists, social workers, and nurses.

In the following chapters, I answer the following research questions:

1. What is the local constellation of ideas and beliefs about dream telling and the perceived capacities to interpret dreams?

2. How are perceptions about dream telling among therapists and staff of the community mental health centers related to preparation for and enactment of roles and designations of status in the institutional hierarchies?

In Chapter 2, I examine the therapist's understanding of personhood. There is a struggle between the public and private aspects of personhood and the personal and professional domains of action. For Americans in general, dreams are a private matter; for American therapists, dreams are understood to be part of the professional domain. There is a relationship of the therapists' approach to their own dreams and to the dreams of their clients. I show that for therapists reflexivity is a social expectation.

Chapters 3 and 4 are investigations in response to the first research question related to the local constellation of ideas and beliefs about dreams, dream telling, and dream interpretation among the therapists and staff in the two community mental health centers. Chapter 3 deals with the research question in relation to dream telling. Dream telling is considered private and intimate; only close family members and intimate friends are told dreams. Therapists are expected to hear private information. They are also therefore expected to have the capacity to hear dreams, "read minds"; therefore, they can interpret dreams. Therapists themselves believe that dream exploration is appropriate only in long-term therapy for "high functioning" clients.

The discussion about ideas and beliefs is continued in Chapter 4 in relation to dream interpretation. Therapist and staff opinions about dream theory and their interpretation of three specific dreams show a "mythology of dream interpretation" that derives from a popularization of psychoanalysis. The dream interpretations also reflect the local concerns of each setting.

In Chapter 5 I analyze the question of how the imputed capacity to hear and interpret dreams relates to designations of status and preparation for and enactment of psychotherapeutic roles. In the first part I consider the agentive capacities of psychiatrists and psychologists, and in the second part I examine those of nurses and social workers. I show that although all psychotherapists are generally perceived to have the capacity to read minds and interpret dreams, not all psychotherapists have the same social entitlement capacities in the local setting, the larger professional groups, and the larger society.

In Chapter 6 I present conclusions drawn from the previous chapters related to *persons* who dream, tell, and interpret dreams.

II

The Psychotherapist: "Simply as a Person"

INTRODUCTION

Joe is a psychotherapist. He has had clinical and research experience and also administrative responsibilities at one of the CMHCs. He was cordial and open to having me do research at the CMHC. He was helpful as one of the gatekeepers to the center. When, after having spoken to many of the therapists and staff, I telephoned him to ask him if he would also be willing to participate in my study, he seemed surprised. He said, "Oh! You want to interview me? As a 'person'!"[1]

During the interview we had an opportunity to talk further about his comment on "person." Joe explained that his work consisted of many different roles. "I see myself as all these together—not separate: I teach, I do therapy, I do administration. I do a lot of that stuff; it's hard to categorize myself." He also explained that at the center key people with whom he worked understood each role, but the situation was more complex in a nonprofessional setting. "I would say that in terms of my role it's hard for them to treat me 'simply as a person,' so that, lots of times I'll get questions about, gee, my grandmother is not feeling well and we think she's depressed, or people will defer in other ways to the professional role rather than remain in the neighbor role" . . . "people respond much more to the role than to the 'person'."

In this chapter I discuss the therapists' understanding of person. There is a struggle to keep in balance the personal and professional arenas of action to minimize incompatibility in the public and private aspects of their roles. For Americans, dreams are a private matter. For American therapists, dreams *and* privacy are understood to also be part of the professional arena. There is a relationship between the therapists' approach to their own dreams and to the dreams of their clients. The concepts used in this analysis, namely, the concepts of *person* and *self*, will help elucidate what they say about dreams. I show that for psychotherapists reflexivity is not only an experience, but also a socially imputed expectation and capacity.

The use of the terms *person* and *self* have been, and in some ways are, part of the native environment of the scholars who use the concepts analytically. Many philosophers, historians, sociologists, and social anthropologists are Western *persons*; and psychologists, social psychologists, and cultural anthropologists who study the *self* also experience role taking and reflexivity. It might be easy when doing ethnographic research in Western societies to fail to distinguish between analytic concepts and emic terms. This could create confusion.

This problem, however, is not insurmountable, especially if it is accounted for rather than assumed not to exist. Moreover, it is essential to understand terms emically in whatever language they are spoken even though, and especially if, the language resembles our own. The task remains to describe and examine field data in the light of abstract analytic concepts to discover patterns and principles of social behavior. The task is also to test and develop social theory by elucidating analytic concepts even though they may also be used as native terms.

ANALYTIC CONCEPTS OF PERSON AND SELF

Mauss (1938) analyzes the concepts of *personne* (person) and *moi* (self) in a historical perspective. He traces the evolution of Western notions of *personne* (person) as historically emerging from the concept of *personnage* (role) and *persona* (Latin for mask or face) to the *personne morale* (social person) who is conscious, independent, autonomous, free, and responsible. Mauss adds that the birth of *moral consciousness* is the originator of conscience, which is an aspect progressively added to the concept of legal right. (*La conscience morale introduit la conscience dans la conception juridique du droit*, Mauss 1934: 278). This evolution continues until a sense of *moi* (self) develops. The self is a psychological person, an *individu* (individual) possessed with metaphysical and moral value (Figure 1).

Fortes (1973, 1983) understands the notion of person in the Maussian sense to be universal, "intrinsic to the very nature and struc-

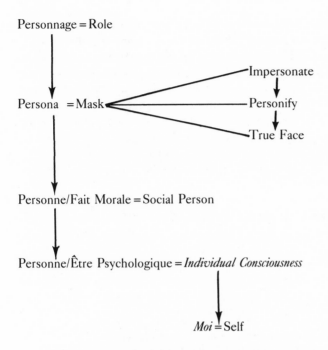

**Figure 1. Mauss's Schema of the Evolution of Person
in Western Society**

ture of human society and human social behavior everywhere" (1973: 288). He perceives the ideas and beliefs about personhood to be channeled into daily activities. More specifically, looked at objectively, persons *show* themselves to be who they are supposed to be by acting with and through distinctive qualities, capacities, and roles; looked at subjectively it is a question of how an actor *knows* himself or herself to be. Fortes calls the objective and the subjective aspects the "*two aspects of personhood*" (Fortes 1973), although he mentions the work of the American social philosopher Mead.

Mead (1934) posits the development of the *self* as the ability to take roles. The self acts in accordance with a generalized set of expectations and definitions that are internalized. This is done by the ability to see oneself from another's point of view. Thus the *self* and the mind are social products.

Harris (1989) also understands the notion of person to be universal and makes analytic distinctions between the *individuals*, conceptualized as human beings as living entities; *selves* as centers of being and experience, and *persons* as members of society with socially imputed agentive capacities and responsibilities; namely, judgmental capacities, social entitlement capacities, and nonpatent capacities that she calls *mystical*. Both Fortes and Harris elucidate their concepts through data from traditional societies. Fortes acknowledges that in these societies it is easy to observe the basic principles of *identification* in *persons* (Fortes 1983: 401). Similarly, Harris states that although the concepts of individual, self, and person could be applied unilaterally in Taita, in contemporary USA there are differing conceptualizations of them within the same society (Figure 2).

Individual: Members of humankind capable of language, discourse, and significance

Self: Locus of experience; product of social experience; capable of reflexivity

Person: Agents in society, with

> *Judgmental Capacities*: locally imputed capacity to embody in conduct the local standard of logicality, factuality, and morality

> *Society Entitlement Capacities*: the capacity to embody in one's conduct the rights, duties, freedoms, and constraints of specific social roles

> *Mystical Capacities*: special capacities that are ordinarily hidden from the ordinary day-to-day processes of construal; assumed to exist; not recognizable in ordinary ways

**Figure 2. Harris's Schema of Analytic Distinctions
in the Concept of Person**

La Fontaine (1985), in an essay commenting on Mauss and Fortes's ideas of *person*, refers to the ethnographic material from four traditional societies, concluding that the concept cannot be considered out of context because the understanding of *person* in each society is shaped by the principles that underlie the major social institutions, the nature of authority, and the succession to office in that society.

Mauss's concept of *person* is relevant to this study because it is in keeping with the subjective way in which members of Western societies describe themselves. Yet his temporal evolutionary progression is not helpful because it implies that the social aspects of the concept elucidated in the early part of the essay are outdated and no longer applicable to synchronic analyses of contemporary societies.

Mead's concept of the *self* is also relevant to this study because of the way Westerners are prone to describe themselves in terms of personal experience. It is also helpful because of the skillful way in which he and symbolic interactionists who have followed him have intertwined the experiencing *self* with the social *role*. Yet although role-theory and self-theory describe, respectively, the context and process of the experience, the aspect of agency is not addressed by them. By *agency* I mean the capacity and intentionality of social actors. The aspect of identity is also problematic as seen exclusively through the concept of the emerging self of symbolic interaction theory.

Harris makes useful analytic distinctions between the concepts of person and self, but chooses not to deal with subjectivity. Fortes retains the aspects of introspection and subjectivity in his understanding of *person*, not straying far afield from Mauss though choosing, unlike Mauss, to emphasize the social aspects of the person. The concept works neatly for Fortes because he is analyzing a "homogeneous" society. He tells us that in these societies the only way you can *know* who you are is to *show* it all the time. However, my data show that Western therapists *know* who they are by *not* showing who they are in certain designated activities some of the time.

Therefore, in my analysis, I will make the useful distinction between person and self that Harris proposes but will work with the subjective and reflexive aspects of self only as they relate to the concept of person in the way Fortes does.

THE PSYCHOTHERAPIST: PROFESSIONAL SETTING AND HOME BASE

I return now to Joe, the clinical psychologist who wants to be treated "simply as a person." On the surface, it seems as though he and his neighbor are having a misunderstanding on the appropriateness of topics of conversation. The neighbor wants to introduce in neighborly conversation the topic of the depressed grandmother. Joe wishes the topic was not introduced. However, there is no social rule designating the topic of depressed grandmothers as inappropriate between neighbors. In fact, if Joe had not been a therapist or if his neighbor had not known that he was a therapist, there would have been less of a problem. However, Joe occupies a role in society that makes him an expert on depression, and the neighbor may be counting on his expertise to get some answers (at least Joe perceives it that way), and in so doing violates the simple reciprocal relationship of neighbor to neighbor. If the neighbor had been a child and had said, "please sir, my grandmother has hurt herself; you're a doctor, can you help us fix it?" Joe would have been less uncomfortable. He might have explained to the child that there are different kinds of doctors, and he might have continued to talk to the child about the grandmother. However, with an adult who should know better Joe probably feels isolated and perplexed. He does not seem to be uncomfortable because he is being asked to play two roles at once. On the contrary, by his own admission, he is used to playing several roles that are compatible with each other. He is known to some people at work as a therapist, as a teacher, and as an administrator. He also thinks of himself as all those things at once. He said to me that he does not like to categorize himself, which I understood to mean that he does not like to think of himself as broken up into different roles that he occupies simultaneously or in sequence. He likes to think of himself as one continuous identity. However, in the matter of being both a therapist and a neighbor to the same person he feels uncomfortable and he tells us why. He tells us two things: first, it is difficult for people to treat him "simply as a person"; second, people respond more to the role than the "person."

I will examine these statements separately along with other similar statements made by therapists. However, I would like to note at this point that this anecdote is similar to several others told to me about how therapists regard being told dreams in a social setting. They find themselves wondering whether the dream is told casually and in fun as a conversation starter, intimately as to a trusted friend, or whether the teller wants an interpretation from an expert. They also have to make a decision about what to do in response. They can join the fun and add to the casualness by making a joke or changing the subject. They can take the trusted friend aside and at least hear the dream (this is more usual when the friend is also in the mental health field). They can also become poker-faced and make evasive maneuvers like statements about not working on vacation or like leaving the room. All of those responses have been used by therapists who have talked to me. This has made me realize that to tell a dream to a therapist is different from telling a dream to anyone else. When I have asked them whether people have actually approached them in social contexts with dream material, I have been given two typical answers: first, that people *do* approach them and want expert answers, being obtuse about their social infringement; and second, that people are more guarded with dream material around them, being sensitive to the inappropriateness of the situation or being unwilling to have an expert stranger know more about them than they want to reveal.

These statements were substantiated by observation in the staff lounge at the suburban Newell site. The day treatment staff who are not, strictly speaking, professional psychotherapists were telling each other and me their dreams. The therapists who came into the lounge for coffee would exchange knowing glances and leave the room as soon as possible in silence and with obvious discomfort. Later in interviews with me, one therapist commented rather condescendingly that he was not surprised at all at the level of dream sharing in the lounge; another therapist said that he was surprised at their lack of guardedness in telling dreams; another that the tellers must not know that dreams were so revealing of self. When I spoke to the dream sharer about the incident he said that the dream he had chosen to share in the lounge was similar to the kind of dreams he shares periodically with his coworkers from the day treatment center, some of whom were in the lounge on that day. He was aware of the fast retreat made by certain psychotherapists because when I mentioned it he explained that they sometimes "get uptight about things like that."

The staff lounge was an open place designated for the use of all staff members, both professional and nonprofessional. The staff members were expected to take a break from work and to exchange general light conversation usually about topical events. There was no shop talk. The protocol was to be friendly, pleasant, and not to get to seriously out of role. It was a place where one can be noticed by professionals in different disciplines, observed by persons in jobs across role boundaries, and contacted, understood, or scrutinized by one's peers.

In the relationship with the neighbor, Joe was primarily in the role of nonprofessional interacting with a neighbor in a place not designated for work, although his professional expertise had become the untimely topic of conversation. In the staff lounge the therapists were primarily in the role of professionals but in a place designated for nonprofessional social discourse, where topics of general concern were allowed. For the nonprofessional staff dreams were a matter of casual conversation, appropriately introduced in that setting. For the therapist the topic introduces a role convergence that made the topic disconcerting, because for him dream telling fell under both categories.

There is yet another scenario that is most upsetting to therapists. It is the eventuality of being in a public place, like a place of recreation in a nonprofessional capacity and meeting one of their clients. The circumstances are eloquently described by a psychologist thus:

> this [city] is a fairly small community, so your "personal life" may be affected by your role and status in the community when you'd like it not to be, so that your degrees of freedom are reduced; for example (this happens much more to some people I work with than to me), they'll describe being out in a restaurant with someone, and they'll want to have fun, and they find people in the restaurant who are their clients, and the clients will be looking at them, reasonably so, recording the behavior and watching. So that there's a sense of being observed, being on stage, or being in charge, or something. That steals something from being spontaneous.

These three examples present the psychotherapists in situations where their actions become problematic to themselves by virtue of being in settings and engaging in activities that might occasion the inappropriate crossing of role boundaries. In these situations they perceive that the role is "too much with them"; they feel scrutinized and constricted. In the words of Joe, their "personal life" is affected and "people respond to the role rather than to the person."

The problem as described can be summarized thus: on the surface it appears to be a problem of role performance, role confusion, role strain, and role incompatibility specifically as it relates to the psychotherapist role and to the activities of dream telling in a complex society. A more comprehensive and discriminating examination of the facts, however, will show that, although role problems are indeed present, they are indicative of the underlying question of how *persons* such as psychotherapists show who they are through their activities and attitudes. This will be reflective of the specific customs and norms of their particular setting within the larger society.

Role theorists have included in their definitions and descriptions of role two important aspects; namely, the aspect of role as a social position, a place in a field of social relations, and the idea of expected behavior associated with the position (Dahrendorf 1968 [1958]; Banton 1965; Emmett 1966; Jackson 1972). The dilemma for role theorists has been to keep in focus and perspective the points of view of both the role position and the role occupant. But, as we have seen from the ethnographic data when the social actor's activities are contextualized in daily activities, certain complexities appear that are difficult to explain. The concept of role, by itself, does not help analyze the data because it is too narrow. It does help describe and compare ethnographic data. It provides a descriptive view of the structure and is helpful only if related to the structuring principles inherent in the system itself. The psychotherapist role can best be understood when it is related to the concept of person as it arises in the professional domain and other domains within the society. I use the concept of domain borrowed from Fortes (1969: 95–97) because it helps organize the analysis of *person*. A domain is a large structural arena of social relations that gives the social analyst the opportunity to derive the social principles as daily activity is observed. The professional domain is a sector of the politico-jural domain. It comprises a whole range of distinctive social relations, customs, roles, and norms apparent in educational preparation, licensing, prestige, professional societies, standardized examinations, fee for service contractual relations, regulatory bodies, peer control, paraprofessionals, record keeping, and legal accountability. The role and setting incompatibilities evident in the therapists' interactions discussed earlier can be explained when we see the role as it is distinguished and signified within the professional domain. From the point of view of a *person* acting in accordance with norms and rules of the professional domain, that domain becomes the locus of a central principle for social action. From within that domain, other domains of social action become external. The intrusion of roles and rules from an external domain cause an odd but predictable assortment of role complexities and contextual problems (Figure 3).

Only one domain can be central and primary in a given context at a given time.

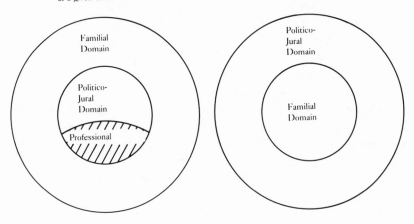

When domains converge the professional aspect remains primary for a psychotherapist.

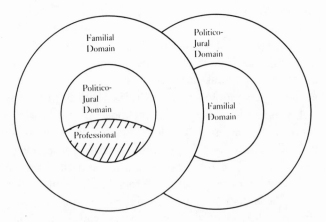

Figure 3. Fortes's Domain Theory

In this section situations are described as they are revealed through therapists' activities and attitudes related to their professional and home settings that show the complexity in their roles and relationships. Dream telling is one of the activities that has different significance for professional and nonprofessonal settings and roles. The concept of role helps describe and further display the complexities in relationships and the problems encountered by therapists as they show their personhood in different settings.

The next part of this section will focus on (1) the professional and (2) the nonprofessional aspects of the *person*, respectively. The expectations, obligations, entitlements, and capacities imputed on therapists are discussed. Fortes's concept of domain helps organize the data.

The Person in Relation to the Professional Role

In complex societies roles are differentiated and specialized to a much higher degree than in simple societies, where roles are multiplex. Therefore, it would follow that the *persons* who occupy the roles are more likely to expect role distinctions and boundaries to be very clear. This is particularly true in the professional arena where roles are distinguished by special regulation, convention, and external signs such as titles that proffer prestige. It is also customary that the professional *person* observe a degree of social distance from the client (Banton 1965: 151–171; Fortes 1969: 99).

I found this to be particularly true of the psychotherapists I interviewed. There was an insistence on the clarity of roles and the need to formulate an understanding of the role boundaries. Most of the people I interviewed seemed to be familiar with the role of subject in a research project. Most people were comfortable in that role: they wanted to fill the answers on the questionnaire; they were tolerant of the tape recorder and perfunctory about signing the consent form. Talking *about* dreams and *about* being psychotherapists were topics they enjoyed, but there was some discomfort when I would produce the text of a dream on a piece of paper and ask them what they thought about it. Most therapists assumed I wanted them to interpret it. When they asked me whose dream it was, I would tell them it was a dream that had been published in a book. One of the psychologists, however, said more: "Where did you get this? I would hate it to be your dream, for example." After I assured him that it was not my dream I asked him why that was important. He said, "because I would feel kind of awkward about that, we don't have that kind of a relationship or a contract. I think a "person" should be entitled by a special relationship to tell a dream." He said he would also have felt awkward if the dream belonged to a person I knew, like a friend or a relative, again "because we don't have this kind of a contract." The role of subject in a research project was compatible with the setting of our meeting, provided it was understood that I was not a client or he a psychotherapist during our interaction, even for a small part of the interview. After that was made clear, he continued the interview with no reservations.

Other examples of the need for clear boundaries and clear role definitions came out in statements that appeared to be efforts to protect their nonprofessional lives from their professional roles. I was told that to be a good therapist it is important to separate one's professional role from home life. A young social worker said, "I'm having a hard time separating my day here at work from my day at home. When I go to sleep at night I'm dreaming of my clients. Not anything dramatic—just a lot of work—I feel like I just worked all night. I think the dreams are telling me I need to separate the two."

The examples abounded in terms of statements about objectivity toward clients. Many therapists said they were not objective enough about their clients; many agreed that the correct blend of objectivity and subjectivity was ideal. One young psychology trainee said that she was sure Freud had been more objective with his patients than she could be with hers. Her comment about objectivity was occasioned by a dream in which the client and she were in a recreational area together and she felt that the client was her sister. She interpreted the dream as a "warning of countertransference." This interpretation was accepted by her supervisor who told her to monitor her relationship with her client so that the feelings would not get too personal. Another psychologist talked about trying to remain an outsider to the situation so that she could remain objective enough to think of a solution to the problem. Some of the therapists responded with alarm when they dreamed about encountering a client in a social setting. I will include only two such dreams.

Dream of a young psychology trainee:

> I dreamed about one particular client I have here; he was in the dream, and it was in a social setting. I think we were in a bar or something (I remember that he was very close to my age). There

was dancing, and I was socializing with friends (I don't remember who the friends were) and the reason the client stood out was because he showed up there at all. Initially when he approached me he was like a friend who was talking and chit-chatting, and then I realized—it dawned on me—I felt myself moving out of the situation, and saying, this is one of the clients I have been working with, what are you doing here! I remember acting friendly but very superficially, and then I remember telling my friends after I realized who he was, and that is all I remember about the dream.

Dream of a nurse who had been a psychotherapist for more than ten years:

I remember at the time I had not paid much attention to how angry I was at this patient for a long time. It seemed he never came to the appointments on time. He came to about every fifth appointment. Very irritating kind of person, very passive aggressive. I just ignored the fact of how angry I was becoming, and, one night I had this dream about him in which he was standing outside my door asking to come in the house—at my home! (I *never* have patients to my house!) Well, he wanted to come in; finally (nervous laughter) in the dream I said, no, I'm not going to let you in; enough is enough, go away, or I'll call the police. I remember I was furious, and then I woke up and said, "whoa!"

Her comments about her dream:

Initially I was appalled that I wouldn't let somebody in who wanted to come into my house—also I was a little scared that I was so angry—this was the last straw. This person was invading my life. Then I started saying to myself: "Wow, you really are angry with this guy, you need to do something different in the therapy to make it tolerable 'cause you're going to end up doing something terrible to him." Well, I did share my frustration with him although I didn't tell him the dream. It was a kind of self-awareness: this dream indicates how close I have become to these people.

These dreams are not unusual for therapists, and although the reaction is not always so intense, the theme usually relates to inap-

58   Dreams and Professional Personhood

propriate closeness with clients and unclear boundary issues in role interaction that point to the possibility of inappropriate action.

None of the dreams that I was told were about inappropriate sexual relations with clients, but most of the many dreams of clients were interpreted as pointing to such unfortunate potentialities. One psychologist said, "there must be something seductive in my relationship with this client which I'm not totally aware of." Her dream was not explicitly sexual.

Clear boundaries in professional relationships, maintaining appropriate distance from clients and patients, and self-inspection appear to be everpresent expectations of the psychotherapy role. They seemed to be standards against which they were continuously checking themselves. One could see in the self-awareness a conscientiousness that, as Mauss pointed out in his essay, was the hallmark of the *social person* with moral consciousness. Dreams were used to make them aware of how they were playing the role.

This use of their dreams was not just an implicit action that I observed, they also talked about it explicitly. Most people told me that dreams were a way of becoming aware of themselves, "a way to self-inspect," sometimes even a way of making them anxious about things that they were not anxious about in order to examine their life.

One social worker who had been a therapist for more than ten years, said it most eloquently. Speaking about his dreams, he said:

I puzzle and wonder about them. It kind of alerts me to maybe some sort of issue or some sort of conflict that I ought to be paying more attention to. Work a little harder at trying to resolve. It's almost like the red light on the dashboard, you know, where a thing goes off where your oil is getting low, or your engine is overheating. Check out the machine to see if everything is OK, or otherwise you're going to have a problem—a warning light indicator that there is something that I need to attend to; some changes I need to make in my life or some sort of decision I need to make, or I'm off on the wrong track and there is sort of some trouble brewing.

Not everyone was as eloquent and not everyone used dreams as intentionally, but many who did not said they *ought* to be more self-aware and they wished they knew how to use dreams better. One young psychiatrist told me that, although he did not pay much attention to his dreams, he thought that they helped process information he already had so that when he awakened in the morning, he would have a solution to a problem. One thirty-year-old man said that he did not remember his dreams and had read that dreams were due to the random firing of neurons so there was *no reason* to remember them. The implication was that he would try to remember them if he had a good reason to do so. Most of the therapists to whom I spoke said that dreams did help them become aware of themselves, and that self-awareness was an important attribute of the therapist role.

The expectation that they have the capacity for "introspection," "insight," "self-awareness," "self-inspection," and "self-knowledge" (these were all words that they used) was accepted and taken for granted, although there were different opinions about the expectation and different degrees of comfort, acquiescence, or compliance with the role. Other expectations, based on the expectations of self-awareness, self-knowledge, and wisdom, were even more difficult or impossible to achieve. One psychologist who was expressing the difficulty of being "observed" by clients in a nonprofessional social setting put it this way: "I think there's some expectation that your own life, that your own issues are resolved completely and there's something you've discovered: a mastery of life, or something! Healed completely! Something like that. There's some fantasies about therapists that they don't have any problems or issues—stuff like that."

Another expectation and capacity they described as being attributed to them was the capacity not only to know themselves insightfully, but also to "analyze" and "know" others. Thus, the capacity to "read minds," which therapists were expected to have, was linked to the expectation that they engage in reflective behavior. When I asked how therapists gained these abilities, I was given one typical answer in many different forms: to be a therapist you need good educational preparation that includes professional experience *and* you need to be the right kind of "person." These two poles describing attributes were important to possess together, and therapists were emphatic about conveying to me the indispensability of each. On the one hand, there were definite, distinctive, predictable, and established norms, customs, and rituals of entry into the professions, such as educational traditions, clinical programs, and licensing and certification requirements designed to protect the public from charlatans and incompetents who would incur legal liability. On the other hand, there were descriptions, at best indefinite, of a "person" who was variously described as empathic, insightful, honest, and possessing a skill for forming interpersonal relationships; not a mere functionary but a person of character. Arguments on both poles abounded, and there was general agreement that the role consisted of both and conferred prestige. One young social worker told me: "Maybe it's just the name outside the door with the initials after it. It's amazing how much respect people give me and I'm no older than their children." This young woman's experience was the same as Joe's who found that people deferred to the professional role. The more a role is interdependent with other roles, the more likely it is to be distinguished by outward signs. Role signs indicate the special rights and obligations in the immediate setting or in all relations in which the parties might be involved (Banton 1965). When therapists spoke to me, they explained carefully the nuances in the differences of their positions. One experienced social worker told me that when he was younger he used to want to call himself a therapist rather than a social worker. A nurse told me she calls herself a therapist rather than a nurse because of the higher prestige connected to being a therapist in comparison to a nurse. A young social worker told me that he was *not* a therapist; he was a *psycho*therapist! He regarded psychotherapist as more prestigious because a psychotherapist does primary therapy, whereas a social worker who does casework can be called a therapist. (He was the only one who explicitly made this distinction.)

Most of the therapists said that a good education was a very important asset, and they did not mind prominently displaying the signs of their expertise. In fact, they were expected to do so. The nuances of rank and prestige went along with the higher education and training. The training for psychotherapy was usually added to traditional professional degrees. There are differences in rank, prestige, and job level between a nurse, a psychiatric nurse, and a certified clinical specialist in psychiatric nursing; similarly between a social worker, a psychiatric social worker, and a certified social worker; and there are differences between a college graduate with a major in psychology, a guidance counselor, a clinical psychologist, and a research psychologist. I was also told that the "premiers" in psychotherapy specialized "in depth" in one approach or school of psychotherapy. They took many years of training in the one area. I was told the importance of continuing in educational programs, but I was also told regularly and in no uncertain terms that education was not, by itself, the most important marker of a good therapist: "It's not the degree that counts, it's the 'person'," or "I think that the degrees and qualifications of the person in terms of what's in a name, quickly dissipate when a relationship is formed." One of the administrative secretaries who had been in therapy herself talked of her therapist in this way: "His credentials were not what I was looking at. I was looking at the person." An experienced psychiatrist told me that when she made a referral, she referred to the "person" not to the kind of training they had had.

On the other end of the pole there was great concern about being associated by reference to people who called themselves therapists and whose credentials were intangibly "personal" but not standardized. For example, one young psychiatrist was emphatic in describing both poles in the same interview. He gave me the following standard description of a good psychotherapist. "I think the individual 'person' and how a 'person' relates to people irrespective of their particular orientation, or dogma, or theory is an essential ingredient in good psychotherapy." Within one minute he was telling me his concern on the other pole of the description. "There are all kinds of quacks, I mean some people would never go to a psychiatrist. They would go to see a psychic, they will spend a fortune telling someone with dubious credentials, interpreting their dreams, reading their palms, and foretelling the future. I think a majority of people think psychiatry is not a specialty of medicine. They think it is a lot of mumbo-jumbo!"

The psychotherapist is expected to be eligible for and successfully complete designated courses of study and experience and pass several levels of examinations, as well as licensing and certification requirements, which are a part of several professional associations. Each level of achievement places the incumbent in a functional and hierarchical position within a professional group. These levels of achievement confer the capacity to practice psychotherapy at different levels of competence with a well-defined set of special privileges and responsbilities. However, another set of capacities, less well defined, describe various qualities including the capacity for introspection, the capacity to separate one's own personal issues from the client's issues, and the capacity to preserve professional boundaries by remaining objective. There is a tradition of interpretation of one's own dreams as a means to self-awareness. Several therapists who did not use dreams in that way said they *should* do so. One therapist had read in the popular and professional literature that dreams were a biological phenomenon with no meaning. He discouraged clients from telling their dreams during therapy and did not pay attention to his own dreams. Others read these same reports about dreams, but did not change their behavior because of them. I did not talk to any therapist or lay person who thought that qualities of introspection and skill with relationships were not important for therapists, although they told of therapeutic approaches in their professional work that did not emphasize or use insight orientation.

Nonprofessional Aspects of the Person

When therapists described their professional role and their actions related to it, they often juxtaposed aspects of themselves related to their work with what they called my "personal life" or "my home life." In this section I examine aspects of the therapist's life that are separate from the professional role. The discussion so far has centered around situations when issues of professional import intruded themselves on "personal life." Therapists also attempted to keep problems and issues of their personal lives separate from their work and to maintain objectivity about clients, as well as awareness of themselves. In this section I explore the influence and relationship of the experiences, social expectations, and agentive capacities learned in the family in the matter of dream telling and the psychotherapy role. It is helpful to return to Fortes's concept of domain at this point.

Human *persons* have a standing in several domains and fields of interaction. They engage in social relations within multiple spheres of activities sometimes all in the course of one day. All human *persons* identify themselves with a particular assortment of roles that are displayed and discharged in appropriate fields of interaction. *Personhood* is acquired wherever agentive capacities are bestowed and responsibilities have to be discharged. A human *self* becomes a *person* within a family structure long before entering a profession. A person occupies family roles that are variously adopted and set aside at different points in the life cycle. The *person* occupying the professional role and the family member are the same *person*. It is absurd to think that family roles do not influence professional roles, more especially because the professional person is *expected* to separate the two roles under particular circumstances. It is the apposition, opposition, and juxtaposition of roles from different domains and the influence they exert on each other that is at issue here.

The concept of the domains can be understood analogically by the image of a highway through which a human *person* travels in life. The highway represents the social and cultural elements and processes that make up a particular sector of a social system. Everything on the highway is linked metaphorically by virtue of its associations with the highway; for example, the pavement, the road signs, the traffic signals, the surrounding vegetation, the buildings on each side of the role, and other landmarks. Each domain comprises a range of customs, norms, roles, and relations that are primary to itself. Other domains of social interaction are analogically represented in our image by parallel or intersecting roads. The protocol for crossings at intersections is highly structured to prevent unnecessary confusion, congestion, or dangerous collisions. When a person is traveling in the professional domain there are frequent interconnections with other domains, some of which are as clear and obvious as an intersection, whereas others are latent or unobtrusive like a gentle percolation of extra traffic caused by roadwork or detours on the other road. However, all domains through which a *person* travels are interconnected. A *person* can travel on only one road at a time. The oral and written traditions of different societies are full of the stories of humorous, tragic, or impossible situations when human *persons* find themselves in circumstances where they have to act according to the expectations of one role while feeling the influences of the expectations of another. The moral dilemmas caused by these circumstances are the material of world mythologies, as well as of daily activities. Although in this study I did not focus primarily on the principles of the familial domain, asking therapists about their own dreams and their experiences of dream telling, I was allowed to learn something about aspects of their life that were familial.

Experiences of dreams and education about them start very early. Most people said that the experience of dreaming remained private and was not a topic about which the family shared. When they experienced nightmares as children, parents comforted them and told them the experience was "just a dream." The experience was rarely granted a value in itself, but was used only to be unfavorably compared with empirical reality. For some the memory was that the subject of dreams was never brought up, for others there were memories of casual conversations about dreams. The few exceptions to this general rule came from black Americans and subjects of recent Italian or Eastern European ethnic background. These told of a folklore about dreams which considered them important; however, not only did these subjects realize that their families were different, but there was a realization that ethnic folklore weakened with gradual assimilation into the mainstream of American society. Thus, whereas grandma from the old country "believed" different things about dreams, the younger generations regarded some of those beliefs to be superstitious. Moreover, subjects who realized as children that other families had a different way of regarding dreams sometimes called those *superstitious*. One woman, a secretary, told me that she engaged in dream talk at a friend's house and added, "they were Italian, you know, and somewhat superstitious. In our family we were not superstitious about dreams." Therapists from other countries who were interviewed (four therapists in my sample were not U.S. natives) told me that the prevailing folklore in the United States seemed to be that dreams are not meaningful. One physician from India said, "Americans must think dreams are childish, or not important; very rarely do people share their dreams." A psychiatrist from the Middle East said: "They must think of dreams as a symptom. They think it's abnormal to dream much."

In spite of these early memories of having dream experiences ignored or minimized, a few of the people who talked to me told me remarkable accounts of dream experiences from childhood. Several people remembered experiences of lucid dreaming and had dreams about upcoming events. One woman told me that when she lost an object as a child, she could dream where to find it. Another woman told me that for her, as a child, dreaming was a way of making things happen which were impossible in waking life, "like being a witch." She added: "Even now I think dreaming is a way of taking risks without paying the consequences." I was also told of "fun dreams" of flying and space travel and of horrifying nightmares of being pursued by large monsters. For the most part these experiences were kept to themselves; only a few people told their deams to parents or close friends.

In adulthood, dreams were treated in similar ways. They were either ignored, treated casually, and occasionally told to a few intimate family members, like spouses, sisters, mothers, or close friends. My observation of being a dream hearer was that people seemed to enjoy telling me their dreams. Most people told me several dreams, even those who claimed not to recall them regularly. The few who could not remember any to tell me seemed vexed by their selective lack of memory. The dreams I was told were dreams from childhood, memorable dreams of different eras of their life, or current dreams they had had recently. Dreamers commented on, or interpreted their dreams. Their interpretations related to present life issues like work, present relationships, or to life cycle issues and transitional crises in their past or present lives; for example, adolescent struggles, marriage, divorce, losing a job, becoming ill, children moving away from home, and the death of a loved one.

It was clear to me from what people said that they told their dreams more frequently to women than to men. There were only two men in the whole sample who preferred telling their dreams to close male friends. People were aware of these gender differences in dream telling and had different explanations for this; for example, one of the receptionists told me, "men just don't like to talk about dreams; they like to talk about business or football." Others simply said, "Oh, it would never occur to me to tell a man." Some men thought that dream telling was generally perceived as a woman's activity, so men were reluctant to engage in the practice: "dreams bring out feelings and men think it's unmanly to talk about feelings," said a male psychologist.

At this point I will contextualize these general comments by giving examples of how two therapists perceived that their early family experiences influenced their psychotherapy role.

Max, in his forties, has been a therapist for more than ten years. He had a remarkable knowledge about his family history, which he told me going back to his great grandmother who came from Germany and built the family homestead. His earliest recollection of dream telling was overhearing his mother and her sister talking about a dream of Grandma who had died recently. He had no recollection of anyone talking to him about dreams at home: "My guess is," he said, "that if I had a dream they kind of squelched it and said 'it's just a dream'." He did, however, share his fun dreams of flying like Superman with his friends.

I asked him how it came about that he became a psychotherapist. "Looking back on it now, I have always been the family therapist on an informal basis." He said this with such matter-of-factness that I, at first, did not realize he was speaking of his role toward his own family. He continued:

> I was the only child in the family, but I wasn't the family standard-bearer. I wasn't seen as the one that carried the family values. I was always a kind of an outsider, a rebel, but I worked behind the scenes, and people in the family who had problems would talk to me even as an adolescent growing up. I would be the family peacekeeper, if I saw trouble going on in the family, I would facilitate a reckoning even as a child. I was always seen as the caring and emotional one; my cousin, the standard-bearer, was the bright, successful, hard-working one; and I was, "well that's just Max; he has a different way of looking at things; he's alright." I became the helper, listener, and facilitator of people talking to other people. So I developed some natural skill there.

Max tried careers in forestry, the military, and technical writing before he realized that he wanted to study psychology. He spent much time telling me that now, in his present nuclear family, he listens to his son's dreams and tells his wife his dreams. These accounts were complete and detailed, with dreams, feelings about dreams, and his interpretations of his own and other's dreams. He ended his story by telling me, "the family system, in one way or another, will carve out some role for you, and you take that into your work."

Rhonda's story was very similar to Max's, in principle, although some of the facts were different. She also was the "different one." She perceived herself more of a dream sharer than her sister. She shared a dream in which both she and her sister were in a dangerous situation. In the dream her parents were able to rescue her sister but not her. She considered herself to be the "strong one," as well as the one who was not afraid to talk about herself: "I was the main one to tell and listen to dreams. My sister did not try to tell dreams. She tried to hold things back. Dreams are a real reflection of things that are going on for you. Her tendency was to repress a lot of her feelings." Rhonda added that her parents became intimidated by her because she was to become a psychologist: "They think you're going to look at them critically or, in some strange way you're going to know all about them. "'You're a psychologist! Oh, my God! You're going to evaluate me!' Yes, even my family!"

Both Max and Rhonda were "different" within their family; not the one to carry the family values, somewhat freer of their family's expectations. But, although Max was considered the unobtrusive peacemaker, Rhonda was seen as the strong intimidating daughter who could know their thoughts and evaluate them. By being the different one, each one was placed further away from traditional gender roles, and each was cast in the role of psychotherapist within the family of origin.

These were not unusual accounts. Many told me similar stories, elaborating on them with specific accounts of a family member who had a mental health problem, an illness, or some other misfortune. They found themselves in a problem solving, mediating, or advising role. Others told me that they were just of an introspective bent unlike the rest of the family. One psychiatrist remembered being somewhat hypochondriacal as a child, always needing to think about his experiences and "wanting to know what was going on in my own head."

To recapitulate, the native term "person" has been explored as it is used by psychotherapists in everyday interactional situations and examined in the light of principles organizing their own social system as it relates to the professional arena. The abstract analytic term *person* is not divorced from the native term "person." The task of anlysis is to retain the local native working construct of the term while disambiguating it from, and analyzing it by, the analytic concept.

Psychotherapists have used the word "person" in three different ways. First, when a therapist like Joe says that, "people defer to the professional role and do not treat me simply as a person," he may be saying that the role is weighty. It is weighty in being prestigious, as well as significant in the professional domain, but it assumes ponderous and burdensome proportions in arenas and situations where it ought not to do so.

Second, when therapists like Rhonda and Max say that they were groomed for their role as psychotherapists by being mediators, listeners, and insightful evaluators within their own family, they are making a statement about what "persons" they consider themselves to be, and how they became such "persons." From the vantage point of the present professional role, they are seeing themselves, not only as a cluster of roles, but also as one continuous identity with rights and obligations in both domains. Moreover, they perceive the curious attendant characteristic of "objectivity" to their position in both domains. In their families they are seen as the special ones or the outsiders, and in their work they have to learn to separate personal and professional issues. They have the social obligation of *becoming* the role while at the same time retaining their separateness from it.

Third, the native term "person" is used to describe the qualities of a therapist that, along with proper educational preparation, are indispensible to the role. These qualities are very well understood by them, although to the outside observer portions of the description remain implicit and unstated. They are variously described as having the capacity to "form relationships," be empathetic, and especially to be introspective. However, the descriptions are not all stated or quite describable, because people keep returning to the phrase "it depends on the person." It is not quite clear how therapists receive the capacity to "know themselves" or "read" others.

In the next section each of these ways of using the native term "person" is examined in the light of Mauss's analysis of the category of *person* (Mauss 1938). Mauss understands the concept in a historical context and discusses its evolution in Western thought. I show that each aspect of the word that Mauss considers diachronically is understood and discussed as it is experienced synchronically by contemporary therapists in the United States.

ANALYSIS: THE ENDURING, EXPERIENCING PERSON

A person is not a passive occupier of roles. Regarding persons in this way would not only imply a reification of society but also a reification of *person*. Nor does a phenotypic explanation of styles of role occupation provide an adequate exegesis of the problem. To be sure there is the reluctant, the eager, the unsure, the masterful, and the rebellious occupier of the same role. There are roles that are inherently too difficult to occupy successfully, like the psychiatric resident who has more than can be possibly accomplished by any single actor; and conversely there is the social worker who prefers to call himself a therapist because he chooses to emphasize a particular nuance of the role behavior required. All of these understandings of the relationship between role and person would see the social actor as a performer behind a mask. It is important to state this because there is an element of this understanding in the native term "person." The therapist who would like to be treated "simply as a person," is also stating a disclaimer: he is not identical to his role.

Conversely, the same statement and others that therapists make also represent a complaint that the role is not a thing that can be shed at will or by choice even when social domains converge. For in a very real sense, socially and personally there are roles that become a part of one's identity, like the senior psychiatrist who says, "I am most myself when I am with a patient or a student."

Mauss describes the evolution from the *personnage* (role) to *persona* (mask) by explaining that a mask was often identified with the name of a clan or a family. Thus, the meaning of the word *prosopon* or face changes from signifying an imposter to signifying one who is legally entitled to wear the mask; that is, from one who impersonates to one who personifies. There is no evidence from my data that these two understandings of person (as mask) are progressive. It is true that when occupying a new role the unfamiliarity might cause the player to feel like an untrained imposter. However, a person plays many roles with different degrees of comfort and compliance. The degrees of comfort have less to do with progressiveness of comfort level with a role than with the context of the situation as when the domains seem to converge. It is certainly not the case that all Western contemporary humans always understand the concept of person in the highly self-conscious and conscientious way that Mauss outlines in the latter part of his essay.

The second understanding of the native term "person" relating to that of being groomed to the therapist role with the family of origin, includes the understanding of person as one continuous identity within a community in a society. The person has a history with a trajectory that is influenced by the capacities imputed to him or her. One sees oneself as destined, because of others' expectations as well as one's own, to play a part such as the black sheep, the leader, the different one, the listener, the therapist. Max understood his family's expectations as a mandate.

Mauss proposes further progressions to the understanding of *prosopon*. In Hellenistic times, the concept was used by the Stoic philosophers to mean one's *true face* (without dissembling). A moral aspect is given to the term, to which the Christian era adds the aspects of unity, indivisibility, and identity. These three descriptors are such important aspects of *person* that there have been many years of theological and social controversy to settle in what ways the term *person* could properly be applied to God and to religious bodies.

Probably a somewhat similar aspect of person is implied when therapists describe the importance of being the right kind of "person." Although the native descriptors are not all explicit there is certainly an expectation of a moral sense related to therapists. Entitlement goes beyond formal preparation for a role. One expects a competent responsible moral being. Whereas one expects all persons in society to understand moral values, the requirements and expectations are especially applied to professional *persons*, and other *persons* who perform a public function, or provide a service in society.

The most "progressed" understanding of person according to Mauss is the *person as psychological being*. Here the *person* is identified with self-knowledge and psychological consciousness. The psychological self that anxiously pays attention to its own consciousness was born after the Reformation and the sectarian movement through the right to stand directly before God unmediated by an institution. The self has an individual conscience, is free to communicate to God inwardly, and is one's own priest. The *person* for Mauss is the same as the individual self with a moral consciousness. Reflexivity is now a social right and an obligation.

We recognize in the native term "person" descriptions of all phases of the evolution of Mauss's category. Mauss presents the phases historically, but they are all part of his descriptions and analysis of *person* (see Figure 1). Yet they are all present synchronically in the understanding of Western psychotherapists.

One could speculate whether anybody could represent an evolutionary picture of each person's life history. The expectation that one will continue to examine oneself remains for young and for old. Complete self-consciousness is a contradiction in terms. The same experienced psychiatrist who told me "I am most myself when I am with a patient or student," also told me later in the interview, "I become anxious when I have a patient who threatens suicide, I wonder if I have done everything as well as I could have done it. I wonder if there is anything I am missing. I will often have an anxious dream about it." The experienced psychiatrist who is totally identified with his role in one situation is also quite uncomfortable and anxious about his role in a different situation; and he knows not only that this is his experience, but also that this is the way it is supposed to be.

In summary, the *person* is an abstract concept that describes a set of relationships within social arenas with all the attendant customs and rules. The person comprises and occupies a variety of roles, with specific clusterings of rights and obligations organized within social domains. For the Western person, particularly in this study of the Western psychotherapist, the understanding of *person* includes aspects of the mask that impersonates, the name that personifies, the identity that endures, the indivisible historical individuality with a biography, the conscience that self-inspects, and the agent that intends.

THE DREAMING SELF AND THE WORKING PERSON

Both Mauss (1938) and Fortes (1973) include in their analysis of *person* the objective as well as the subjective aspects. However, each makes clear in his analysis that the *person* is an agent-in-society and not just an experiencing entity. The *person* is understood to be capable of and responsible for being self-aware. Mauss attributes this capacity only to Western persons. Fortes understands the concept of *person* to be universal. Harris (1989) also understands the concept to be universal and proposes a useful distinction between the *self* as experiencing being and the *person* as agent-in-society. The distinction is especially useful in this research because the dream can be explored as a phenomenon of experience as well as a social communication. Although both are related it is not helpful to confuse them. In this section I investigate the relationship between how therapists experience their own dreams and how they work with deams in their professional practice. Although the dream is an experienced phenomenon, the choice to explore it to gain self-awareness involves agency. The objective and the subjective aspects of *person* are related as closely as the outer and inner surfaces of a glove. However, when the glove is worn only one surface is visible to the outsider, the inner surface is felt only by the wearer. An example of this can be demonstrated by the fact that the success or failure of the *person* in a social role can be a matter of public record; however, how a self experiences the role is not an open matter at all times either to the observer or to the participant. The *self* could disguise the feelings or be unaware of them. Yet *person* and *self* are inextricably related; for the *person* has dialogues with and formulates intentions regarding *itself*, even as the *self* experiences *personhood*.

I discovered that therapists' understanding of dreams and their actions related to their own dreams corresponded to their understanding of themselves as persons and the way they used dreams in their work. In fact, it is not hard to demonstrate a relationship between what they said about dreams and their understanding of the aspects of *personhood* as elucidated by Mauss (1938), namely *personnage* (role), *persona* (mask or face), *personne: fait morale* (social person), and *personne: être psychologique* (psychological person). In my analysis, all of these aspects are synchronous and interconnected, rather than progressive and historically discrete. The aspects are separated only for the purpose of analysis. They can all be concurrent aspects of one *person*.

The Intentional Use of Dreams: The Person as Agent

Agency means the capacity to perform an intentional action to an end or for a reason; or the capacity to refrain from action for a reason (Beck 1965). Agency involves the capacity to produce an effect. The word *agent* is also used to signify one who acts for another by being granted authority to do so, usually by the person represented. To say that persons are agents is to imply responsibility and capacity for action by the principal actor or a substitute. Psychotherapists' understandings and actions related to dreams involved the aspect of agency in these two senses. Intentionality was related to both one's own dreams and to the dreams of clients, for whom there was a perception of responsibility by virtue of the role. There was an expectation that therapists would make a decision regarding their own dreams and the dreams of their clients. Even if the decision was to do nothing about them, because they were meaningless or because it would not be therapeutic to the client, therapists made comments that indicated they had thought about it intentionally or were expected to have done so.

This attitude toward dream telling was so prevalent that sometimes it was assumed rather than stated specifically. The topic of my research was not unfamiliar to my informants. It was acceptable that a researcher should ask them about dreams, because they ought to know something about the topic. I was told, sometimes apologetically, that they did not remember their dreams, and that they ought to pay more attention to dreams than they actually did; I was told that they were working with the kind of population with whom it was not therapeutic to talk about dreams, or they might have done more dream work with clients; several therapists told me that I would "not get anywhere with behavioral psychologists" who do not listen to dreams. They had had only one course in college related to dreams so they were not good enough as interpreters. I ought to speak with a psychoanalyst; he would tell me what I needed to know. Both lay informants and psychotherapists agreed that therapists were persons to whom you could tell a dream, even though, more often than not, they may not have done so with their own particular therapist. Many therapists told me they were "upset" by the recent reports in popular and professional periodicals that dreams were meaningless. They did not tell me why the report was upsetting. Some of the therapists said it was inconceivable that the brain should do anything meaningless.

The two most obviously intentional statements made regarding dreams were as follows. The first statement came from a young counselor. He said that after reading the reports about dreams being caused by random firing of neurons in the brain, he had decided that the scientific evidence did not warrant dream exploration or dream tell-ing, so he made no effort to remember his dreams and actively discouraged clients from talking about dreams. The second statement, which was much more typical, was made by a social worker. She said she tried to remember her dreams and actually put pressure on herself to do so. Here is a part of her comments:

> I didn't get a lot of training in the use of dreams, and even in my own therapy it's not really that encouraged. When it comes up it's something I initiate. It's not stated as an option by my supervisor or something to look into, say when I may encourage someone to keep a journal; I haven't thought that this is something I can in-corporate in an educational way for clients. . . . I think there's a

whole mystification about what dreams are. . . . I'd like to remember my dreams better. I haven't actually a way in which I can actually record—I've tried that. *I put pressure on myself to remember*, and when I can't I just have to let it go.

I included these two examples not only because of the intentionality involved but because in both of them the therapists moved freely from talking about their relationship to their own dreams to what they did with clients. Both examples demonstrate an expectation that as therapists they ought to have an opinion about dreams with regard to themselves and their clients although each therapist made a different decision. There were many more instances similar to the second example than to the first.

Knowing about Dreams and Teaching Dream Work: Entitlements and Responsibilities of the Person

I was told by many therapists that people expected them to know something about dreams even though they had had very little training related to them. The expectation that they should know something about dreams was part of the expectation that they have insight into themselves and know how to analyze others. Many were amused by this expectation assuring me that they could not really analyze people's minds but that people thought they could. It was part of the job. They had this capability imputed to them in professional and nonprofessional situations, as soon as it was known that they were therapists. It was clear that the perceived capacity came with the office rather than the training. Even those who thought this was a ridiculous notion took it with good nature and humor. Most did not think it was a ridiculous notion. Some told me that dream work was "part of the work" whether it was used for many patients or a few.

However, what was most interesting to me about this special knowledge of dreams was a perception that the therapist ought to also be responsible *not* to use it with all clients and to teach only a few selected clients how to derive self-knowledge from it. In general, therapists thought that the low income, schizophrenic, chronically psychotic, and people with little insight were *not* helped by examining their dreams. (This was not a consensus because a few did dream work with clients in these categories.) There was even a feeling that harm could be done by dream exploration of these people. On the other hand, they thought some people who had the capacity for intuition and insight could learn. Those who could learn had to be taught gradually. One psychiatric nurse specialist said:

> Some people I don't do anything with dream material immediately, and it may be months before I do anything with dreams. Let's say, if I've got a person who's really *not ready* for interpretations, someone fairly new in therapy—someone who's been only dealing with survival, not necessarily with internal growth, kind of thing. So, in a sense I have to work with these women 'till they're ready to deal with that; I may keep the content of the dreams in here [pointing to her head] or in the record, and then when I think they are at a point where they are ready to at least begin to make some interpretations themselves, I will go back to it.

This was not an isolated comment. A social worker thought that when clients first came to therapy they wanted the therapist to interpret their dreams for them, but she added, "I don't do that. I think *you can train patients* into a way of understanding their own dreams which is helpful to them." Two psychiatrists told me wistfully that young people today were not interested in being insightful or turning toward the inner life: "Young people in the 1960s were more interested in dreams, but today kids are interested only in material success, not insight." However, as people continued in therapy they could be taught insight that would involve the capacity to work with their own dreams.

There was a consensus that therapists not only had or ought to have knowledge of dreams but also had a responsibility to make a decision whether dreams would be part of the therapy. This was done by drawing attention to the subject or away from it.

Thus, therapists were expected to have special knowledge of dreams and the responsibility to use this knowledge with the right kind of patients. Selected patients could be trained to learn about dreams when they were ready. The psychologist who talked to me earlier summed it up by saying: "I think a person should be entitled by a special relationship to tell or hear a dream, and dream work is not for everyone."

Practicing Your Role in Your Dreams: The Person as Role Player and Occupier of Office

The title therapist seemed to confer expectations of capacities that might or might not be learned in training. The role itself seemed to raise expectations of insight and expertise. It was a difficult role to play. One social worker who had recently graduated said that it seemed pretentious for her to identify herself as a therapist although she thought of herself as a therapist. In her opinion therapists had a higher status than social workers and were expected to know more, and at the moment she felt ill-trained and unprepared. "It's pretentious because it's not real yet; it's like taking on an identity that I haven't yet earned." This therapist felt that although she ought to personify the qualities of a good therapist it seemed to her that she was, in fact, impersonating one. She did not "know enough," and the role felt contrived although she had spent much time learning it. She said that being in therapy herself was absolutely essential training for being a good therapist. When she worked with a client's dreams she asked the same kind of questions that her therapist would ask her.

Another social worker corroborated her statements by saying that dreams were a way of learning about life and about herself. When I pressed her to explain further she said: "dreams are a *safe way of role playing* or enacting events with thoughts and feelings that you would not normally have or do in waking life, because you are unsure, or because it would be too risky. If I am having some kind of anxiety, I hope the dream will shed some light on it."

I asked therapists to tell me their own dreams, the dreams of their clients, and to comment on dreams I brought to them. I observed that therapists who worked with their own dreams, were also open, in general, to working with their client's dreams, and those who did not, were not. This was not surprising. I expected this similarity in the *process* of dream work. However, the surprising finding was that in many cases the *content and interpretation* of their own dreams which they chose to tell me were similar to the content and their interpretation of the client's dream that they chose to tell me. A few examples will illustrate.

A social worker who told me her own dream of her uncle's death, also described her client's dream of the death of her father. A psychologist who told me her own anxiety dream about introducing her boyfriend to her parents, also told me a similar dream of a client, adding that her client had anxieties about her boyfriend. A psychiatric nurse who said that she had been separated from her mother by death when she was very young, and afterward had "separation dreams" herself, also told me a dream of a client who had anxiety dreams of being separated from her. Another nurse who told me that her dreams expressed her grief about the fact that her children had grown up and recently left home, interpreted the dream that I gave her as that of a woman who had lost her children. A psychiatrist who dreamed of abandonment in a love relationship in her own life, also told me the dream of one of her clients who dreamed of being abandoned by her. One could only speculate about possible reasons for all these similarities, but one can conclude, at least, that there is a relationship between the therapists' work on their dreams and the work on the dreams of their clients. It is possible that more therapists than the ones who have explicitly said so, look on their dreams as ways to role play or rehearse their different roles, including the role of psychotherapist. They had no difficulty in producing dreams about their work: their clients, their colleagues, their supervisors, their teachers. They seemed to learn about their clients by learning about themselves and vice versa.

Thus, many therapists regarded their dreams as opportunities to role play situations, impersonate unfamiliar roles and rehearse events. The *process* of reflecting on their dreams made them aware of thoughts and feelings associated with situations in their lives to which they might not pay attention in waking life. Several therapists said their dreams made them aware of their anxieties, fears, and anger; when their roles or life situations were difficult; and when their awareness of these were limited. Those who reflected on their own dreams also reflected on the dreams of their clients. Moreover, the *content* and interpretation of their own dreams were similar to the dreams of their clients. If they noticed this similarity they did not comment on it.

Dreams as a Means to Honesty: The Person as Social Moral Consciousness

In Mauss's analysis one aspect of *person* (prosopon) is showing one's *true face* without dissembling, or pretense. Mauss traced the development of this understanding to the Stoic philosophers: "sculpting one's mask in truth" meant to be true to one's role. He introduced two words from the Stoic literature to illustrate his point. The word *caractere* means the moral and ethical qualities of the person as well as the person occupying a role in society. The meaning of the word *conscience* (Greek: *sunaidysis*), which could be translated literally as

"one who witnesses" or "joint knowledge," is now changed to consciousness as in the knowledge of good and evil. Thus, the aspect of
honesty or authenticity was added to the aspect of legal and social
responsibility. Therapists talked about honesty in two ways; namely,
honesty toward others and honesty toward oneself.

They were expected to be who they represented themselves to
be. This was a complex expectation because although training was
valuable they could not *just* imitate the masters or their teachers; it was
expected that competent therapists would not only reflect their education but also their personal qualities. An experienced social worker says
it in this way:

> You learn about all these masters in psychotherapy, but then you
> can't do exactly what they do. If you try to be someone else it's
> never that effective. It never works, because unless you're very
> *honest* with people in therapy, I don't think they're very im-
> pressed. When you're asking them to change, you're asking them
> to do a pretty risky thing, and if you're sitting here as somebody's
> puppet, they will know it, and I don't think they'll feel safe to do
> what you are asking.

She continued to explain that although she had much respect for a
special school of psychotherapy (which she named) that had been inspired by an excellent master, he was impossible to imitate or impersonate. To be authentic what is learned from the master must change
the learner first. Training is not enough, it has to be complemented by
personal qualities. This is why a good therapist learns the role best by
being in therapy.

This understanding of person is extended to the client. To learn
from therapy the client must be the kind of "person" who can tell
another the truth about himself or herself. The capacity to tell one's
dreams to another person is part of the process. The clients who lie are
not the ones who make progress. Another social worker corroborated
this by saying explicitly that therapy requires that clients "are gonna be
completely honest about intimate thoughts and feelings, and dreams are a
part of that."

When I asked why the telling of dreams required honesty of the
teller, the typical answer I received was that dreams are revealing to
others and to oneself, and telling one's dreams required the ability to
tell others intimate and private things about oneself. Several therapists

told me that their dreams diminished self-deception. If you are unaware of a feeling a dream will reveal it. They gave me examples of dreams that helped them know they were frightened, angry, or anxious. The dream told in the context of psychotherapy provides a "witness" to oneself and "joint knowledge." This understanding of dreams as "searching one's conscience" was compared to the confessional. Several informants, both lay and professional told me specifically that the therapist was not only a counselor, teacher, and healer, but, sometimes, also a confessor. Some suggested I talk to clergy as well as therapists.

Dreams as a Means to Individuality: The Person as Individual Consciousness

According to Mauss, since the Protestant Reformation the Western individual no longer has a confessor. With the right of each individual to communicate freely and directly with God comes the anxious need for self-scrutiny. Examination of conscience becomes examination of consciousness as each "person" becomes his or her own priest. The person is now compelled to be a psychological being. Reflexivity is not only an experience but also a social responsibility.

At this time I will present three examples of how dreams were intentionally used to increase self-knowledge. The first two examples will show how two therapists derived self-knowledge from their own dreams and the third deals with how a psychologist understood and worked with the dreams of one of his clients.

The first dream was presented by a young female social worker:

> I had a dream in the past couple of weeks which I still think about a lot, because it was about my mother. She had won an award like a Mother-of-the-Year award. She got up on stage and she was presented with this award and we were happy for her. The next day they called everybody together to tell them that there had been a mistake, that she didn't win the award, that somebody else was supposed to win. She had to give the award back and present it to the other mother. She was quiet and smiling and nice. It was so sad. And I was so upset about it, and I'm shouting "you can't do that to a person." The dream has stuck with me.

The dream made such an impression on her that she shared it with her sister. She understood the dream as an opportunity to become aware of thoughts and feelings suppressed during waking life. The dream was showing her the two extremes related to her feelings toward her mother. She called those "the two personalities inside me." One part of her defends her mother and the other part does not give her credit. She was troubled by the whole situation with her mother, and the dream was reminding her of it. She did not tell me whether her dream caused her to make a decision regarding her relationship with her mother.

The second instance is about a therapist who had made an important decision regarding his work after reflection on a dream. I was encouraged to speak to him by two of his trusted friends and colleagues with whom he had shared the momentous dream. He spent most of the hour of our conversation telling me the background to the dream, the time of dreaming, the dream content in great detail, the interpretation to the dream, his conversation with two friends about it, and finally the decisions he had made in waking life related to the dream. He had the dream when the institution of his employment was making changes in goal direction and administration. He perceived that his own future in the institution depended on a choice he had to make about a new position he was being offered. The dream made him aware of the complexity of his feelings toward the new goals and the new administration. After prolonged reflection on the dream and discussions with close friends he realized that he would "lack integrity" if he accepted the position, *because he did not really want to do so* without reservation. So he made the decision not to accept it and is satisfied with his decision several years later.

He said: "The dream was so compelling that I almost used it as an oracle, actually it was like a metaphor for what was going on. The dream really helped me make a decision about what I should do about my position in the agency. I was very conflicted about my role." When I asked him whether people did indeed make decisions on the basis of the information they received from dreams, he responded that he thought people occasionally did that, but if they did they would not tell too many people about their decision-making process because people had a tendency to "pathologize" dreams.

The third example is a client's dream told to a psychologist who was her therapist, about the client's relationship with her boyfriend.

The dream: "She and her boyfriend are sitting on a couch and the mail arrives. She goes out to pick up the mail and then discovers that he has received nice letters from friends and the only mail for her is a stack of bills."

The therapist's comments on her dream: "the way she developed the dream was that that was how it was in their relationship. He was getting all the good stuff and she was doing all the responsible things. She cried. It obviously penetrated her denial about issues in this relationship but at the same time she wasn't ready to make those changes. She just left. She never came back after that dream."

These three illustrations show therapists interpreting their own dreams and dreams of their clients as ways to become aware of their feelings on issues in which they feel divided. The telling of the dream to another person gives them an opportunity to reflect on the issues further and may help them choose a course of action. In the first example the therapist shared her dream with her sister; she felt divided in her feelings about her mother. She did not talk further about whether the dream had subsequently influenced her actions regarding her mother. In the second dream the therapist shared his dream with two colleagues; he felt divided in his feelings about his role in the institution. On the basis of that reminder from his dream he decided not to accept the new position. In the third example the therapist perceived that the client was divided regarding her feelings about her boyfriend, and she made a decision to act on her new awareness after she talked about her dream. That decision caused her to end the therapeutic relationship and continue her relationship with her boyfriend.

The second therapist expressed his decision as one that decreased his divided attitudes and feelings and restored "integrity" or "oneness." Social consciousness was expressing itself in individual consciousness. A person divided against himself can not be honest, or in the social sense a moral individual consciousness—a *moi* (self).

The *moi* (self) as analyzed by Mauss is not just a processual internal experience nor simply an intellectual experience; it is rather an individual consciousness capable of moral decision and action within a social context. He says: "It was not among the Cartesians but in other circles that the problem of the *person* which is no more than a consciousness found its solutions. . . . it was Spinoza, because he put the ethical problem before all else, rather than Descartes who had the soundest view of the relations between the individual consciousness and the things of God" (Mauss 1938: 280).

SUMMARY AND CONCLUSION

In this chapter I examined therapists' understanding of "person." Situations have been described as they are revealed through therapists' activities and attitudes related to their professional and personal lives that show the complexity in their roles and relationships. Dream telling is an activity that has different significance in professional and non-professional settings.

In their professional lives therapists are expected to have the competence conferred by proper educational preparation and as the "kind of persons" who possess special qualities and capacities variously described as the capacity to possess a knowledge of their feelings, the capacity to inspect their motivations, the capacity to be caring and responsible in human relationships, and the capacity to be objective enough to be able to distinguish between their own issues and their client's issues. A knowledge of dreams, their own and other peoples', is part of the expectation that they can "analyze" themselves and others. These capacities are imputed to them when they become therapists whether or not they have had the training for them and whether or not they possess them.

The professional role is weighty. It confers prestige, and often the demands of the role assume primary importance in their activities and attitudes even in nonprofessional contexts. Thus the psychotherapist's *personhood* as it arises in the professional sector of the politico-jural domain is the locus for the central principle for social action (Figure 3). This domain comprises a whole range of distinctive social relations, customs, roles, and norms apparent in daily social interactions. One example of the primacy of the locus of the professional domain in their social interactions can be seen in dream telling: telling a dream to a psychotherapist is different from telling a dream to any other *person* whether in a professional or in a nonprofessional context. The psychotherapy aspects of one's *person* take precedence over the other aspects of one's *person* in the matter of dream telling or other interactional topics about which there is a perception of special capacity or special relationship.

Therapists perceived themselves to be groomed for the therapy role by their roles in their families of origin where they were perceived to possess special qualities and capacities. For some these were the capacity to be caring and willing to listen; for others they were the capacity to be strong and objective and to solve problems. For most of them, it made them "different" from the rest of the family. They perceived themselves as standing apart from their families. This accentuated their introspection and reflexivity. Most therapists also perceived themselves to be more likely than others in their families to pay attention to, and reflect on, their thoughts, imaginings, dreams, motivations, actions, and regrets. Because of these combinations of capacities they perceived themselves to function as therapists within their families of origin. In telling their stories many of them saw themselves to be destined to function as therapists in their families, and subsequently chose to become professional therapists. Their present understandings of their personal history indicates further that the professional aspects of their person is the locus of the primary principle for their personal and social relations.

In further analyzing these social data regarding the understanding of the native term "person," Mauss's analysis of the category of the Western *person* was used. Mauss understood the concept in a historical context and traced its evolution in Western thought. I have shown that each aspect of the category of *person*, which he considers diachronically as historically discrete, to be a part of the contemporary concurrent understanding and experience of the therapists in the two community mental health centers examined.

In examining the relationship between how therapists experienced their own dreams and how they worked with dreams in their professional practice, I found that therapists understood themselves to have special knowledge of dreams, and to have the responsibility to use this knowledge in their own experience and with the right kind of clients. Only selected clients could be trained to learn about dreams "when they were ready." Many therapists who did not work with their own dreams thought they ought to do so or remembered wistfully a time when they did so. Therapists who worked with their own dreams were open, in general, to working with the dreams of their clients; those who did not, were not. There was a curious but notable similarity in the *content* of the therapists' own dreams and their reports of their clients' dreams.

In conclusion, dream exploration was to increase their awareness of themselves. Reflection on one's dreams could show persons how they were feeling and what their motivations were, even when they were tempted to deceive themselves. This awareness included situations in which they felt divided within themselves. As Western *persons* they were alone with their conscience, and they were expected to think independently. To be a *person* is to stand apart; be aware; reflect about one's thoughts, dreams, and actions; and to choose a course of action that will reflect responsible undividedness (individuality). A fragmented self cannot be a responsible agent and therefore cannot be a *person*. For a Western therapist to be a *person* is to be independent, individual, and reflexive. Reflexivity is an expectation. Personal dream exploration is a part of the reflexivity.

However, there is a constellation of ideas and beliefs about dream telling and dream interpretation that considers dreams to be private and intimate, and dream work with certain clients to be at best useless and at worst dangerous. In Chapters 3 and 4 these ideas are investigated.

III

The Contexts of Dream Telling

INTRODUCTION

In Chapter 2 the concept of person was used to describe and analyze situations and contexts in the lives of therapists that reveal a variety of roles and relationships, with specific clusterings of obligations and capacities. These were organized according to social domains of interaction. For psychotherapists, the professional sector of the politico-jural domain emerges as the central structural influence in their activities and attitudes. Dream telling is one of the activities that has different significance in different contexts: professional or nonprofessional.

In this chapter the first research question related to the local constellation of ideas and beliefs about dreams and dream telling in the two community mental health centers is addressed. Although most of the fifty-eight informants interviewed in the two community mental health centers would agree that dreams are "personal" and that few people talked about them, there were many opinions about who told dreams to whom, in which contexts, and for what purposes. In many of the descriptions and opinions the native terms "person" and "personal" were used by informants to say what they meant.

In this chapter the analytic concept *person* is used to describe and observe the contexts in which dreams are told. Thus, the etic perspective is incorporated with the emic perspective to organize the data received from informants.[1] Dreams are told and heard by *persons* with distinctive qualities, capacities, and roles. For example, persons both professional and nonprofessional were expected to use their *judgmental capacities* to ascertain the appropriateness of certain contexts for the telling of certain dreams. Therapists were considered by all concerned to have nonpatent (*mystical*) *capacities* to know themselves, read minds, and analyze dreams. There was a general expectation among them that they would exercise professional clinical judgment, a responsibility derived from their social role and involving their *social entitlement capacities* to decide when to draw attention to the dreams they hear and when *not* to (Harris 1988). What emerges is a strong belief among therapists that "psychological mindedness" (a native term) is a prerequisite for dream work. I show that psychological mindedness is related conceptually to the concept of *personne: être psychologique*, as analyzed by Mauss in his essay on the Western person (Mauss 1938).

DREAMS ARE "PERSONAL": EMIC PERSPECTIVES

Although most of the therapists and other staff members who spoke with me at the two community mental health centers would agree that dreams are "personal," the word *personal* was used in different ways. The word was also observed to be spoken with different degrees of emotion, from dispassionate indifference to intense concern. A few examples will illustrate.

Kate is in her early thirties. She works in the Day Treatment Center at Newell. She has a bachelor's degree in social work. Although she is not a professional primary therapist, she is engaged in therapeutic activities, such as planning and participating in socializing activities such as outings with clients from the Day Treatment Center and in group meetings with coworkers and clients. Kate enjoyed talking to me about her dreams. She tells her dreams to her sister and to a few close friends and coworkers.

I think most people don't remember or don't give any thought to their dreams. They just erase them after they wake up. Then, people think it's kind of *private*, you know, *strongly personal*. I'm sure people think other people don't care about their dreams.

[In social circles] I tell dreams only if I think its something interesting or funny . . . but to somebody real close to me like my sister who lives with me or a close friend, I would tell a scary or sad dream.

I tell my dreams to a few people I work with. I think sometimes they're surprised that I tell my dreams so frequently. . . . I get the impression when telling *such dreams* that they think I have a lot of conflicts—that would probably tie in with why a lot of people don't talk about dreams.

Kate's explanations about dreams being personal were typical. Most informants used the word *personal* in one or several of three ways: to signify subjectivity, to classify dreams, and to connote normative evaluation.

Kate and others said that the reason why people do not tell their dreams is primarily because dreams are "strongly personal." The adjective in front of the word *personal* illustrates the emotional intensity attached to the word. Other informants have used the words *highly personal, really personal,* or *deeply personal.* The description refers to *subjectivity* and privacy. Certain activities are not engaged in publicly. Dream telling is "personal" in the way certain bodily functions are personal. It is inappropriate to share personal dreams in the presence of people before whom one would not undress, even partially.[2]

Kate continues by classifying dreams into ones that are told openly and casually and others that are not. She screens her dreams, using a protocol that she and others know. She tells funny dreams or dreams of general interest without reservation, but she should be discriminating with personal dreams. Another informant says it in a similar way: "I've had this funny dream that I've shared with my boss. But I've had dreams I wouldn't share with him. It depends on the dream. I wouldn't share a *personal dream* with a message-type thing." The word *personal* is used here as a descriptor and *classifier* of dreams. When using the word *personal* in this classificatory sense, informants spoke in a matter-of-fact dispassionate tone, as one does when talking about the obvious: this is a personal dream and this is not.

However, Kate continued to explain that she is concerned about what her close friends might think about her if she shares dreams too frequently. Maybe she *should* not share dreams as frequently as she does. If "such dreams" (presumably personal ones) are shared, people might think she has conflicts and problems. To tell dreams too often or in the wrong contexts would be inappropriate and might cause people to think that she uses poor judgment or even that she might be emotionally unstable. The rules about dream telling are generally known, but unspoken and not always clear. Because the rules are not stated, Kate is not always sure when she might be breaking them. This increases her concern, and she concluded quite astutely that: "that would probably tie in with why a lot of people don't talk about their dreams." Thus, the use of the word *personal* to describe dreams and dream telling signifies not only subjectivity and classification, but also connotes normativity and appropriateness.

"MY PERSONAL LIFE": EMIC AND ETIC PERSPECTIVES

In anthropological analyses it is important to keep emic and etic perspectives separate, yet difficult to do so. An emic statement is an insider's perspective but the observing analyst imposes preferences and perceptions by choosing to focus on certain aspects of that statement. It is important, therefore, that the analytic or etic perspective be clear before it is used to clarify the emic data. In this section I use Fortesian domain theory to organize the material on dream telling to and by psychotherapists. According to Fortes, a domain is a large structural arena of social relations that gives the social analyst the opportunity to deduce social rules behind daily activities (Fortes 1969). The general principle is that one domain is central or internal and primary in a given context at a given time. The professional sector of the politico-jural domain comprises a range of distinctive social relations, customs, roles, and norms apparent in daily activities and interactions. For psychotherapists (and possibly for personnel in other professions) the demands and perceptions of the professional role assume primary importance in their activities and attitudes even in nonprofessional settings. Their *personhood* as it arises in their professional life emerges as the central influence in their activities and attitudes (Figure 3). Therefore, when therapists say "my personal life" they mean *everything that is not a part of their professional activities* (Figure 4). Thus, activities like paying taxes and voluntary involvement in the community are considered parts of "personal life," when they do not derive from professional activities. Even so, it is hard to ignore the professional identities of private citizens.

Dream telling is an activity that has different significance in professional and nonprofessional contexts. A *context* is not simply a setting,

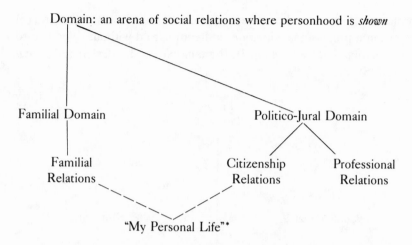

*"My personal life" usually refers to all social relations that are not professional; all relations in the familial domain and nonprofessional contexts in the politico-jural domain.

Figure 4. An Adaptation of Fortes's Domain Theory

but rather an arena of social interactions involving the setting, roles, relationships, and all the attendant rules for interaction as perceived by all those involved. Thus, when a therapist is told a dream, the norms related to professional interactions and activities become part of the context even in a nonprofessional setting.

Not only is the professional role a central aspect of therapists' personhoods and actions, but also they expect distinct and clear boundaries between professional and nonprofessional aspects of their person. Therefore, domain theory is helpful in distinguishing recurrent patterns and different contexts for dream telling.

As the emic perspectives on the "personal" or "nonpersonal" aspects of dream telling are examined in the light of whether they are professional or nonprofessional (etic perspective), four contextual categories emerge: (1) when telling a nonpersonal (not private) dream in a nonprofessional situation the context can be designated *casual*; (2) when telling a "personal dream" in a nonprofessional situation the context can be designated *intimate*; (3) when a "personal dream" is told in a professional situation the context can be designated *confidential*; and (4) when, in a professional situation, a dream is told without reference to the dreamer (i.e., nonpersonal), the context can be designated *formal* (Figure 5).

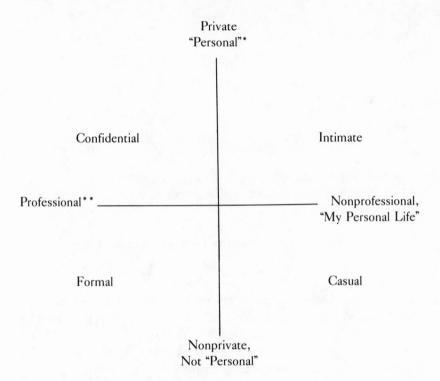

*The horizontal axis represents an emic perspective, a native understanding of what is considered personal or private.

**The vertical axis represents an etic perspective, a social observer's understanding of social domains and contexts.

Figure 5. Typology of Dream Telling Contexts

TYPOLOGY OF DREAM TELLING CONTEXTS

A context is not simply a setting. It involves social roles, relationships, and rules for action, as well as the setting. A context is designated *casual* when a nonprivate dream is told in a nonprofessional context.

Casual Context: Normal Dreams

Although American therapists and lay persons would agree that dreams were not a frequent topic of serious conversation in public settings, most of the people with whom I spoke also agreed that dreams were a frequent topic of incidental conversation in a casual context. This has been corroborated by the readiness with which dreams are brought up in general social gatherings among people who do not know each other well. For example, the topic of dreams was discussed in the staff lounge, and people did not hesitate to talk to me in the hall or other public areas about my study and their dreams. Sometimes there was apologetic reference to their "crazy dreams," and sometimes a scene from a funny dream might be described. I was told that the topic of dreams was introduced at parties and other entertaining social gatherings. The dreams were described as amusing, funny, silly, entertaining, and nonsensical. They were told as social openers, ice breakers, conversation pieces, and mixers, as having no important consequence in themselves. In a casual context dream telling is somewhat similar to joke telling (Figure 6).

This joking way of telling dreams is not only engaged in by nontherapists but also by professional therapists when not in a professional context. Two psychiatrists described it thus:

Dream telling is to illustrate a clinical point, to get a good laugh. (female psychiatrist)

Dreams are told to fellow workers in a jocular sense to make a point, like, well I dreamt about Dr. So and So the other night, and he was wearing these awful clothes and this and that. How much is an authentic dream and how much is an indirect way of poking fun at an authority figure, I don't know. (male psychiatric resident physician)

Casual contexts assume relationships of equality. Although these psychiatrists were talking to their coworkers, they were doing so as peers. When they talked about dreams in this joking manner, they

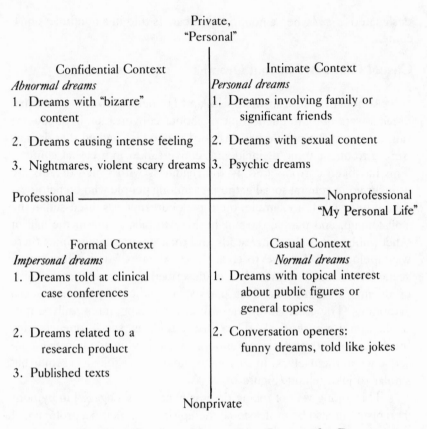

Figure 6. Classification: Appropriate Context for Dreams

were not having case conferences nor were they telling personal dreams. It is doubtful that they would engage in such joking conversation in front of their superiors, unless it was at a school party to "roast" them.

Dream telling in casual contexts seldom crosses lines of social hierarchy. This could be seen when dreams were told in the lounge. The psychotherapists shared very little and looked uncomfortable, while paraprofessionals and staff members were sharing their dreams. If lines of social hierarchy are crossed it is more acceptable for a person in an inferior position to tell a superior a dream than vice versa. However, many informants told me they would not tell their supervisor a dream. One of the administrative assistants told her boss a dream in a joking sense, but she hastened to tell me that there were many dreams she would *not* tell him. One of the nurse administrators said it very explicitly in this way: "It is inappropriate to tell your dream to someone you're the boss of. If a boss will tell you their dream, you think 'what am I supposed to do with that?' *I* don't discuss dreams with my boss."

Because casual contexts assume relationships of equality and because it is more unusual for a dream to be told by a person in a superior position than otherwise, it follows that psychotherapists who have a higher position in the social hierarchy have less opportunity to participate in a casual context. This was a common theme discussed at length by many psychotherapists, wistfully wishing they could be regarded "simply as persons" instead of primarily as psychotherapists when they were in a nonprofessional setting.

The categories of dreams that can be shared in casual contexts are very restricted. One secretary, who told me it was all right to tell dreams as a joke, added that this was so providing the dreams did not "go off on the social taboos like sex and religion." This was corroborated by many others. In fact, a social worker told me that a male acquaintance once told her a sexual dream, which she thought inappropriate and seductive (Figure 7). However, the proscription on categories of dreams that could not be told in a casual context did not involve only generally inappropriate topics but also "personal dreams" of any kind, especially dreams that were frightening, sad, or in any way "abnormal." A female psychologist said: "I would not tell a casual acquaintance my dream unless it was a silly dream; entertaining but not *personal*. It is not appropriate to tell a *personal* dream to a casual acquaintance, *especially a dream that is troubling you*."

Intimate Context: Personal Dreams

"Personal dreams" can be told in an intimate context. A context is designated *intimate* when neither the teller nor the hearer is in the role of a professional to the other one. Spouses, intimate friends, close allies, close relatives, or confidantes satisfy these relationships for dream telling. There was consensus on this point. When I asked questions about neighbors or coworkers, I received predictable answers. For example, one psychologist drew a circle of intimacy with "personal relationships" in the center and other relationships around that. Only people who qualified to be in the center could be told "personal

94

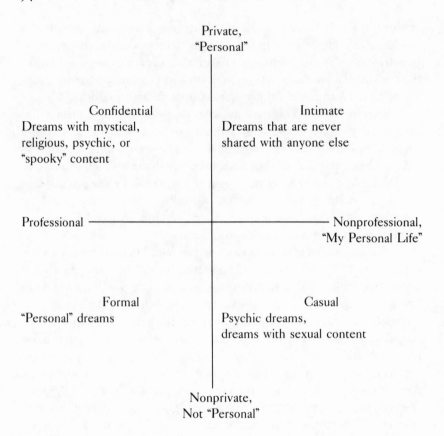

Private,
"Personal"

Confidential
Dreams with mystical,
religious, psychic, or
"spooky" content

Intimate
Dreams that are never
shared with anyone else

Professional ———————————————— Nonprofessional,
"My Personal Life"

Formal
"Personal" dreams

Casual
Psychic dreams,
dreams with sexual content

Nonprivate,
Not "Personal"

Figure 7. Classification: Inappropriate Context for Dreams

dreams." He said: "So I think that you might not tell a dream to a
neighbor or someone you didn't have a personal relationship with. You
might not tell just an acquaintance or your work coworkers with whom
you didn't have a personal relationship. The thing would be that if you
had some personal relationship that was developed, then those would
be OK, and other people would not be, those you didn't know to some
further degree than just an acquaintance."

Dreams were shared in an *intimate context* more than in other contexts. Also, except for spouses, most respondents, both men and
women, therapist or not, said that they were more likely to tell dreams
to close friends and relatives who were women. Even in an intimate

context certain male therapists were reluctant to tell their dreams. This was explained by saying that the level of disclosure required to tell a personal dream left the person "exposed" emotionally. A male social worker put it this way: "I find that even with people I know well it's a little risky sometimes because I wonder if other people see things in it, that I'm not aware of. But, I think, just generally that I'm going to end up talking about how I'm feeling, in some sense, and I think women that I know do that more often than men."

One category of dreams told only in an intimate context were psychic dreams. Twenty of the fifty-eight people I interviewed said that they had psychic dreams or knew someone intimate (a sister, an aunt) who had psychic dreams. A psychic dream is described as a dream of an event that later happens in waking life. This kind of dream was most disturbing to most people who experienced it. One woman who dreamed of the death of her father-in-law a few days before it happened was reluctant to tell anyone the dream for a long time; she told her husband after the funeral. While she was telling the story she assured me several times that she was not superstitious and would rather not have these experiences. Two therapists told me their dreams of patients who had, or were about to, commit suicide. In the former case the dream was simultaneous to the patient's action, in the latter case the dream allowed the therapist to intervene and prevent the suicide. These experiences were surprising and disconcerting to them. They told those dreams only to a few close friends and called the dream a "weird" experience.

Formal Contexts: Impersonal Dreams

When, in a professional situation, a dream is told without reference to the dreamer (i.e., impersonal), the context is designated *formal*. In this context a dream can be discussed at length as long as the identity of the dreamer is not directly connected to the dream.[3] Dreams could be presented formally at case conferences and in professional publications, but the identity of the dreamers are protected and held in confidence.

Therapists, who considered their relationship with me to be professional and therefore to provide a *formal context* for our interviews, told me their clients' dreams; but they were very careful not to reveal their clients' identities. In fact, some therapists made a point of asking me not to publish their clients' dreams. One psychology trainee put it this way: "I want to say that I'm *worried*. I know that you said that everything is confidential, but if my client knew that I had told anyone her dream, she would not be able to trust anyone any more. I don't care about myself, but I don't like the idea that her dream would be published."

When I assured her that the client's identity would be protected she relaxed. The issue of protecting the identity of the dreamers was important. Therapists told me their own dreams but needed assurance that I would not reveal their identity. When I was told "don't quote me on this," I would respond "I am going to quote you, but no one will know who you are." This answer would bring a smile. It immediately made the context a *formal* one, and that was acceptable.

Part of my data gathering on dream interpretation included presenting respondents with three dreams and asking for their opinions on one of them. When they asked me where the dreams had come from, I would answer that they had come from a publication. This was acceptable to them. One psychologist added that if the dreams had been dreamed by me or even by someone I knew, it would be inappropriate for him to interpret the dream because we had no proper contractual agreement to do so. It would put me in a position of being a researcher and a client at the same time. It would change the context from a *formal* one to a *confidential* one, or it would merge these two contexts in a way he considered inappropriate. Thus, in a formal context the only dreams that are told are those that are *impersonal* or that have been rendered so by separating the dream material from the person of the dreamer.

Confidential Context: Abnormal Dreams

When a personal dream is told by the dreamer (or a person with whom the dreamer has a close relationship) to a professional therapist, the context is designated *confidential*. This was the context in which therapists were most comfortable. It was understood that in such a context the client and the therapist have a contractual agreement and that the therapist will keep the content of the interaction confidential. In this context dreams could be told by clients to their *own* therapist. A distinction was made between therapists in general and one's own therapist. "I'd be hesitant to tell a therapist I'd just met a dream. I'd tell my own therapist," said one secretary. In fact, it was generally thought to be *less* likely that people would tell a dream to any therapist (that is, one with whom they had no contractual agreement of confidentiality). An expert stranger would be even more threatening or embarrassing. It would be as inappropriate as undressing in the presence of a physician who was not one's own physician. A psychology trainee emphasized the privateness of the context in this way: "A client is with a therapist and the client is telling his dream, because it might mean something very significant or important. It is a private thing and you keep the door closed."

Therapists told me that the conventional thing was to tell your therapist *all or most* of your dreams *only* if it was an analytic type of therapy. However, I was told that, because most therapeutic treatments were not analytic, it was thought that normal dreams were not brought to a therapist, only those that were problematic. The words used to describe these abnormal dreams were *dreadful, nightmarish, morbid, bad, frightening, recurrent, crazy,* and *bizarre.* When people had these dreams they felt "out of control" and were fearful of going insane. They wanted dream interpretations and assurance. They wanted the therapist to "fix them" and to "take care of them."

Most of the therapists I interviewed thought that the general public confused therapy with psychoanalysis, and that popular opinions related to dreams were also confused with psychoanalysis. All the therapists thought this was naive and untrue and spoke with amusement of caricatures of therapists in the popular press and in movies. However, many of them used the word *analysis* for "interpretation of dreams." Many were apologetic when they told me they did not know enough about dreams, and that I should talk to a psychoanalyst, because psychoanalysts were experts on dreams and would be ideal resources for my research!

One medical technician told me with great assurance that, "therapists want to hear your dreams. They ask a lot of questions about dreams." This was an opinion she could not corroborate in her experience! She had never been in therapy or had known of anyone whose dreams were explored, or had been explored in the past, by a therapist!

Because *abnormal dreams* are generally brought to therapists, the telling of dreams to therapists in a confidential context is generally associated with mental illness or emotional disturbance. One of the intake coordinators, who receives the initial phone calls requesting therapeutic help at one of the community mental health centers, said she believed many of the people who phoned her associated both dreams and therapy with mental illness. In fact, to the amusement and occasional dismay of many therapists, the connection to mental illness or "craziness" was extended to include the therapists themselves. This was one of the reasons a social worker was reluctant to tell people in her social circle that she was a therapist. She said: "Therapists are authority figures; there's some of that. But there's also a joking quality about psychiatrists or psychologists that they are sort of, you know, cuckoo, 'crazy'! At the same time they think that you're interpreting all the time!" (see Appendix B).

This perception of how the general public regarded them was held by many therapists. In fact, the word *crazy* was used very frequently when talking about dreams, dream telling, and therapy. The word was used in one of four ways; to signify (1) nonsensical, (2) mentally ill, (3) emotionally disturbed, or (4) eccentric. These meanings were carefully distinguished from each other, but they were also clearly interconnected, sometimes by the same person (Appendix B).

1. I was assured that the adjective *crazy* to describe dreams did not mean mental illness; it just meant nonsensical or silly. The word was used to describe dreams that could be told in a casual context. People who said a dream was crazy meant only that it did not make rational sense and was somewhat bizarre or strange.

2. However, people added sometimes in the very next sentence that having frequent bizarre nightmares might make people afraid of becoming "crazy"; that is, mentally ill. One staff member said she was cautious of telling dreams to strangers because they might think she is "nuts." She added, "They might associate the bizarreness of the dream with my state of mind. I think some people might think that if I have this *crazy* bizarre dream then something must be *wrong with my mind*."

3. The third way in which *crazy* was used in relation to dreams also started with a disclaimer. Dreams were not so much an in-

dication of craziness (insanity) as of problems, turmoil, or conflicts. So that a person was not so much insane as emotionally disturbed. Yet, one could be so disturbed by nightmares and such problems as to become really "crazy."

4. The fourth way in which the word *crazy* was used occurred when some therapists applied it as an adjective to describe therapists. The connotation to this meaning was positive. One social worker said that he had met many "crazy" people doing therapy. He added that *crazy* here did not mean mentally ill but interesting and eccentric! This seemed to be an idealized view of a therapist who is not prosaic and uninteresting but creative and intuitive. Thus the word *crazy* could be applied to therapists if it was applied in that positive sense. The amount of energy evident in describing this word was an indication that the word was emotionally charged and that, despite most of the disclaimers, dreams were indeed connected with mental illness when they were told and heard in confidential contexts.

Thus, each context was created by the setting, roles, and relationships of those involved, and in each context only certain dreams and not others were appropriate to tell. The actors were expected to use social judgment in knowing which to tell in the right context. Social blunders always involve issues of personhood. For therapists, the convergence of contexts created social and ethical dilemmas.

WHEN CONTEXTS CONVERGE

Any of the four contexts just described can become uncomfortable for social actors when they experience a confluence of roles. The discomfort is felt because a confluence of roles makes the context unclear. In this section the more usual convergences in contextual situations will be discussed, as well as the primacy of the professional domain for psychotherapists.

When persons in a casual context tell or hear a "personal dream," the casual context is changed as some of the actors perceive that the casualness is breached by unwanted intimate information. Sexual and psychic dreams are examples of dreams classified "personal" by participants. Telling a sexual dream in a casual context is considered in poor taste. A social worker explained to me exactly why this was. She said: "I had a friend once—a man—we were not very close. He would tell me certain dreams in order to become more intimate. I thought it was seductive." (She told me later that the dreams were of a sexual nature.) A psychologist told me he never told sexual dreams in mixed company. However, most male and female informants told more personal dreams to close friends and relatives who were women. Some of those personal dreams were of a sexual nature. These contexts were intimate.

Psychic dreams represented a different problem. These dreams were regarded by the dreamer to have foretold a future event in waking life. Telling such a dream in a casual context might earn the teller a reputation of being superstitious or, worse, peculiar. Audiences for psychic dreams were very carefully chosen. Hearers either had to be "believers" in precognition or intimate enough to be included in the telling of such an unexplainable mystery. Another difficulty with psychic dreams was that they were usually disturbing to the dreamer, and it was felt to be uncomfortable, and even deemed inappropriate, to let casual acquaintances see such a personal and private part of one's life.

Professional therapists were most comfortable with clear unambiguous confidential contexts. However, they were often placed in the situation of having (1) to disambiguate confidential contexts from formal ones, or (2) to distinguish confidential contexts from intimate ones. In the former cases, the general method of redress was to tighten confidentiality by making further efforts to disguise the identity of the dreamer. Breach of confidentiality is not only an ethical problem but also can become a legal one. In both situations the *confidential context* had to be protected and preserved. In every case when dreams were told and the hearer was known to be a therapist, the professional identity of the therapist became a primary consideration. The examples to illustrate this type of situation from interviews and observations are too numerous to list. The professional sector of the politico-jural domain of personhood is the primary structural principle in therapists' activities, attitudes, and interactions.

Judgmental Capacities: The Understanding of Context and the Fear of Craziness

Judgmental capacities are defined as the locally assumed, imputed capacities to show in one's activities that one understands the local standards of propriety, morality, factuality, and logicality (Harris 1989). When a dream is told or heard it is assumed that adult, responsible, moral persons with good sense will understand the social context and will act appropriately. Judgmental capacities mark humans as *persons* who are able to exercise social judgment by understanding social prescriptions and proscriptions. Children are not held capable of understanding certain social rules and therefore are not held accountable for breaches in social judgment. The process of socialization is a painstaking process of teaching children social judgment until they can be held accountable for their actions. Children who break social rules and laws are treated differently than adults who do so in the same society. However, people who are deemed to have lost their senses are also not expected to be capable of understanding social contexts and also treated differently from sensible adults when they have behaved improperly or broken the law. Social blunders, immoral conduct, absurd behavior, or illegal actions always call into question the judgmental capacity of the actor. Is the person naive and ignorant but well meaning? Is the person knowingly in breach of social conventions and laws? Or does the person lack judgmental capacities? In the first case, persons are expected to receive further education in social skills or social sophistication; in the second case, they are expected to apologize, make amends, or pay their dues to society; in the third case they are relegated to a position of marginal personhood and expected to have mental health care.

The recognition of proper contexts to tell dreams involves judgmental capacities, and therefore, social blunders in the matter of telling dreams involve issues of personhood, like all social blunders. However, those happen with different degrees of seriousness. A breach in propriety might cause eyebrows to rise, a breach of morality might cause a scandal or even a lawsuit, but a recognition that someone lacks judgmental capacities although it excuses the actor from consequences, also acknowledges the loss of personhood.

For all persons, professional or otherwise, the display of lack of good judgment in the telling of dreams makes the stakes higher in a *confidential context* because this is where clinical judgments usually are made about whether a person is mentally ill.[4] It is not surprising that the word *crazy* elicited such emotional ambivalence. A young staff member of the Day Treatment Center, who had a bachelor's degree in psychology and intended to pursue a career in clinical psychology, assured me that he thought dreams were a normal everyday happening, but he thought most people connected them to being mentally ill. He explained:

> In high school and college dreams are usually categorized by drug experiences. They are lumped in with hallucinations, and hearing voices, and drug taking (I, myself, always got the impression that dreams were very elusive for scientists to study). Well, they used to say that what dreams are . . . dreams are a lot like what people do when they hallucinate, then they got into the biochemistry of hallucination and statistics of people taking drugs. . . . They looked at dreams as something strange, and dreams were associated with schizophrenia. When they [textbooks] showed paintings done by patients who were schizophrenic, they would always describe the paintings as "dreamlike" and "nightmarish"; that they didn't make any sense; that they were *crazy*. I remember being taught that people with schizophrenia are actually living in a "dreamstate," and that they see the world as dreamlike.

Thus, although dream telling in different contexts spanned the gamut from jocular and inconsequential to frightening and crucial, in every context the word *crazy* was used to describe dreams. The word itself was used in all of these ways. I hold that even when it was used in its most innocuous sense, to denote harmless irrelevant nonsense, actors spoke with veiled anxiety about what others might think of them for having such a dream. This anxiety was increased when the dreams were considered abnormal because of the potential threats to personhood. The people who can make such determinations of people's mental health or craziness are psychotherapists. Among psychotherapists the general consensus was that people imputed to them the capacity to "read their minds" and "analyze their dreams."

Mystical Capacities to Read Minds and Interpret Dreams

Mystical capacities are defined by Harris (1989) as alleged capacities, imputed to social actors, assumed to exist but not recognizable or assessed by ordinary means. This description can be accurately applied to the perception and expectation that therapists can interpret dreams.

Therapists' alleged capacity to interpret dreams was deemed to be part of their capacity to "read minds," "know human nature," "analyze what people are thinking," "see through people's defenses," and "break into their secrets." (These are all literal comments made by informants.) The lay staff I interviewed corroborated these perceptions in three ways. First, they made comments that assumed these capacities; second, they believed that these capacities were not all acquired through education, other capacities being not-quite-definable accruing from their "person"; third, some lay staff members acknowledged their reluctance to tell therapists certain dreams for fear the therapists would make interpretations that would judge them to be, if not mentally ill, not quite mentally healthy either: as in "engaging in magical thinking," "lacking stability," or "having hangups."

Therapists sometimes impute this capacity to each other as well. A nurse said it clearly in this way:

> People in a social situation have told me that they have watched what they have said to me because I am a therapist. People think I can know about them and solve their problems—I can't really solve anything for them. I can help them maybe.
>
> I have to tell you—I do it, too! I understand that [smiling] because two weeks ago while I was making rounds with the psychiatrist, he was rough and gruff, and I thought he was analyzing me! His questions were uncomfortable!

Therapists accepted these imputed capacities in two different ways. The first way was to become embarrassed, unassuming, and to minimize them. The other way was to take them for granted and make the most of them. These capacities were specifically applied to dream interpretation in these two ways. A clinical psychologist took the unassuming position when he said: "I would guess that probably the bulk of therapists don't know any more about dreams in general than the rest of the general public. They think we can read their minds and their expectations don't often coincide with reality."

Another psychologist had an opposite opinion of these capacities. She said: "When patients come in and tell me the dream, they're expecting me to know all about it and to give them some kind of analysis. I think there is a certain power that goes along with doing this work, and a therapist can make this work in the best interest of the patient or not. A lot of that kind of work rests on the fact that the patient thinks the therapist is up on a pedestal."

However, regarding their own capacities, therapists knew that they were expected to exercise clinical judgment to make decisions about how to use these capacities properly, ethically, and competently. One of the clinical decisions discussed was the decision whether to draw attention to dreams in specific clinical situations. The capacity to make this decision derived from their professional entitlements and responsibilities.

Social Entitlement Capacities and Responsibilities

Social entitlement capacities are defined as the capacities to embody in one's conduct the rights, duties, freedoms, and constraints of specific social roles (Harris 1989). The role of professional psychotherapist conferred on them the capacity to act as agents on behalf of themselves and their clients. There was an expectation that therapists would take responsibility about what to do regarding their own dreams and the dreams of their clients, even if the decision was to do nothing about them. With regard to their own dreams there was generally a vague uncomfortable feeling among them that they did not do as much dream work as they wanted, or felt they *ought*, to do. All but one therapist I interviewed regarded dream exploration and dream work as a way to achieve self-knowledge, reflect on one's feelings, and gain insight. These were qualities they expected of themselves and others expected of them.

With regard to the dreams of their clients, therapists' social entitlement capacities included the capacity to know when dream work with clients was therapeutic and when it was not. The criterion that most of them used in making this clinical decision was what they described as "psychological mindedness."

Psychological mindedness is a term that was introduced spontaneously and frequently by therapists to describe a general inclination and disposition to attend to one's mental and emotional processes and experiences. In this section I describe the attribute only as it was related to dreams. Psychological mindedness was related to dreams in the following ways: first, it was correlated to interest in and valuing of dreams; second, it was related to successful psychotherapeutic use of dreams; third, it was described positively as a quality that only certain persons possessed and that was related to other attributes also regarded affirmatively. A few illustrative examples of how the term was used might elucidate.

1. One psychologist said that his interest in dreams started with his relationship and dialogue with people who were psychologically minded. He continued to define the term thus: "people who did a lot of thinking about life, about experiences, about perceptions and dreams, and could talk about them in a particular way. Those are the people I would kind of group as *psychologically minded.*"

A psychiatrist related her interest in her own dreams to her capacity to be psychologically minded. She talked about her dreams to selected members of her family, whom she described as also being psychologically minded. Another psychiatrist said that people who expected the psychiatrist to listen to their dreams were psychologically minded: "I guess what I mean by that is that they are people who are used to thinking in terms of introspection, reflecting on their own experience, not just living in the world but thinking, self-conscious and self-aware, and saying 'how is my living in my world affecting me'—a heightened self-awareness. That's what I call *psychologically minded.*"

2. Not only was psychological mindedness related to having an interest in dreams, but also it was related to the successful use of dreams in psychotherapy. Because patients who were not psychologically minded would not be disposed to reflecting on their lives, their mental processes (including dreams), and their emotions, it was deemed unlikely that they would profit from the use of dreams in therapy. According to some of the therapists, patients who were not psychologically minded would not be likely to even remember their dreams or tell dreams to the therapist.

Another psychiatrist said that in his work with teenage anorexic girls he had discovered that those who could remember their dreams had a better prognosis than those who could not, because "they have a greater capacity for psychological mindedness or for looking inside and are not so highly defended."

The patients who improved with psychotherapy were valuable to therapists. It made their work more rewarding than working with patients who were not psychologically minded. One of the psychiatrists insightfully explained to me that because of his capacity to prescribe medication he was assigned most of the sickest patients. He said that probably psychologists were assigned the kind of patients with whom dreams could be used in psychotherapy; his patients could not because they were not "insight oriented."

3. This quality of psychological mindedness was cast in a very positive light by therapists. It was a quality that, at best, they liked to attribute to themselves and, at least, they thought they *ought* to acquire. An interest and valuation of dreams was deemed to be the hallmark of a person inclined to introspection. I was also told that this was a rare quality that most people did *not* possess. A psychiatrist made this point very clear: "I went to a school system that was not psychologically minded. . . . I think the lay public is nowhere as near involved with dreams as I am, because thinking about dreams, valuing them, is correlated with psychological mindedness, and an awareness of the intrapsychic life, and the general mass of the lay population are not as a group psychologically minded."

But *insight, introspection*, and *recall of dreams* were not the only adjectives correlated to psychological mindedness. The psychologically minded were also described as brighter, more educated, more highly motivated, more sophisticated, and higher functioning. (See Appendix C.)

For those people the exploration of dreams in psychotherapy was expected to be rewarding and beneficial, but for "low-functioning" people the exploration of dreams was considered at best not helpful and at times harmful. (See Appendix D.)

"Low Functioning Patients" and the Art of "Not Messing With Their Heads"

There was agreement among many of the therapists that patients who functioned at a higher level would profit by dream talk and dream exploration, and that it was "unadvisable," "tactically incorrect," "not helpful," "painful," and even "harmful" to explore dreams with patients who were classified as low functioning.

The classification into levels of functioning is a part of the diagnostic assessment of patients in the *Diagnostic and Statistical Manual of Mental Disorders* (DSM III) published by the American Psychiatric Association.[5] Therefore, all therapists would be acquainted with that terminology. The guidelines in DSM III stipulate that a person who functions at a higher level immediately prior to the time of his or her mental illness will be considered to have a better prognosis for recovery. However, most therapists did not think dream work appropriate with low functioning patients.

In this section I describe therapists' ideas about low functioning patients, and their reasons for not introducing or focusing on dreams in their therapy. I also show that a few therapists do indeed listen to the dreams of patients whom they judge to be low functioning, and they use dreams in different ways to effect therapeutic outcomes.

Patients who were functioning at a lower level were deemed to be "unhealthy" and "more emotionally disturbed," Patients who were "psychotic," "prepsychotic," or "chronically mentally ill" were seen as functioning at a lower level. These people were probably unemployed and hospitalized, or had been hospitalized in the past, for a mental illness. They were said to have come from "more disadvantaged backgrounds."

In trying to explain why the use of dreams would not be advised in low functioning patients, therapists used descriptions and analogies that were mechanistic. I was told that their egos were "not intact," their defenses were "faulty," their "functioning was impaired," and one wanted to "shore them up" not "break them down." It was important when working with these people that the therapist focus on their relationships, their daily activities, but *not* on their dreams, their fantasies, or their imaginings. Only people who were "well put together" could stand to deal with their dreams. Because they were "too loosely wrapped" already, dreamlike experiences would have the effect of "loosening them up" further. The correct approach would be to "seal them over" not to disturb and distress them further.

One psychiatrist explained to me that if patients have violent, distressing, and gory fantasies, it is "not helpful" to focus on those fantasies. Another psychiatrist was much more emphatic about the harm that could be caused by focusing on dreams:

> I would not use dreams with psychotic persons, schizophrenic persons. *You mess around with dream material* in schizophrenic persons, you usually make them worse. You want to suppress that material, because that's unconscious material, put the lid on that. It's dangerous unless you're specifically trained for it, *to mess with dreams* in borderline patients, because it loosens them up too

much, and you want to tighten their defenses rather than have all this unconscious material out in the open.

Most of the therapists were not as emphatic as this psychiatrist about the harmfulness of using dreams with psychotic patients but most would agree that with low functioning patients it was not helpful to encourage talk about dreams in therapy.

One social worker believed that she used dreams in her therapeutic work more than anyone else in the center. This social worker said that she almost always brought up the subject of dreams and told her clients that dreams were important and that she was interested in them. However, even she was emphatic about not using dreams with psychotic patients: "I think dreams are extremely powerful and I think it would be easy to *mess around with people's heads*. . . . For myself, I wouldn't touch a dream with anyone who is psychotic. When someone is psychotic you don't want to uncover, you want to help them cover as much as possible. I've read things about doing dream work with psychotics, but I feel like I would need more training to do that. I wouldn't touch it." There were other categorical statements about not pursuing dreams with psychotic or low functioning patients, but none as emphatic as this one.

Nevertheless, seventeen of the forty-nine therapists interviewed said that they saw no harm in listening to dreams of patients whether they were high or low functioning. The reasons given for listening were (1) the therapist could gain much information about the patient from the dream without pursuing the topic; (2) the therapist could focus on the affect as the dream was told; and (3) sometimes telling the dream could help the patient talk about other things. This was thought to be especially true of children. The attitude of these therapists was that if the client chose to bring up a dream there might be a good reason to take the time to listen even if the dream itself would not be the topic of focus or comment (see Table 1).

Only eleven of the forty-nine expressed an active interest in their patients' dreams. These therapists made their interest known in the following ways: (1) they asked questions about the dream when the topic was brought up, (2) they made empathic comments about the feelings within the dream, (3) they took notes of the dream, and (4) they told the patients that they were interested in their dreams.

Eight therapists told of patients who they described as "low functioning," "chronically mentally ill," "disadvantaged," "schizophrenic,"
and "psychotic," respectively, with whom they had used dreams to effect therapeutic outcomes. For the most part those were reported as
exceptional or atypical cases. A more detailed description of these
reports will illustrate.

A social worker, who told me "schizophrenics are *not* the right patients to be using dreams, because with their delusional thinking they
don't make it easy to decipher what is a dream and what is reality," added that nevertheless there was a schizophrenic patient who told other
patients in group therapy that he was having dreams of being physically
abused by his alcoholic father. In this case the other group members
gave him understanding, support, and comfort and helped him talk
about his fear of his father, which was very real (see Table 1).

Similarly, a psychiatrist reported the case of a psychotic woman
who on a series of occasions when her medication was changed would
have nightmares about dead people, especially her dead mother. He
added:

> She reproduced her mother, who is dead, and actually found it
> comforting that her mother comes in her dream—comforts her.
> This woman is reality oriented. She knows that her mother is
> dead, but during sleep her mother comes to comfort her. . . .
>   *I thought that was in context*; she needed someone to comfort
> her. Since she is fifty-one she thinks it's childish to go to people
> for comfort. She does not seem frightened of her dreams but
> since there are dead people in them, she calls them nightmares.

This psychiatrist was the only one in the sample who reported a
case in which he thought the dream and the telling of it was comforting
to a psychotic patient (see Table 1). He was not a U.S. citizen and had
told me earlier that in his country of origin the folklore was that you can
visit people in your dreams. It was apparent to me that he was well
educated in and aware of Western psychiatry as well as Western ideas.[6]
He wanted to assure me that the woman was "reality oriented during
the day"; that in this case, even though she was psychotic, she was,
nevertheless, deriving comfort from this dream; and that this dream
was the topic of numerous sessions until the medication was changed.

Table 1

Local Ideas about the Use of Dreams in Psychotherapy: Therapist's Approach

Subjects			Use of Dreams in Psychotherapy					
ID	Site	Sex	Never Use	Therapist Has Insufficient Knowledge	Only with High Functioning Patients	No Harm in Listening to Dreams of All Patients	Active Interest in Dreams for All Patients	Use Dreams to Confirm Patient's Feelings, Support, Comfort
D1	Ri	M				X		
D2	Ri	M		X	X			
D3*	Ri	M						
D4	Ri	F		X	X			X
D5	Ri	F			X			
D6	Ri	M			X			
D7*	Ne	M			X	X		
D8	Ne	M			X			
D9	Ne	M			X			
P1	Ri	M		X	X	X		
P2	Ri	F			X	X		
P3	Ri	F		X		X		
P4	Ri	F			X	X		
P5*	Ri	F		X		X	X	
P6	Ne	M				X		
P7*	Ne	M				X		
P8	Ne	M			X			
P9	Ne	F			X			
P10	Ne	F				X	X	
P11	Ne	M			X			
P12	Ne	M					X	X
P13	Ne	M	X					

Table 1
Local Ideas about the Use of Dreams in Psychotherapy: Therapist's Approach (cont.)

| | | | | | Use of Dreams in Psychotherapy | | | |
| Subjects | | | | | | | | |
ID	Site	Sex	Never Use	Therapist Has Insufficient Knowledge	Only with High Functioning Patients	No Harm in Listening to Dreams of All Patients	Active Interest in Dreams for All Patients	Use Dreams to Confirm Patient's Feelings, Support, Comfort
P14†*	Ne	M		X	X			
P15†	Ne	F			X			
S1	Ri	F			X			
S2	Ri	F				X		
S3	Ri	F		X	X			
S4	Ne	M			X			
S5	Ne	F			X		X	
S6	Ne	F		X		X		
S7	Ne	F				X		
S8	Ne	M				X		
S9*	Ne	M						X
S10	Ne	M				X		
S11*	Ne	M		X				
S12	Ne	F			X	X		
S13	Ne	F				X		
S14	Ne	F		X	X			
S15	Ne	F			X			
N1	Ri	F		X				
N2	Ri	F					X	X
N3	Ri	F					X	X
N4	Ri	F				X		

Table 1

Local Ideas about the Use of Dreams in Psychotherapy: Therapist's Approach (cont.)

Subjects			Use of Dreams in Psychotherapy					
ID	Site	Sex	Never Use	Therapist Has Insufficient Knowledge	Only with High Functioning Patients	No Harm in Listening to Dreams of All Patients	Active Interest in Dreams for All Patients	Use Dreams to Confirm Patient's Feelings, Support, Comfort
N5	Ri	F					X	X
N6	Ri	F		X			X	X
N7	Ri	F				X	X	
N8	Ne	F					X	
N9	Ne	F					X	X
N10	Ne	F				X		

*These were of foreign nationality; came to the United States as adults.

†These had only an undergraduate education in psychology.

Ne = Newell; Ri = Riverpool; D = Psychiatrists; P = Psychologists; S = Social Workers; N = Nurses.
M = Male; F = Female.

He added "now her medication is changed so she does not need those dreams any more." He seemed to wish to emphasize that he was practicing good Western psychiatry and that in this case the comforting dream was *in context*!

Two nurses reported cases of patients telling nightmares that became the focus of therapy. In each case the nightmare turned out to be reliving memories of a traumatic experience: in one case witnessing a murder; and in the other, a rape. In both cases, although the symptoms increased for awhile, they eventually diminished and disappeared after many therapy sessions when the dreams were topics of focus. Similarly, another nurse told of a patient who was having a recurrent nightmare, which disappeared after she spent time talking about it in therapy sessions.

Because these were not high functioning patients, I asked the nurses whether they talked about dreams to other low functioning patients. All of them told me they focused on dreams with *any* patients who wanted to bring them up. One nurse explained as follows: "Usually if someone brings in a dream I'll address it in some way. But the way in which I address it is different, depending on the person and how impaired they are, what kind of pathology they have, and whether I'm doing supportive therapy or not." She added that one of her most "dysfunctional" patients had become reassured when she understood that her violent dreams were expressions of her own anger and that, because she was dreaming about all these violent acts, they did not need ever to be expressed in real life.

Another nurse, who was a black American told me that her black patients whether schizophrenic or not enjoyed talking about their dreams with her. She added: "Black people have not traditionally been in psychotherapy, but dreams are really a way in which they can do some internal work. They, perhaps, do not realize it as such, but I see it as a real positive thing."

Two nurses spoke of dreams as emotionally cathartic even for schizophrenics; and one added that dreams "were normalizing experiences." She continued, "it's always a relief for me to hear that they have dreams and that they want to tell about them" (see Table 1).

Finally, the only psychologist who thought it was helpful to use dreams with schizophrenics said that he thought it was helpful to "join" the patient in his experience even if it was a delusion, a dream, or a hallucination (see Table 1). It seemed important to him to understand the patients from inside their own frame of reference or language. The purpose of this is to "build rapport" and "trust." He had gained his insights from his experience of working exclusively with schizophrenics in a previous job. He maintained emphatically that when patients were constantly coached in becoming "reality oriented" all the time, "in essence what was happening there was that the patient was learning to play the game of not telling their dreams or hallucinations, and not telling their delusions because they realized that the staff didn't believe them or want to hear them. They played the game so they could get off the unit."

Thus, therapists were expected to know when dream work was therapeutic and when it was not. It was generally agreed that clients who were psychologically minded could gain insight from their dreams, and for them dream work was helpful and beneficial. However, patients who were not able to receive insight from their dreams were not helped by focusing on dreams. This was especially true of patients who were assessed as low functioning or chronically mentally ill. For those people focusing on dreams was believed to be harmful, painful, or distressing. Many of these patients were also described as low in education and income level.

Seventeen of the forty-nine therapists who were interviewed nevertheless saw no harm in listening to the dreams of patients who wanted to tell them. Eleven of the therapists interviewed had an active interest in pursuing dreams with patients; and eight of those gave examples of patients who were considered low functioning or chronically mentally ill with whom dreams were used with therapeutic outcomes, such as diminishing symptoms and receiving support and comfort. These cases were treated as exceptional even by four of the eight therapists. Only one of the fifteen social workers reported such a case (Table 1). Similarly only one of the nine psychiatrists reported such a case (Table 1). He was not a U.S. citizen. One of the fifteen psychologists reported such a case (Table 1). He had worked exclusively with schizophrenics previously. Five of ten nurses interviewed reported such cases (Table 1). One was black, and she found that black Americans were, in general, helped by dream work. The five nurses had experience working with schizophrenics and other low functioning patients with poor prognoses and found focusing on the patients' dreams could be "normalizing," "reassuring," "emotionally cathartic," "supportive," and "comforting," even when the patients could not gain insight from them.

CONCLUSION

The concept of *person* has provided a method for observing and analyzing the ideas and attitudes about dream telling of forty-nine therapists and nine staff members in two community mental health centers. As emic perspectives on the "personal" or "nonpersonal" aspects of dream telling were examined in the light of whether the dreamers were therapists or not, four contextual categories emerged: the casual, the intimate, the confidential, and the formal. Social actors were expected to use their judgmental capacity to know which dreams to tell in the right context. When contexts became unclear actors became uncomfortable about dream telling; and therapists, because of the primacy of the professional role for their personhood, preferred to place the interaction in a *confidential context*.

However, for all persons, therapist or otherwise, the lack of good judgment in the telling of dreams make the stakes higher in confidential contexts because in those contexts clinical judgments are usually made about whether a person is crazy (mentally ill). The label of "crazy" is feared because of potential loss of personhood. It was not surprising that the word *crazy* was applied to dreams in all contexts to span a whole range of meanings from inconsequential to crucial, from harmlessly facetious to psychotic. Therefore, even when the word was used in its most innocuous sense, actors spoke with veiled or obvious discomfort about what others, including professional peers, might think of having such a dream or telling it in that particular context.

The general consensus among therapists was that people ascribed to them the capacity to "read minds" and "analyze dreams." Therapists accepted the social entitlement capacities and responsibilities of knowing in which cases to hear dreams, pursue dreams, make them the topic of focus, or ignore them. The therapists in the sample generally agreed (all but one) that exploring dreams was a beneficial thing to do when the patient was *psychologically minded*.

The description of *psychologic mindedness* as the capacity to be self-aware, introspective, and self-searching is similar to Mauss's *per-*

sonne: être psychologique. Therapists valued that understanding of personhood. The capacity and responsibility for self-knowledge and insight were deemed to be among the criteria for being a good therapist. Psychological mindedness was a quality and ideal that they liked to attribute to themselves or sought to possess. Therapists also valued psychologically minded patients because they were perceived as having good prognoses for recovery with psychotherapeutic treatment.

It was apparent, however, that dreams were seen as valuable almost exclusively in this sense, for receiving insight. Dreams were seldom seen as valuable for other therapeutic purposes. For patients who were not psychologically minded it was not considered helpful or even possible to do insight-oriented work, so what would be the use of pursuing dreams? Dreams might stir up unwanted and unwieldy unconscious material that could distress and further disturb patients who were already disturbed by unconscious material. For patients considered emotionally disturbed, psychotic, chronically mentally ill, or otherwise disadvantaged who had a low level of functioning, the use of dreams was generally believed to be harmful. It could make crazy patients crazier, confused patients more confused, and cause patients who were not very articulate to be more frustrated. The community mental health centers serviced a large number of such patients, and those patients were not considered suitable for the use of dreams in therapy.

Consequently, although in theory dreams were valued for their part in increasing self-awareness and were considered useful for psychoanalytic methods or for long-term, insight-oriented therapy, practically speaking dreams were not considered valuable resources for the kind of therapy done in their present jobs.[7] Also, long-term, insight-oriented therapy was considered expensive and effectively out of the reach of all but a few people, even those who were psychologically minded. Theoretically and ideally, dreams were considered resources in psychotherapy; but practically and actually, this was not the case.

Regarding dreams as valuable only and exclusively for the psychologically minded to gain insight and self-knowledge is analogous to Mauss's ideas regarding the psychological individual as the most developed concept of *person*. Mauss understood this concept to have been achieved only in rudimentary form in earlier and more primitive societies, but to have been fully developed only in Western thought.

The understanding of one's personhood only as a role (*personnage*) and mask (*persona*) was designated as occurring earlier and being less developed than the understanding of person as a moral and psychological individual (*moi*). The psychological individual was one whose communications could no longer be mediated by priest and community after the Reformation. The psychological individual began, by necessity, to communicate directly and inwardly with self and God. This, according to Mauss, made the Western person intensely concerned with individual consciousness.

Mauss's concept of *person* represents an extremely thought-provoking historical analysis of the evolution of an idea. It is an abstract theoretical category that brilliantly and accurately, albeit very generally, describes the preferred dispositions of the modern Western individual. However, one can argue with much evidence, when looking at particular cases, that not all contemporary Western persons understand and exhibit personhood in the highly self-searching and self-conscious way that Mauss outlines in the latter part of his essay. Nevertheless, it would be hard to argue that this understanding of person was not very highly prized in the West.

I have shown earlier (in Chapter 2) that the different aspects of the category of person that Mauss considered diachronically as historically discrete are part of the concurrent understanding of personhood for the therapists who spoke with me. Although they liked to see themselves as introspective, self-searching, and self-knowing (*être psychologique*), they also at times saw themselves as playing unfamiliar roles or roles that were prefigured by their families or their social environments (*personnage*). At times they seemed to be wearing masks that felt external and extraneous to them, and at other times the masks (*persona*) seemed to express a social persona like a face or a name. They repeatedly said in their talks with me that many people were *not* psychologically minded. However, none of them described themselves as lacking this quality. There seemed to be among them a clear preference for psychological mindedness. Psychologically minded persons were also described as more intelligent, articulate, educated, sophisticated, high functioning, and motivated; and for those who were thus endowed dreams were seen as a valuable resource.

The association of dreams with the lofty ideals of self-discovery, on the one hand, and with the disturbing thoughts of the "crazy," on the other, tended to cause the more prosaic and commonplace interactions about dreams to appear trivial and inconsequential. Dream telling was usually accompanied by either an apologetic or a cautionary comment. But it was considered unlikely that those who were "crazy" could be helped by talking about their dreams. Four of the eight therapists who found the use of dreams helpful with psychotics tended to minimize the incidents, consider them atypical, or call the therapeutic outcomes "limited." Because gaining insight was the most important outcome, other outcomes were by comparison "limited."

Only five of the therapists (one psychologist and four nurses) who reported using dreams with "low functioning" patients talked about the incidents as valuable with matter-of-fact acceptance. In Chapter 5 the question of how perceptions about dream telling among the staff was related to their role preparation and enactment will be addressed to discover why nurses might have been more disposed to use dreams with "low functioning" patients. But first, in Chapter 4, the question related to the constellation of ideas and beliefs about dreams will be explored in relation to dream interpretation.

IV

Dream Interpretation: Freudian Mythology and the American Mystique of Dreams

INTRODUCTION

A notion based more on tradition than fact, which nevertheless essentially captures the local ideas, beliefs, and important issues of the people who hold it, is generally known as a myth. The notion that dream telling is valuable only for gaining insight, but of little use or value to those who are not psychologically minded and harmful for those who are mentally ill is such a notion. In Chapter 3 that notion was related to the Maussian category of *person* as *psychological individual* (*être psychologique*), which he understood to have evolved historically in the West from the notions of *person* as *role* (*personnage*) and *mask* (*persona*).

In this chapter the local ideas and beliefs about dream interpretation are examined. I show that the mythology about dream interpretation at the two community mental health centers exhibits the influence of Freud and the psychoanalytic tradition. Perceiving dreams as a means of insight and self-discovery is not far from Freud's view that dreams are the "royal road to the unconscious." However, I also discovered that, among the therapists and staff, very few had read the Freudian literature, many had not read *any* of Freud's works, many did not mention him, and a few, although they referred to Freud, were misinformed about his work. Thus, Freud was variously understood, misunderstood, quoted, misquoted, rejected, or ignored. Yet a popularized version of Freudian ideas and terminology was generally assumed as obvious.

THE EXPLORATION PROCESS AND METHOD

The method used to explore the local beliefs and ideas about dream interpretation was to ask the therapists and staff why they thought people had dreams and to ask their opinions about one of their own dreams and one of the dreams of another person (a client, a friend, a coworker, or a relative). They were also shown three dreams and asked to give their opinions about one of them. They were subsequently asked where they had learned about dreams. The nonprofessional staff were asked the same questions as the therapists, except, of course, for the questions about clients' dreams. I tried not to use the word *interpretation* myself. But very often they used this word as well as the word *analyze*. For example, when I showed them the dreams, various comments were often made as follows:

"Oh! You want me to analyze this?"

"It's not right to interpret a dream without asking the dreamer's associations."

"O.K.! but I'm not very confident about dream analysis."

"Some people would say these are all Freudian symbols, but I don't go for all that Freudian stuff."

A similar method of presenting dreams to dream interpreters was used by Benjamin Kilborne in his work in Morocco (1981a). He chose dreams from Freud's works. Kilborne's focus was on the dream interpreters and on the social context of the dream telling, as is mine. He was looking for their perceptions of the dreams and for similarities in their reactions to the dreams. The dreams as interpreted by the Moroccan interpreters provided an emic account of their ideas about dreams, about themselves, and about the dreamers. Then Kilborne provided the etic analysis by considering the dream *and* the interpretations from a Freudian perspective. Among the many other values of his methodology is the instructive demonstration of the differences between the Moroccan interpretations and Freud's own interpretations of the very same dream.

In this study three dreams were selected from Freud's work *The Interpretation of Dreams* (1965 [1900]) and presented to each of the people I interviewed at the two community mental health centers. I asked their opinions about one of the dreams and also asked: "If someone told you this dream, what would you think? What would you say?" The professional therapists and the nonprofessional staff were given the same dreams. It gave each subject a chance to select a particular dream and to give reasons for their selection if they wanted to do so. Some of them did not select but commented on all three dreams. It also gave them an opportunity to form their own ideas about the alleged dreamer. Most, but not all, of the therapists assumed that a client would bring this dream. Other therapists distinguished the contexts, "If a client were to tell me this I would think and say this, but if a friend or stranger told me this it would make me think thus." It gave them a chance, while in the *formal context* with me, to comment not only on the dream interpretation but also on other social contexts of the dream telling.

My method of analysis is in three steps. First, I describe the therapists' and staff members' ideas about why people dream, and their interpretations of their own and others' dreams; second, I trace the influence of Freud by comparing and contrasting their use of Freudian terminology and interpretations with Freud's theory and interpretations of the same dreams; third, I analyze their ideas of themselves and dream interpretation by examining them in the light of Mauss's understanding of the category of person.

LOCAL IDEAS ABOUT DREAM INTERPRETATION

Every person with whom I spoke had an opinion about why people dream. Even though two of the therapists said they thought no one really knew why people dream they nevertheless gave their own opinions about it.

Distinctive features of their ideas about dreams were (1) that dreams mean something that is discoverable by analyzing the symbols, (2) that analyzing dreams is related to self-discovery, (3) that what is discovered about the self has to do with unconscious, hidden, and unacceptable feelings, conflicts, and wishes that the dreamer is either unaware of or unwilling to face.

In this section I discuss only a few of the many statements made by both professional therapists and lay support staff. The statements indicated that many of the therapists were unaware of the general Freudian influence in their beliefs whereas only a small number of them acknowledged this influence. Finally, some of their misconceptions about Freudian theory of dreams are addressed.

Fifteen of the forty-nine therapists had read Freud, were well acquainted with his work, acknowledged Freud's influence on them, and were able also to acknowledge minor differences they had with Freudian theory. Four were psychiatrists, six were psychologists, three were nurses, and three were social workers (see Table 2). In fact, one psychiatrist would not complete the exercise of telling me her opinions of the dreams because the dreamer was not there, and she said Freud would call analyzing the dream without the dreamer's associations "wild analysis." A very large percentage of the therapists (all but nine) also said that the right way to do it would be to get the dreamer's associations. However, that did not prevent them from commenting on the dreams and giving quite detailed interpretations. All the therapists' *and* most of the lay staff's opinions about why people dreamed were delivered in Freudian terminology, even though some of those were misconceptions of Freudian ideas. (Only two of the lay staff did not talk about dreams in this way, see Table 2). The words *symbol, sexual symbols, unconscious desires, unconscious conflicts, internal anxiety, wish fulfillments, hidden emotions, disguises, distortions, associations*, and *analysis* were frequently used to describe their theory of dreams and their ideas of dream interpretation (see Table 2). An example of a typical statement will illustrate.

Paul, a social worker, is a seasoned therapist who has been practicing his profession for more than ten years. He is confident of his professional ability. He seemed to enjoy talking with me about his own dreams and of his belief that they had alerted him to things that needed attention within himself and in his life. He did not remember having formally learned anything about dreams, yet he referred to many works in the fields of psychology and religion, some of which he was currently reading with curiosity and excitement. He said he had not read anything by Freud. This is what he said about why people dream:

> I think people dream to resolve *conflicts* the person is struggling with, which their conscious mind has not resolved in their daytime awakened state. The *unconscious* mind attempts to

resolve *the conflict* in the dream. There is another type of dream, too. I guess I would call it the *erotic dream* or the *pleasure* dream, but I guess in a way you can think about that as a conflict, too. Some sort of erotic impulse that we tend to *gratify* in the dream. Dreams are *symbolic, unconscious*, and poetic.

I don't remember any formal discussions in the academic setting [on dreams]. I think I learned it in a more pervasive way—well, you know, about the Freudian thing, that dreams are significant, people's dreams *are supposed to mean something*. The person may benefit by *reflecting* on it and talking about it . . . [the dream] is an indicator of something that *needs attending to.*

Paul's statements represent the expressions of a large number of therapists who recognized knowing Freudian ideas without remembering where they had learned them.

There were also a large number of therapists who did not recognize that their ideas resembled Freud's. For example, a psychology intern, who said without hesitation that she believed dreams were *wish fulfillments*, could not tell me the source of her knowledge. She said, "that's a pretty good theory, but I don't remember where I learned it." As another example, a nurse said that dream symbols incorporated physical symptoms that would otherwise have aroused the dreamer in such a way that the dreamer could *continue to sleep*. She used the example of the needs of a full bladder to which Freud had made specific reference (Freud 1965 [1900]: 402, 668), again without any idea of her source. When I pressed her by asking if she had made up that example herself she said, "no I must have read it somewhere, but I couldn't tell you where right now." Similarly a psychiatric resident physician who allegedly had not read anything in or about Freud said that he thought dreams provided a *"release"* or a way of vicariously experiencing things that could not be experienced in *real life*. When I asked him whether he might have learned this in college, he replied that he remembered having the same opinion about dreams in high school!

A few of the therapists were convinced that they had not been influenced by *any* dream theory. For example, a social worker who had just told me that the "emotional content, people, places in the dream might be *displaced* onto other people or places" (a Freudian idea), told

Table 2

Local Ideas about Dream Interpretation: The Freudian Influence

Subjects			Use of Freudian Ideas and Terminology							
ID	Site	Sex	Interpretation by Dreamer	Symbols	Sexual Symbols	Unconscious	Disguise	Wish	Internal Anxiety Conflict	Read Freud
D1	Ri	M	X	X	X	X	X			X
D2	Ri	M	X	X	X		X			
D3*	Ri	M						X		
D4	Ri	F	X	X	X	X	X	X		X
D5	Ri	F	X	X	X		X	X		X
D6	Ri	M	X			X	X	X	X	
D7*	Ne	M	X	X	X	X	X	X		X
D8	Ne	M	X	X	X		X	X		
D9	Ne	M	X	X	X		X			
P1	Ri	M	X	X	X	X	X		X	X
P2	Ri	F	X		X	X			X	X
P3	Ri	F	X		X	X		X		
P4	Ri	F	X	X	X	X	X		X	X
P5*	Ri	F	X		X	X		X	X	X
P6	Ne	M			X		X		X	
P7*	Ne	M	X	X	X	X		X	X	X
P8	Ne	M	X	X	X	X	X	X	X	
P9	Ne	F		X	X			X		
P10	Ne	F	X		X					
P11	Ne	F	X	X	X	X	X		X	X
P12	Ne	M								

Table 2
Local Ideas about Dream Interpretation: The Freudian Influence (cont.)

Subjects			Use of Freudian Ideas and Terminology							
			Interpretation by Dreamer	Symbols	Sexual Symbols	Unconscious	Disguise	Wish	Internal Anxiety Conflict	Read Freud
ID	Site	Sex								
P13	Ne	M	X	X		X		X		
P14†	Ne	M	X	X	X	X	X			
P15†	Ne	F	X	X	X			X	X	
S1	Ri	M	X			X			X	
S2	Ri	F			X				X	X
S3	Ri	F			X				X	X
S4	Ne	F	X	X	X		X	X	X	
S5	Ne	F	X	X						
S6	Ne	M	X		X	X				
S7	Ne	M							X	
S8	Ne	M	X			X				
S9†	Ne	F				X		X		
S10	Ne	F		X	X				X	
S11†	Ne	M	X	X			X			
S12	Ne	F	X	X		X	X			
S13	Ne	F		X	X					
S14	Ne	F	X			X	X			
S15	Ne	F	X	X		X				X
N1	Ri	F	X		X			X	X	X
N2	Ri	F	X		X		X	X	X	
N3	Ri	F	X	X		X			X	X

Table 2

Local Ideas about Dream Interpretation: The Freudian Influence (cont.)

	Subjects			Use of Freudian Ideas and Terminology							
ID	Site	Sex	Interpretation by Dreamer	Symbols	Sexual Symbols	Unconscious	Disguise	Wish	Internal Anxiety Conflict	Read Freud
N4	Ri	F	X	X		X		X		
N5	Ri	F	X		X	X			X	X
N6	Ri	F	X							
N7	Ri	F	X	X			X	X		X
N8	Ne	F	X			X			X	
N9	Ne	F	X			X	X		X	
N10	Ne	F	X			X			X	
L1	Ne	F						X		
L2	Ne	F								
L3	Ne	F		X	X			X		
L4	Ne	F							X	
L5	Ne	F								
L6	Ne	F								
L7	Ne	F				X		X	X	
L8	Ne	F	X	X		X		X	X	
L9	Ne	F		X	X				X	X

*These were of foreign nationality; came to the United States as adults.

†These had only an undergraduate education in psychology.

Ne = Newell; Ri = Riverpool; D = Psychiatrists; P = Psychologists; S = Social Workers; N = Nurses; L = Support Staff Members. M = Male; F = Female.

me a few minutes later that his ideas about dreams came from himself because he did not remember reading anything about dreams. He said, "I make up my own idea of where dreams come from. But I've never read other stuff to confirm that. If I watched a T.V. program about that, it probably just supplemented what I had thought about it myself." This young man was not as arrogant as his statement seemed to indicate; he said repeatedly that he wished he knew more about dreams, and also that he was wishing he had learned more in his training.

A young psychiatrist who had read many theories about dreams, including Freud's insisted that he was not influenced by any of them. He said, "I'm not a dogmatist, I try to approach the topic with almost a blank screen approach. I don't subscribe to any one theory of dreams." When I pressed him by asking which of the many theories he had read were the most plausible, he said this:

> If someone came to me with a dream I would ask a lot of questions. Someone might dream they love a person, but they don't—to couch uncomfortable feelings. It's a *reaction formation*. But sometimes it's simple and straightforward. Let's say, if someone has a craving for a particular food they haven't had in a long time, and they can't find it in the city, they might see that in their dream. This is a simple *wish fulfillment*. It does not always represent something else. Sometimes a cigar is only a cigar.

While protesting his neutrality and lack of "dogma," he was not willing or able to express his views without Freudian terminology and without quoting Freud.

The therapists were not the only ones who presented their dream interpretations in Freudian terminology. I interviewed nine staff members who were not therapists. Although Freudian ideas were less explicit, they nevertheless were clearly present (see Table 2). These are the thoughts of Victoria, a secretary in her forties. She has completed high school, but all of her formal continuing education experience was in accounting, secretarial skills, and word processing. When I asked for her thoughts about why people dream, she said:

> I believe it's the subconscious working. When all day long we keep control over many things we want to squash down in our subconscious. When we're sleeping things come out and we have no control; it's the subconscious doing its things without it having any barriers on it.

It puts me in touch with myself—often my dreams are pieces of what I've heard or done during the day. All jumbled together. I can pick out—it was a fleeting thought I had and this can all be put together in a dream—like a mishmash of my whole day. This will not make any sense whatever, but I have also had dreams where I can look at them and know what the deeper meaning is. I can find whatever the deeper meaning [is].

When she interpreted her own dream, she talked of the symbols and what each meant to her. Then she added, "I think the dream showed me what I wanted and what was troubling to me." I asked her where she had learned about dreams. She was not sure about her sources but she vaguely remembered reading something in a woman's magazine a long time ago.

Thus, both staff members and therapists were influenced by Freudian ideas about dreams but most had not learned these ideas directly by reading Freud; the influence was more indirect and pervasive. In fact, most people did not know that their own ideas resembled Freud's. Because of this, they were also unaware when they had misunderstood or simplified Freud's theory. In the next section Freud's theory of dreams will be summarized and his interpretation for three dreams presented, as well as the therapists' and staff members interpretations of those dreams.

FREUDIAN INFLUENCE ON LOCAL DREAM INTERPRETATION: THREE DREAMS

In this section common misconceptions of Freudian ideas are examined against Freudian theory of dream interpretation. Then the local interpretations of three dreams by therapists and staff members are compared with Freud's interpretations of the same dreams.

There were many subtle and obvious misunderstandings of Freudian theory. The most common was related to the use of symbolism. The misconceptions occurred at all educational levels. Three examples of this will illustrate.

A doctorally prepared clinical psychologist told me: "If you look at the analytic literature, it's fraught with symbolism, and, if you see this, then it means this, and if you saw a barn then it means this, or if you had a real big dream when you're in a house with a lot of rooms, it, you know, I'm unfamiliar with it, I don't even know the exact correlations." This psychologist was very impressed with the knowledge of psychoanalysts, and she seemed to impute to them the capacity to translate dreams according to some kind of code that she did not know.

Similarly, a young psychology trainee who had just started graduate school expressed to me the same misconception of Freudian understanding of symbols in dreams. He said, "The only thing I remember learning about dreams in school was one thing; it was a Freudian idea that there were universal symbols, that they were, you know, you could interpret a dream based on the universal symbolism." When I asked if he knew any of the symbols and their meanings, all he could tell me was that he thought there were "a lot of sexual overtones."

I discovered from statements such as these that any sexual content in dreams, as well as attaching sexual meanings to other content was considered Freudian. A master's prepared graduate nurse described her therapeutic relationship with a client who had "Freudian kinds of dreams." She said she was referring to the sexual content of the dreams. She said, "I remember thinking that if I really knew how to do Freudian analysis I could have really helped her. She had all sorts of conflicts bubbling up to the surface. I ended up referring her because you could do a lot of damage if you didn't know what you were doing."

These were not the only three people who had this misconception of Freud, and when after these interviews I asked what "Freudian dreams" were, even those who did not misinterpret Freud understood that misconception. They would say something to the effect that "others" would classify those as sexual dreams, but the responder knew better.

Before Freud wrote *Interpretation of Dreams*, he made thorough studies of how dreams had been interpreted in ancient Mesopotamia, Greece, and Rome. The works of Artemidorus of Daldis stood out in particular contrast to other works because of his suggestion that the interpreter should discern the dreamer's circumstances and should interpret the dream symbolically. This was not the major thrust of Artemidoros' work, but it was one that Freud seized upon (Freud 1965 [1900]: 130) and that depends on the dreamer's associations for the interpretations of the dream. On this particular methodological point,

Freud based much of his theory of dream interpretations that led eventually to his theory of sexuality and his theory of personality structure. The emphasis is on the particular dreamer and the particular dream. Dream code books therefore are useless for interpreting dreams unless the dreamer is aware of the dream code. The dreamer makes use of a symbol as a disguise for latent thoughts. The manifest dream content comes from the residue of thoughts and experiences of waking life, especially as it is lived on that day. The latent thoughts are transformed into images that the conscious mind might not accept because of its tendency to censor. Therefore, the symbol is represented by something other than what it is. The emphasis may also be displaced from an important to an unimportant issue or event in an effort to hide the true meaning from the dreamer. This is necessary because the dream is always a "disguised fulfillment of a suppressed or repressed infantile wish" (Freud 1965 [1900]: 160). The dreamer cannot accept the explicit dramatization in his dream of sexual or aggressive wishes. The work of the dream is therefore to transform the latent dream thoughts, which might be unacceptable, into acceptable dream images in order to offer the appearance of fulfilled repressed wishes while safeguarding the sleep, rest, and health of the dreamer.

For Freud, any attempts to interpret a dream by dealing directly with the manifest dream contents must be erroneous. The true latent thoughts behind each dream symbol must be first uncovered. The translating or decoding is done by a process called *free association*. Every symbol or phrase of the dream is repeated and the dreamer gives associations to those words. The choice of associations will give clues to the latent thought behind the manifest dream content. The unconscious is the repository of the unremembered, the unknown, and the repressed.

His theory that the basic life instinct is the same as the sex instinct introduced into his dream interpretation the appearance of giving sexual meanings to many symbols. It was conceptualized in the following way. Because the basic life instinct is the sex instinct, it follows that most dreams are wish fulfillments of repressed sexual desires. Therefore, most of the manifest dream contents are disguises for latent thoughts of a sexual nature. Elongated, sharp, and penetrating objects must be symbols for the penis, whereas hollow, rounded, and enclosing objects are symbolic of the female genitalia. In his technique of dream interpretation, Freud did not apply his interpretation of symbols inflexibly like a code. In *Interpretation of Dreams*, he tells us how carefully he asked the dreamer to report not only the dream but all associations to symbols. Freud guided his understanding by what the dreamer said. He said, "the technique which I describe in the pages that follow . . . imposes the task of interpretation upon the dreamer himself" (Freud 1965 [1900]: 130).

It is important to note that even for Freud the interpretation of dreams was a social experience. It was dependent on the telling of the dream by the dreamer to the interpreter. Freud put an emphasis on the individual dreamer in his dream theory, but in his process he put just as much emphasis on a specialized kind of dialogue between two social persons who have specialized reciprocal roles; namely, the analyst and the dreamer.

The Dream of the Little House between Two Palaces

The following dream is from Freud's *The Interpretation of Dreams* (1965 [1900]. It is in a chapter on typical dreams. The dream is included here with Freud's interpretation of it.[1] I presented only the dream to the therapists and staff with the question, "If someone brought you this dream what would you think? What would you say?"

Standing back a little behind two stately palaces was a little house with closed doors. My wife led me along the piece of street up to the little house and pushed the door open; I then slipped quickly and easily into the inside of a court which rose in an incline. Anyone, however, who has had a little experience in translating dreams will at once reflect that the penetrating into narrow spaces and opening closed doors are among the commonest sexual symbols, and will easily perceive in this dream a representation of an attempt at *coitus a tergo* (between the two stately buttocks of the female body). The narrow passage rising in an incline stood, of course, for the vagina. The assistance attributed by the dreamer to his wife forces us to conclude that in reality it was only consideration for her that restrained the dreamer from making attempts of this kind. It turned out that on the day-dream a girl had come to live in the dreamer's household who had attracted him and had given him the impression that she would raise no great objections to an

approach of that kind. The little house between the two palaces
was a reminiscence of the Hradshin [Citadel] in Prague and was a
further reference to the same girl, who came from that place.
(Freud 1965 [1900]: 433)

Twenty of the fifty-eight people to whom I presented this dream
gave comments or interpretations. Six were psychiatrists, seven were
psychologists; two were nurses; three were social workers; one was a
secretary; and one was involved in financial management for one of the
programs (see Table 3).

It was remarkable how many comments about the dream were
delivered in Freudian terminology and how many interpretations were
similar to Freud's. Only half of the sample had read any Freud, and
only a small portion of them had read Freud's dream book. No one
identified the source of the dream; however, almost all (all but one)
said that dreams should be interpreted by getting the dreamer's
associations. Fourteen of the twenty made explicit reference to the
sexual significance of the symbols in the dream. There were also
references to the "unconscious," to "disguised, distorted or hidden"
material, "wish fulfillments," and "internal conflicts."

Only two of these twenty interpretations will be specifically
presented here: the first one because it was typical of most of the
others, and the second one because, although it still illustrates the influence of Freud, it is different from the others.

The first one was from an experienced clinical psychology trainee
(within a few weeks of defending her doctoral dissertation) who
remembered learning about dreams in high school and in freshman
psychology courses, but who had not read Freud's works. She said in
response to the dream:

> This dream of the stately palaces has a lot of *sexual symbols*
> and connotations. It is about intercourse. She's accepting him
> into her world. It's important in terms of how welcoming she is to
> him. Maybe the fact that it's about palaces and courts is that there
> is some intimidation by the wife.
>
> In the process of working out *internal conflicts* dreams are
> useful in terms of *giving insight*. Also they give a glimpse of the *un-
> conscious*, and *primary process* thinking. I would want to know how
> accepting the wife is of him and what he thinks of her.

Other interpretations were equally close to Freud's. Some of them were more specific in relating different symbols to body parts; other respondents smiled circumspectly and simply made a general comment about this being "full of sexual symbols," or simply being a "sexual dream."

Both of the nontherapist staff members described the dream as a "Freudian dream," and then one of them, who claimed to have read the *Interpretation of Dreams* (Freud 1965 [1900]), had much more to say: "If someone told me this dream I would not comment" (smiling). I asked why. She continued: "If Freud interpreted this it would be very sexual." I asked her how she would interpret it. "I don't know, that's why I didn't choose that one. I wouldn't know what the heck he was dreaming about if it wasn't Freudian. That's why I wouldn't want to tell my dream to a psychiatrist. I wouldn't want them to interpret it in a Freudian way. Because I personally don't believe in that. That's just my opinion, and I don't want somebody telling me about my sex life because, you know, that's *my* business."

This particular dream was identified as full of "sexual symbolism" by all but two of the respondents (see Table 3). The therapists used Freudian terminology in their interpretations, and the staff members who were not therapists identified the dream as a "Freudian dream" without interpreting it. One staff member who had read Freud's book did not accept Freud's interpretation but was unable to give the dream any interpretation different from Freud's.

The Dream of the Three Lions in the Desert

The following dream was introduced by Freud in a chapter on affects in dreams. It was introduced as an example of dreams where the manifest content in the dream does not match the affect of the dreamer, because the ideational material has undergone displacement and substitutions: "*I saw three lions in a desert; one of them was laughing; but I was not afraid of them. Afterwards, however, I must have run away from them, for I was trying to climb up a tree. But I found that my cousin was up there already*" (Freud 1965 [1900]: 499).

The young woman whose dream it was told Freud that she had a visit from her husband's supervisor and had not been afraid of him, although she expected that she might be. The analysis of the dream revealed that the dreamer's affect pointed to her latent thoughts that what appears frightening (the three lions) is not always really so.

Table 3

The Freudian Influence: Interpretation of the Dream of Little House between Two Palaces

Subjects			Use of Freudian Ideas and Terminology							
ID	Site	Sex	Interpretation by Dreamer	Symbols	Sexual Symbols	Unconscious	Disguise	Wish	Internal Anxiety Conflict	Read Freud
D1	Ri	M	X	X	X	X	X			X
D3*	Ri	M	X							
D4	Ri	F	X		X	X		X		
D5	Ri	F	X	X						X
D6	Ri	M	X	X	X		X			X
D9	Ne	M	X	X	X		X			X
P1	Ri	M	X	X	X				X	
P4	Ri	F	X	X	X	X		X	X	
P5*	Ri	F	X	X	X	X	X	X	X	X
P7*	Ne	M	X		X		X		X	X
P8	Ne	M	X	X	X	X	X		X	X
P11	Ne	M	X	X	X	X				X
P12	Ne	M	X		X					
N1	Ri	F	X		X			X	X	
N4	Ri	F	X	X	X	X		X		
S12	Ne	F	X			X	X		X	
S13	Ne	F	X	X	X				X	
S15	Ne	F	X	X	X	X	X		X	X
L3	Ne	F	X							
L9	Ne	F								X

"Freudian"

X "Freudian"

*These were of foreign nationality; came to the United States as adults.
Ne=Newell; Ri=Riverpool; D=Psychiatrists; P=Psychologists; N=Nurses; S=Social Workers; L=Support Staff Members.
M=Male; F=Female.

Ten therapists and one secretary commented on this dream (see Table 4). Two were psychiatrists, three were psychologists, two were nurses, and three were social workers. Again, the comments and interpretations were delivered in Freudian terminology. Eight of the eleven commented on the fact that the affect as reported in the dream was inconsistent with the content. Five of them recognized issues of status or competition. One social worker said:

> They are lions, but I'm not afraid of them! I'm not afraid, but I must have fled from them! I have to climb the tree, but my cousin is up there! It doesn't add up. I would ask some very concrete questions not only about the content of the dream but also the feelings. Like, "How were you feeling in the dream? How did you feel when you woke up? What was going on with you?" something to that effect—and I would watch if she tried to change the subject.

An experienced nurse therapist was similarly concerned with inconsistent affect.

> Well, let's look at the one with the lions. Knowing nothing else about this person, I would say that this person is grappling with something which seems to be causing him a lot of ambivalent feelings. The person saw three lions in the desert. One of the lions was laughing (maybe at him?) and yet he's not afraid. Then, however, he says I must have fled from him. OK? So you've got I'm not afraid but you've also got I must be fearful because I must have fled and I tried to climb this tree; so maybe he doesn't want to be afraid but back there there is some fear.

Not all the respondents assumed the dreamer was afraid; however, they said they would want to check into the affect, and eight of the eleven gave a word or explanation of Freud's concept of displacement or disguised content. One of the best explanations of displacement was given by the secretary; she said:

> If the person fled from the lions and was trying to climb a tree, then they were trying to solve a problem or run away from something probably *totally unrelated* from lions or trees. Maybe they would go to bed worrying about what was really bothering

Table 4

The Freudian Influence: Interpretation of the Dream of The Three Lions in the Desert

Subjects			Use of Freudian Ideas and Terminology							
ID	Site	Sex	Interpretation by Dreamer	Symbols	Sexual Symbols	Unconscious	Disguise	Wish	Internal Anxiety Conflict	Read Freud
D1	Ri	M		X	X	X			X	X
D8	Ne	M	X	X	X	X	X	X		X
P6	Ne	M	X	X		X			X	
P10	Ne	F	X	X						
P14	Ne	M	X	X		X	X			
N3	Ri	F	X	X		X			X	
N9	Ne	F	X			X	X			
S1	Ri	F	X			X	X		X	
S7	Ne	F	X			X			X	
S15	Ne	F	X			X	X		X	X
L8	Ne	F	X				X	X		

Ne = Newell; Ri = Riverpool; D = Psychiatrists; P = Psychologists; N = Nurses; S = Social Workers; L = Support Staff Members. M = Male; F = Female.

them, and subconsciously maybe they would dream about the problem or trying to get away from it. Even if you're not consciously saying before going to bed "Ah, this is bothering me," yet you're apt to dream about things which are really bothering you.

The two psychiatrists who had both read Freud gave more elaborate and longer interpretations of what the dream could mean. Each discovered "sexual symbolism" in it. The first one had this to say after exploring possible threats, themes of status and competitiveness, and inconsistent affect: "So you see there's a threat behind the smile and there's fear behind the courage. There's less sexual imagery in it than in the other one [the dream of the little house between two palaces]. But you know you can find it anywhere if you want to look for it. You know sexual imagery is so rich. Trees, caves, tunnels, trains, lions, almost anything."

The other psychiatrist was more methodically Freudian. In the last part of his interpretation he explained the method of finding the puns, jokes, and plays on words so typical of Freud's work: "Dreams often have jokes in them or puns. In the American language to be 'up a tree' means you're in some sort of trouble, so I would ask him 'why was your cousin up a tree.' Then he'll say, 'I haven't a clue.' Then I would say, 'do you see the pun? Why is your cousin *up a tree*? Is he in some sort of trouble?'" He said this with humor and obvious enjoyment at his artful questioning. Then with an enthusiastic flourish he gave me this final interpretation: "Well, you see, he wants to get up the tree, but his cousin is already up the tree. So what's happened? Well, the cousin's been discovered in bed with someone or is in some trouble; and he is vibrating to that also."

It was clear that these two psychiatrists were enjoying the dream. They delivered their interpretations with accomplished glee with the confidence of someone who had guessed a difficult riddle. This was definitely their territory of expertise; and I felt like Sherlock Holmes's less astute assistant being told, "Elementary, my dear Watson. If I have the clues then I can deduce the answers." Thus, in the absence of the dreamer, and with a good knowledge of Freudian ideas and methods, they gave me interpretations which were more "Freudian" than Freud's!

The Dream of Watching the Small Boy in the Water

The following dream was presented by Freud in a chapter on typical dreams. He introduced it as a birth dream in which the dreamer had inverted the order of the content. The first part he analyzed as a birth fantasy and the second part as a fantasy of flight from her husband: "*I stand at the seashore watching a small boy, who seems to be mine wading in the water. This he did till the water covered him, and I could see his head bobbing up and down near the surface. The scene then changes to the crowded hall of a hotel. My husband is not with me, and I enter into conversation with a stranger*" (Freud 1965 [1900]: 436).

More of the therapists and staff chose to comment on this dream than on the other two dreams. Those who chose to comment on their choice were women who said they chose this dream because the dreamer was obviously a woman, with whom they could identify. Many said they were also captivated by the small boy in the water. Thirty-eight respondents commented on this dream (see Table 5). Six psychiatrists, eight psychologists, six nurses, nine social workers, and eight staff employees. Twice as many women as men chose to comment on this dream. This was a higher percentage than the women who responded to the other two dreams.

Again, the interpretations were delivered in Freudian terminology. People spoke of the "unconscious," of "uncovering the true feelings," and of "internal conflicts" and "hidden unconscious wishes, for example, death wishes toward herself, or her husband or the child."

Most of the respondents said there were themes of separation, loss, disconnectedness, danger, loneliness (see Table 5). However, it was remarkable that, without having the dreamer's associations, four of the therapists identified it as a childbirth dream. One psychiatrist said it sounded like a woman who remembered what it was like to have a baby in the hospital. In hospitals there would be many crowded halls, and a woman meets many strangers. A social worker said she remembered having such a dream when she was pregnant. A nurse who was pregnant at the time I spoke with her said this was a very pleasant dream and that the mother and the boy were going to be all right. The fourth interpretation made by a psychologist is presented here because of how thoughtfully and tentatively he made it. This interpretation also contains some of the themes that others identified as well.

She's talking about a small boy that seems to be mine. There's a lot of information that I don't know about this woman. In order to make a good interpretation I need details. I wonder if she is married or if she has a child? She says the child *seems* to be hers. She might not have a child. Maybe she wants a child, maybe she doesn't. What does she *really want* and what is she *feeling*? There are some issues of closeness, distance, and separation. Words are symbolic and metaphorical. What's going on under the surface? Under the water? The issue seems to be an issue of closeness, the issue of intimacy perhaps in having a child, in giving birth. I would ask about how she feels about the water. Is the water cold? Is the boy coming out of the water or going in the water? Is she pregnant now? I wouldn't make any definite interpretations, but those are the kinds of hypotheses I'd make.

He made his comments thoughtfully and slowly, as though he were speculating while he was commenting. He said that he had not read the Freudian literature; and it was clear that he did not know that this was supposed to be a typical childbirth dream. He seemed to arrive at the conclusion by deliberation.

This dream was not recognized as a typical childbirth dream by most of the therapists and staff who interpreted it. In the absence of the dreamer's associations only four of the therapists identified it as a childbirth dream. However, many of the therapists *and* staff members said they recognized in the dream the experience of separation, disconnection, loss, and anxiety that Freud connected with fantasies he traced to the act of birth[2] (see Table 5). In these interpretations as in the ones to the other dreams Freudian terminology was evident.

THE CONTEXTS OF DREAM INTERPRETATION

In Chapter 3 the contexts of dream telling were explored. Contexts for dream telling are created by the settings,[3] roles, relationships, and all the attendant rules for interaction as perceived by all the actors involved. Four contextual categories emerged: the casual, the intimate, the confidential, and the formal.

In this chapter the investigation of the local ideas and beliefs about dream interpretation revealed the influence of a popularized version of Freudian ideas in all contexts. In the two nonprofessional contexts, the *casual* and the *intimate*, the influence of Freud was hardly

Table 5

The Freudian Influence: Interpretation of the Dream of Watching Small Boy in the Water

	Subjects		Use of Freudian Ideas and Terminology							
ID	Sex	Site	Interpretation by Dreamer	Symbols	Unconscious	Disguise	Wish	Internal Conflict	Recurrent Themes	Read Freud
D1	M	Ri	X	X	X		X		Childbirth	X
D2	M	Ri	X	X						
D3*	M	Ri	X			X			Loneliness	X
D6	M	Ri	X							
D7	M	Ne	X	X	X	X	X	X	Fear	X
D8	M	Ne	X	X	X	X	X	X		X
P2	F	Ri	X	X						X
P3	F	Ri	X	X						X
P4	F	Ri	X	X	X			X	Danger	
P7*	M	Ne	X	X	X	X	X			X
P8	M	Ne	X	X	X		X	X		X
P9	F	Ne	X	X			X		Fear	
P12	M	Ne	X	X	X	X	X		Childbirth	
P15	F	Ne	X	X				X	Separation	
N2	F	Ri	X			X	X		Childbirth	X
N5	F	Ri	X						Loss	
N6	F	Ri	X						Alone	
N7	F	Ri	X	X		X			Separation Alone	X
N8	F	Ne	X				X	X	Loss	
N10	F	Ne	X						Separation Loss	

Table 5

The Freudian Influence: Interpretation of the Dream of Watching Small Boy in the Water (cont.)

	Subjects		Use of Freudian Ideas and Terminology							
ID	Site	Sex	Interpretation by Dreamer	Symbols	Unconscious	Disguise	Wish	Internal Conflict	Recurrent Themes	Read Freud
S2	Ri	F	X					X	Loss	
S3	Ri	F	X	X		X			Separation	X
S4	Ne	M	X	X	X	X	X	X		X
S5	Ne	F	X	X						
S6	Ne	F	X						Alone	
S8	Ne	M	X		X				Loss	
S9	Ne	F							Alone	
S10	Ne	M	X	X	X	X	X		Disconnect	
S15	Ne	F	X	X	X	X			Separation Childbirth Fear	X
L1	Ne	F					X			
L2	Ne	F							Loss	
L3	Ne	F		X						
L4	Ne	F		X				X	Danger	
L5	Ne	F								
L6	Ne	F							Barrier Separation	
L7	Ne	F			X		X		Loss	
L9	Ne	F	X					X	Separation	

*These were of foreign nationality; came to the United States as adults.

Ne = Newell; Ri = Riverpool; D = Psychiatrists; P = Psychologists; N = Nurses; S = Social Workers; L = Support Staff Members.

M = Male; F = Female.

ever acknowledged. Among the professional therapists in the *formal* and *confidential* contexts, the influence of Freud was acknowledged only by a small percentage of therapists. Most of the therapists did not seem to be aware of the influence of Freud *on their interpretation* of dreams; however, they knew that Freud was connected to dreams and psychotherapy. In fact, there were many anti-Freud comments and protests and disclaimers of adherence to Freudian "dogma." Therapists also acknowledged, sometimes with disgruntlement, that the popular understanding of psychotherapy was still linked to psychoanalysis. Many said that some clients expected to find a couch in their office and that high functioning and psychologically minded clients expected to be asked about their dreams. A young female social worker sounded irritated when she said: "They're surprised by me because either they've expected somebody much older or a man with a beard and glasses. They have told me this and they have made comments like: 'OK, I'm supposed to tell you whatever pops into my head, right?'"

The association of dreams with Freud and psychoanalysis affects not only the telling of dreams but the interpretation of dreams. This influence is felt not only by the dream tellers but also by the therapists themselves. Dream interpretation is connected with psychotherapy. Therefore, if one is not talking to a therapist, one cannot expect an interpretation. In a *casual* context dreams are treated as jokes or social openers, and in an *intimate* context interpretation is probably common but not expected or recognized as interpretation or analysis. The non-therapist staff members who gave me interpretations in a context that can be designated *formal*, in relation to this study, did not call them interpretations. They just responded by saying this is what they would tell the dreamer or this is what the dreamer was probably feeling. Only in a *confidential* context were interpretations as such expected. These were deemed to be appropriate only to psychologically minded patients, who could gain insight from them. The interpretation of dreams was therefore regarded as an idealized, specialized, and restricted activity. Although all the therapists recognized it as an activity expected of them, most made implicit allusions to their limited training in dream interpretation. Twelve therapists in the sample mentioned explicitly their lack of sufficient knowledge about dreams (see Table 1), and many told me that a psychoanalyst would be much more helpful to me as a researcher of dreams than they could be.

One effect of this way of regarding dream interpretation was that the serious pursuit or interest in interpreting dreams was expected to be restricted to psychotherapists, who were reluctant to talk about them in any context but the professional *confidential* one. Psychics and spiritual mediums were mentioned by both staff members and therapists, with embarassment and contempt, respectively, as occasionally giving dream interpretations to the unenlightened, the uneducated, and the superstitious.

Another effect of regarding dream interpretation as an activity that therapists engaged in only occasionally, when they had the good fortune to have a psychologically minded patient, made the pursuit of dreams seem like an elitist activity that only a few could afford and from which only the fortunate could profit. Although psychological mindedness was not *directly* related to a high level of social functioning, education, or comfortable economic means, I was repeatedly told that low functioning patients who were described as the mentally ill, not verbally articulate, uneducated, or otherwise disadvantaged could not profit from dream interpretation.

THE POPULARIZATION OF FREUD AND THE AMERICAN MYSTIQUE OF DREAMS

It is not surprising that therapists in the latter portion of the twentieth century should have been influenced by Freud. Freud's influence on the twentieth century can hardly be overestimated. However, the notable fact that emerges from this study is that they were *still* influenced by an oversimplified popularization of Freudian ideas of which there was not much awareness. Popularized Freudian ideas about dreams functioned as a part of the Freudian mythology. These ideas affected and were affected by the beliefs about dreams, psychotherapy, and about themselves as *persons*. To be therapists they had to have the capacity for self-searching, self-knowledge, and the knowledge of other persons. To be responsible persons, they had to be willing to know themselves. In Mauss's analysis, the *personne morale* became *être psychologique*. This psychological mindedness is not merely the Socratic or Stoic understanding of a person with a sincere demeanor responsible to the body politic, this is the authentic individual who has to answer to the self. Reflexivity is now an expectation of the loftiest ideals of what it means to be *personne morale*. Hence, the expectation that dreams could make us aware of what was unconscious. There was an optimistic belief that consciousness could be *achieved*. This optimistic achievement of personal, individual self-consciousness and creativity is an exaggeration of Freud's claims that dreams could provide a road to the unconscious.

It is the focus on self-searching and the unbridled preoccupation with the individual self which made way for the ambivalent mystique of dreams in this century in the United States. This self-searching involves making conscious the individual moral and "authentic self within," but at the same time involves a disconnectedness with older and outer traditions and a belief that those who *find themselves within* are more highly evolved than those with an earlier or "less-developed" consciousness.

William Domhoff's (1985) thesis is that the American mystique of dreams, as it has been manifested since the 1960s by adopting methods allegedly learned from the Senoi, is an allegory about the nostalgic search for community and authenticity. This mystique sees dreams as a source of creativity, interpersonal closeness, and personal and social insight. Domhoff points to the eager adoption of the Senoi method by Americans as revealing more about the Americans than about the Senoi. Dentan (1983), who also did fieldwork among the Senoi and whose findings did not corroborate Stewart's (1969), said that "Senoi dream therapy" became "a solution of Western social and psychological problems" (Dentan 1983: 46).

I hold that this mystique of dreams would not have emerged at a time when the understanding of what it means to be a *person* was less influenced by psychological individualism, and in a place where it could not be infused with the optimistic belief in the capacity to individually shape and control one's own destiny.

Thus, dream telling and dream interpretation are connected with the lofty ideals of self-searching and the "finding" of the individual self that is related to a culture of psychotherapy, where psychological mindedness is not only a characteristic of the mature individual but also an expectation of the psychotherapist. However, this ideal cannot be achieved by those who are not psychologically minded, and dreams are neither of use to them nor of use in any communication that is not intensely insight oriented. The more prosaic, less intense, and less consciousness-seeking communication about dreams is devalued and trivialized. Most Americans show an ambivalent fascination with dreams that idealizes them on the one hand and trivializes them on the other. Psychotherapists are part of the mystique because of their roles, their relationships, and the rules that shape the *confidential* context of dream telling. However, whereas all therapists are expected to be capable of "reading minds" and "interpreting dreams," some are expected to have this capacity to a higher degree than others. In Chapter 5 the relationship between the capacity to interpret dreams and the social hierarchy is examined.

V

Psychotherapy, Dream Telling, and Hierarchy

INTRODUCTION

We have established that the dream as a communicated report is inseparable from the particular social situation of its telling. Moreover, ethnographic studies of other societies suggest that dream telling and dream interpretation are connected to issues of social role, status, social power, and socialization (Hallowell 1942; Spier 1933; Devereux 1957; Meggitt 1962, 1965; Charsley 1973; Tedlock 1978; Kilborne 1978, 1981). The ability to tell, hear, and interpret dreams is related to the attributes and capacities that constitute a social person.

In Chapter 3 the analytic concept *person* was used to describe and observe the context of dream telling among the psychotherapists and staff members of two community mental health centers. Dreams were told and heard by persons with distinctive qualities, capacities, and roles. Persons, both professional and nonprofessional, were expected to use their *judgmental capacities* and to understand the appropriateness or inappropriateness of certain contexts for the telling of certain dreams. Therapists were considered by all concerned to have *mystical capacities* (Harris 1989) to "read minds," and "analyze dreams." There was a general expectation among them that they would exercise professional clinical judgment, a responsibility derived from their social role and involving their *social entitlement capacities* to make the decision when to pay attention to the dreams they were told and when not to do so. What emerged was a strong belief among psychotherapists that "psychological mindedness" (a native term) is necessary for dream work to be useful to the dreamer. Moreover, although there was general agreement on this point, there was no general agreement on whether it was helpful or harmful to listen to dreams of persons who were not psychologically minded and who were classified as "low functioning" and chronically mentally ill (Table 1).

In this chapter I consider to whom the imputed capacity to hear and interpret dreams is related: their designations of role status, hierarchical position, preparation for, and enactment of psychotherapy roles in the community mental health centers. I show that the imputed capacity to hear and interpret dreams is embedded in the *context* of the dream telling. This involves not only the setting at each community mental health center and the reciprocal roles of the particular actors, but also a host of interconnected perceptions of social capacities that particular actors represent. These derive from the norms and traditions of their original practice disciplines. Psychiatrists, psychologists, social workers, and nurses told their perceptions and understandings of their own and each other's professions. The rigors of training, the models they admired, the images they valued, and the challenges they experienced were part of those perceptions. I found that the simple question, Who is most likely to ask about and listen to dreams? yielded long answers related to the complexities of professional traditions, relationships, and hierarchies. For although all psychotherapists are perceived by others and themselves to have the mystical capacity to "read minds" and "interpret dreams," not all of them have these capacities imputed to them *to the same degree.*

WHO IS A REAL DOCTOR?

The exploration of the local ideas and beliefs about dream interpretation revealed the influence of a popularized version of Freudian ideas. Therapists and staff members at both community mental centers also acknowledged that the popular understanding of psychotherapy was still linked to psychoanalysis. So, to the question, Who is most likely to listen to dreams? I would be told the popular understanding first along with their own opinion, which was usually acceptance, rejection, or qualification of public opinion. A few examples will illustrate: "The conventional wisdom would be that a psychiatrist would be more likely to be versed in Freud and would be more likely to want to interpret a dream and consider it important, but that might be a fiction."

This was said by a psychiatric resident physician who also had much to say about the competition between psychologists and psychiatrists.

Another psychiatrist, this one older and more seasoned, also started with the popular perception about a psychiatrist's interest in dreams:

> I've had patients who tell me: "I thought you would be more concerned about my dreams." I've heard them say that. They think that's the number one thing that a psychiatrist will want to hear. And if you're not producing dreams, then you're not really doing what you ought to do.
>
> I believe that the more highly trained—that would be someone at the doctoral level, be it psychology or psychiatry—that the more highly trained, the more able to deal with the severely impaired. There is something about training and experience that kind of allows one to keep perspective in situations like that, which someone with fewer years of training and less experience doesn't do as well. But that's just a generalization with many exceptions.

An experienced psychologist had similar perceptions, and she had more to say about the similarities and differences between psychiatrists and psychologists.

> I think there is probably a greater tendency to want to tell dreams to a psychiatrist because psychiatrists are connected in the public mind with an analyst, and everyone knows from the public press that analysts are people who want to hear dreams. It's not necessarily an adequate perception, but the public is quite confused about psychologists—don't know what it is they do.
>
> The first thing people want to know is if I'm a doctor. They mean a physician. That's a frequent question. "Are you like a psychiatrist? What's the difference?" So you see their perceptions shade over their views of that. So although we labor in the shadow of physicians, we are accorded great authority; we ride on their coattails.

These three examples illustrate the multiple layers of understanding that the actors had of their situation in response to the question about the likelihood of dream telling and dream interpretation in their psychotherapy practice.

1. They could not answer the question without telling me about the capacities ascribed to them. Whatever their own perceptions about dream telling, they were aware that the clients' perceptions or the perceptions of the general public affected the situation.

2. They perceived that the capacity for and interest in dream telling was ascribed primarily to psychiatrists because of their alleged relationship to Freud and psychoanalysis, even though the relationship between the psychiatric discipline and Freud reflected traditional and symbolic associations rather than educational expertise and actual practice.

3. One of the psychiatrists indicated that he thought that in actual practice, both psychologists and psychiatrists who were more highly trained *at the doctoral level* would be more capable of knowing what to do with dreams than others. In that statement he acknowledged the expertise of psychologists and the reality of their presence in psychotherapy situations.

4. There were two other assumptions in his statement. The first was a connection between dream telling and the more highly trained and dream telling and the more severely impaired. The second was the use of the words *doctoral preparation* to describe the training of both physicians and psychologists. This conflation of meanings of the word *doctor* was not unusual. Although the therapists occasionally treated this popular misunderstanding of the word *doctor* with disgruntlement, it was not unusual as in this case for psychotherapists themselves to connect both meanings to make a point. When I pressed the point with another psychiatrist, he explained to me that one who was trained as a physician and one who holds the highest academic degree in a university both have undergone such rigorous training that they have demonstrated a commitment to their profession probably lacking in someone with less rigorous training.

The doctor is the holder of a social office invested with capacities for healing as well as expectations that the holder has advanced learning in a specialized field. The office confers social capacities and responsibilities, and the holder acquires and exercises the customary skills, attitudes, and values peculiar to that office (Fortes 1973). The person shapes the office, and the office shapes the person. Because the word *doctor* describes a social office or a social status, the actor is invariably affected by the name, whether as a psychiatrist or psychologist.

This understanding of doctor as a status is further explained by the psychologist who said, "although we labor in the shadow of physicians, we are accorded great authority; we ride on their coattails." The status of the *physician doctor* is higher than the *clinical academician doctor*, yet the name *doctor* seems to raise the status of a psychologist and confer on her or him a portion of the capacities bestowed on a physician. But the recipient of the services wants to know if the therapist is a *real doctor*, to determine if that person is *really capable* of delivering the care.

This local understanding of the capacities of a doctor was operational in the very structure of each community mental health center. A receptionist explained it in this way:

> People come in and say, "I want to see a psychiatrist," flat out, and you say, "Well, in our agency you are assigned a primary therapist first and then we have psychiatrists available on a consultation basis," but they don't understand.
>
> Well, to some extent, when they send the insurance referral over, it always has a psychiatrist's name on it, even though they may never see the medical director and have no idea who it is. But everybody here is still covered by insurance *because they work under the doctor.*

The Hierarchical Structure at the CMHCs

Community Mental Health Centers (CMHC) are federally funded institutions that received their impetus from the conclusions compiled by a Joint Commission on Mental Health and Illness in 1960 (Veroff, Kulka, and Douvan 1981). The goals were to make mental health resources available to all people including poor and middle-income families. Community Mental Health Centers imply a change in the focus for mental health; namely, a general belief that people could manage ordinary mental health problems on their own with minimal support from mental health clinics and a belief that people needed intervention from community sources during crises in daily living. This changed the focus of mental health treatment in two ways. It allowed for the use of professionals who were not psychiatrists and the use of paraprofessionals in treatment. It changed the emphasis from long-term in-hospital psychiatric treatment to short-term crisis intervention and community outreach including educational and developmental projects. Nevertheless, the recipients of mental health treatment were people with crises of daily living as well as people with long-term chronic mental health problems who were no longer in need of complete hospitalization.[1] Community Mental Health Centers became extensions of hospital care. In fact, the Riverpool Center was not only affiliated with the University Hospital but was located in it. The Newell Center was soon to increase its affiliation with an area hospital by moving one of its clinical sites onto the hospital campus.[2]

The recognition that psychiatrists were the officially designated specialists in the care of the mentally ill was reflected in the hierarchical structure of both CMHCs. The chief executive administrative director of each CMHC was a psychiatrist. However, in both CMHCs psychologists were placed in very high positions that could be characterized as second in command.[3]

At Newell the coordinator of services at each one of the three sites was a social worker. These were middle-management positions, with the lines of authority and communications connecting to the psychologists and psychiatrists who were in higher positions. Two administrative positions were held by nurses at Newell. One was director of the two partial hospitalization programs. Her superior was another nurse who was director of extended care. This position held responsibility for the care of long-term chronic patients and provided a link between the center and the chronic hospitals in the area. This position also can be defined as a middle-management position with the lines of authority and communication connecting above to psychiatrists and the few psychologists who were in higher positions.

Thus, the two CMHCs were staffed by psychiatrists, psychologists, social workers, nurses, and paraprofessionals. Both the

CMHCs were affiliated with area hospitals. Psychiatrists held the highest positions. Some psychologists also held very high administrative positions. A few middle-management positions in the CMHCs were held by social workers. Nurses held a few administrative positions that linked them to other area hospitals. However, the positions held by social workers and nurses were not top executive positions.

Perceptions of Hierarchical Issues about and by Psychologists

There were fifteen psychologists in the sample from both CMHCs. Seven were clinical psychologists who had their doctoral academic and clinical degrees. Four were psychology interns at different levels on the way to completion of a doctorate. Two had master's degree preparation; they had been clinicians for many years and risen through the ranks but had not completed their doctorate. Two had not completed their master's degrees. I counted them in this group because both of them had a sense of themselves as psychologists. One had assisted a clinical psychologist in research projects, learned from his mentor, and was in the process of applying to graduate schools. Both, who had only bachelor's degree preparation, were involved in the partial hospitalization programs and in group psychotherapy with other therapists. They did not do primary psychotherapy.

I was told that the discipline of psychology was considered to be the "second mental health profession" after psychiatry. The education consisted of four to five years of academic, research, and clinical graduate work at an accredited university including many hours of supervised clinical work and a research project and dissertation. Many had completed or were engaged in post doctoral projects. The experienced clinicians were supervisors for the psychology interns. However, some psychologists were supervised by psychiatrists.

Psychologists were very confident that their education equipped them with the knowledge to be competent psychotherapists. Two of the doctorally prepared psychologists saw no difference in psychotherapy skills between psychologists and psychiatrists:

> You could not tell from a therapy audiotape if it was a psychiatrist or a psychologist unless a prescription is being handed out.

> A lay person coming from the outside world sees no difference in

terms of psychology or psychiatry, probably because they call both of them doctor. People often relate to me as though I had some medical background as any other doctor.

Many of the psychologists did not think psychiatrists in the general course of their medical training received adequate preparation in psychotherapy. Psychiatrists were alleged to go through the kind of training that would inundate them with large numbers of very sick patients that they would have to medicate. Unless they received specialized training in psychotherapy they were not perceived to have good listening skills, or much practice or time to devote to listening. This kind of opinion was given to me in impassioned speeches like this one from a doctorally prepared psychologist:

> I'm a *doctor*, it helps to have that title; people are more apt to listen to me and maybe do what I suggest and allow me to enter into their lives. However, doctors are also perceived as uncaring and as not having enough time to listen. The physicians seem rushed and sometimes they give advice that just makes your hair curl. I have a lot of my own personal feelings about physicians; also people come in with a lot of expectations based on the role of how the doctor functions for them, as well as what doctors have told them in the past about these problems, and then I have to struggle with that.

There were many perceptions about why psychiatrists ranked higher; however, the capacity to prescribe medication was one of the most important reasons offered. A psychologist explained the procedure:

> Basically, in this setting psychiatrists are used as psychopharmacologist. They do little psychotherapy. If a therapist such as myself or the psychiatric nurse across the hall, if we think one of the patients needs to be evaluated for medication, or would benefit from medication, we would set up an appointment with the psychiatrist who is here every day, and maybe we would talk to the psychiatrist for a few minutes and say why we wanted this person to be evaluated for medication.

This capacity to prescribe medication placed psychiatrists in general at the highest hierarchical spot in comparison to other therapists. At Riverpool, the psychiatric residents provided "medical backup" for all the therapists who were not psychiatrists. This put a heavy burden on psychiatrists in terms of responsibility and working hours, but it also made all the other therapists dependent on them. A few of the therapists considered themselves to have more training and experience in psychotherapy than those psychiatrists who were backing them up. At Newell the psychiatrists were also responsible for the medical condition of the patients including prescribing medication; however, the psychiatrists there had all completed their residency training.

Because the capacity to prescribe medication was traditionally accepted and legally sanctioned, insurance companies who covered patients required that psychiatrists be responsible for cases even when other psychotherapists actually did the work. This made psychiatrists not only more indispensable but also more valuable financially to the center. One psychologist put it this way: "Psychiatrists are usually seen on top of the totem pole, and that's largely because of third party payments. Almost all insurance companies want things cosigned by a psychiatrist, even if that psychiatrist never sees the patient. They just want to know there is a psychiatrist in the clinic. So psychiatrists are usually seen [points up]. You see, it comes down to money!"

The competition and hierarchical issues between psychologists and psychiatrists were noticed by all the professional groups (see Table 6) and were the subject of comment by most therapists (see Appendix F). Some were more emphatic than others. One psychology intern was explaining to me that she was working with a psychiatrist on a case in which they were not coequal because it was the psychiatrist's case and he was in charge. She explained later that in terms of pay and power psychiatrists were higher but it was more than that: "It's more a traditional split in our society between physicians and the entire rest of the world! *Anybody who is a doctor is a different sort of a human being;* and anyone who is not isn't. So because a psychiatrist is an M.D., there's a lot of status that goes along with that."

A psychiatric resident offered a complementary point of view:

There's a feeling that psychology is overreaching and grabbing turf, and I'm sure psychologists think the psychiatrists are a bunch of pompous fuddy-duddies who really don't know what they are doing. I think the psychologists are jealous of the ability to prescribe almost to the point of becoming politically obstruc-

Table 6

Hierarchical Perceptions within CMHCs and among Therapists

ID	Site	Sex	Statements Made Regarding Perceived Hierarchy
D1	Ri	M	D>P>others
D2	Ri	M	D>P>others
D5	Ri	F	D>P>N>Sw
D6	Ri	M	D>others
D9	Ne	M	D>others
P2	Ri	F	D>P>others
P3	Ri	F	D>P>Sw>N
P4	Ri	F	D>P
P5	Ri	F	D>P>Sw>N
P6	Ne	M	D>P>Sw
P7*	Ne	M	D>P>Sw
P13	Ne	M	D>others
S2	Ri	F	D>P>q
S5	Ne	F	D>P>Sw
S10	Ne	M	D>others
S13	Ne	F	D>others
S14	Ne	F	D>P>Sw>N
S15	Ne	F	D>P>Sw
N3	Ri	F	D>others q
N4	Ri	F	D>N>Sw q
N5	Ri	F	D>N>Sw
N6	Ri	F	D>N>others q
N7	Ri	F	D>P>N>Sw
N8	Ne	F	D>P>Sw>N
N9	Ne	F	D>Sw>N
L2	Ne	F	D>others
L3	Ne	F	D>others

*Of foreign nationality, came to the United states as an adult.
Ri = Riverpool; Ne = Newell; D = Physician; P = Psychologist; S = Social worker;
N = Nurse; L = Support staff member; q = qualified answer; M = Male; F = Female

tionist to psychiatry. There was a legal case this summer. It was the position of the American Psychological Association that psychiatric medications were overprescribed. There was definitely an aroma of: 'we can't prescribe so we'll make sure that no one will prescribe either'."

Psychiatrists guarded the right to prescribe medication very jealously. One of the senior psychiatrists told me this after a long discourse about the fact that the general public was confused about the distinctions between psychiatrists and psychologists and had to be reminded constantly that psychiatrists went to medical school and had M.D. degrees. She said: "There are some states where psychologists are allowed to prescribe medication. There's a push to get this passed in this state. I don't know where the legislation is at this point. But if psychologists prescribe medication, that feels dangerous to me."

To summarize, psychologists were considered the second mental health profession after psychiatry. The authority of psychologists was enhanced by their association with physicians because they were both called *doctors*. There was a perception of confusion among lay people about the distinctions between psychologists and psychiatrists. This was irksome to most psychiatrists and even to a few psychologists. Psychiatrists were quick to point out the distinctions between themselves and psychologists who did not go to medical school; that is, they were not real doctors because they were not physicians.

Patients who came to the centers usually asked to see a doctor. They usually meant a physician because he or she would be considered the expert on mental health and illness. Patients were told that they would be seen by a therapist who was not a physician, but that the psychiatrist would be available for consultation. Psychiatrists' names were usually entered on official records and insurance forms as being responsible for the cases along with the names of the nonmedical therapists. Most of the forms had to have the name of a psychiatrist on them.

Psychiatrists held the highest executive positions at each of the CMHCs. A few psychologists had high executive positions that were analogous to being second in command.

Psychologists told me that with regard to interest in listening to dreams and interpreting them, those among them who were research psychologists and behavioral psychologists would probably *not* be interested in dreams. However, none of them described himself or herself in this way. The typical answer given by psychologists in response to that question was made *with qualification*. Psychologists would say that psychologists would be more interested in listening to dreams than psychiatrists. However, some psychiatrists, who studied Freud, therefore would listen, too; and psychiatrists would be told more dreams because of the traditional connections to psychoanalysis—*but* that psychologists actually listened better. Some thought that psychologists and psychiatrists were equally likely to be interested in dreams (see Appendix G). Their answers reflected the constant comparisons, distinctions, similarities, and competition that they perceived between themselves and psychiatrists. Like all therapists they had imputed to them unexplainable (mystical) capacities to read people's minds and interpret their dreams. Moreover, like psychiatrists they were called *doctor*, so they were expected to have capacities to heal the mind by virtue of their profession and their association to the profession of psychiatry. These capacities included the ability to interpret dreams. Well, not quite like psychiatrists *because they were not physicians* and, therefore, were one level lower on the hierarchy even though they thought that sometimes they could actually listen better than psychiatrists.

Perceptions of Hierarchical Issues about and by Psychiatrists

There were nine psychiatrists who spoke with me from both CMHCs. Four were psychiatric residents and five had completed residency.[4] Two were connected to the CMHC by virtue of their position as clinical instructors, and two held administrative positions. Four of the nine psychiatrists were seasoned clinicians who had finished residency more than ten years earlier.

All the psychiatrists had no doubt that they were in the highest positions at the CMHC. I was told in no uncertain terms that psychiatrists had the last word at CMHCs, but that they also had the ultimate responsibility.

In fact, one of the administrators, a psychiatrist, outlined the traditional roles different psychiatrists play at the CMHCs. All were leadership positions that placed psychiatrists in positions superior to other professionals and paraprofessionals. The functions were executive director in charge of administration, medical director in charge of clinical services, clinician and leader of the clinical team, consultant to nonmedical professionals, and psychopharmacologists for prescribing medication. There was little doubt in their mind that they were presumed to be more competent than any of the other professionals at the CMHC about most issues regarding mental health and mental illness including dream telling and dream interpretation.

Psychiatrists understood that they commanded much prestige and authority from the general public because of the capacities they were preceived to possess. Some of these were clearly delineated social or legal entitlements, such as the capacity to prescribe medications, whereas other capacities were less clearly defined or understood, such as the capacity to see into someone's mind. Yet each of these capacities derived from their roles and were composed of and expressed their *personhood*. Here is an example of how a psychiatrist described these capacities:

> In a *formal way*, psychiatrists have enormous power in the society. I can throw someone in the hospital in the absence of criminal and civil charges, and people get mad at me if I make a mistake about that. If someone is seen in Psych ED and goes out and kills somebody or themselves, why didn't I know! they expect a great deal. So they give us *formal power*. We are asked to predict violence, asked to be the people who understand and to some extent control violence, in ways different from the police. But we also have some *informal power* like people—well—I get this all the time. Especially if I go to a party and someone finds out you're a psychiatrist. "Oh, have you been analyzing what I've said all evening?" That's *mythical power*. (Italics mine)
>
> But lots of times people don't know the difference between a psychologist and a psychiatrist, and some people won't give psychiatrists the power they give to other MDs, because they don't perceive that we're M.D.s—some of them.

I asked if general M.D.s had the power to commit people for psychiatric hospitalization; the response was that they could, although they didn't like to do so because of possible lawsuits; they would rather call in the expert, the psychiatrist, to do it.

Here is another example of how another psychiatrist perceived the capacities others ascribed to him:

I think psychiatrists to a degree are like policemen. Some people are a little afraid of them, that they can figure things out. That they're going to figure out that I'm crazy. I think to a certain degree for some people, psychiatrists have that aroma of being able to see inside you. People don't like that—it's like being a witch doctor. I mean it's something that people don't really know what's going on. Sometimes I suspect the psychiatrist does not know what's going on either. It's like in ancient Rome when they used to read the entrails of the animals, and know that something must be there. For the lay public this is very important. But if I may generalize the status of psychiatrists in the profession of medicine is low—for a variety of reasons. Well, we might as well talk of this. Are you interested?

Every psychiatrist with whom I spoke had much to say about the capacities attributed to them. But these capacities, some of them clear and formal and some unclear and informal, yielded mixed reactions from others. The lay public perceived them as very powerful because of this mixture of formal and informal capacities *except* when people forgot that they were really M.D.s. The other professionals at the CMHCs recognized the uniformly higher position of psychiatrists in the institution and their own dependence on the psychiatrists for medications and signatures, and they resented the psychiatrists or actually tried to "grab turf" and undermine their authority.[5] However, among other physicians the status of psychiatrists was low. The issue of how they were regarded by other physicians was an extremely important topic to psychiatrists, which they all talked about at length and most of the time with passion. For example, the two psychiatrists whom I quoted earlier told me of experiences that illustrate this point. At a meeting of clinical instructors on clerkships for medical school, general physicians made jokes about whether a psychiatrist could teach physical diagnoses to medical students, because they were perceived to have lost their physical medical skills through disuse.

The other experience is an illustration about how often people forget that psychiatrists are M.D.s. The psychiatrist said that his patient was actually surprised when he suggested that he could draw blood in the examining room since the laboratory was closed. The patient became terrified and asked him if he could do that. He responded calmly that he could but then added to me, "I didn't want to tell her I don't do it very well."

Psychiatrists were perceived by their medical colleagues to be lesser doctors because they did not keep up their physical diagnosis skills, and this perception sometimes was held even by patients, who always wanted *a real doctor* to treat them.

This impassioned speech was delivered by a highly experienced psychiatrist who had a high clinical position as a clinical consultant in both CMHCs:

> But psychiatrists have such a hard time with our medical col-
> leagues, because if we can't measure something or prove it, they
> say it isn't there. See, the internists and so forth think we're all
> weird because we even look into people's feelings and all that;
> you're not supposed to do that, you're supposed to just stiff upper
> lip and do it; all these dark motives or unconscious drives, that's
> all subjective, and you can't measure it, so to hell with it [raising
> his voice] . . . if you can't treat it with a drug it doesn't exist. You
> find this split here, but it's worse in England and Germany.

The fact that psychiatry is subjective—"amorphous," not "con-crete" (their words), related to interpersonal skills and even to those vague mystical capacities to see inside people—is what makes it so different from other medical specialties. A young psychiatrist who had finished his residency added this dimension of people's perceptions of psychiatrists: "I went into medicine because I wanted to become a psychiatrist, but I think a majority of people think that psychiatry is not a specialty of medicine. They think it's a lot of mumbo jumbo. Some people would never go to a psychiatrist. They might think only crazy people go see a psychiatrist while some people might even see a psychic to foretell the future."

Psychics are perceived to possess mystical capacities to foretell the future. This psychiatrist perceived that being connected to those kinds of capacities caused people to forget that psychiatrists were specialists of medicine. It was surprising to me that most of the psychiatrists, especially the young residents and the young psychiatrists, spoke freely about their perceptions that they were *not regarded as real doctors* and that they found themselves colluding with this ridiculous opinion themselves. I would say, "but what do you mean? Who is a real doctor?" The response in this case was:

> A *real doctor* is a non psychiatrist. I guess the *real hard core doctor* would be family practitioners, internists, pediatricians, obstetricians. It's a kind of joke that psychiatrists are not real doctors. We play on that all the time ourselves. We joke about it a lot because we get those vibes from others. I can't quite define it but within the medical culture, there's a certain amount of respect accorded these other specialties, and the rest of us kind of feel inferior about these specialties and have to defend ourselves. (Italics mine)

Another resident added to this the perception that others had about psychiatrists by saying that *real doctors* belong in the *real world*. He said: "I've come to terms with it, you know—*that I'm not a real doctor*! You know, it is acceptable that you should go into a specialty that will keep you in the *real world*: medicine, surgery, and so on. I just tagged along, I went into surgery until I thought it wasn't what I wanted to do. The real medicine is surgery, gastroenterology, urology, endocrinology. Psychiatry is not real medicine. It's a socio-anthropological thing." (Italics mine)

To check whether this notion that psychiatrists were not real doctors was a perception only of psychiatric residents who were struggling with professional identity issues related to their education, I asked the five experienced psychiatrists what they thought about this notion (see Appendix E). One said it was part of the educational experience that most psychiatrists overcame. However, psychiatric residency caused psychiatrists to fear that it would cost them their identity as real physicians: "They want to reassure themselves that they haven't turned their back on their profession. They haven't lost face, status; they're conflicted. They want to be a psychiatrist, they want to believe in psychotherapy, they want to interpret dreams."

One of the psychiatrists told me it was a ridiculous notion, protesting (too much) that he stayed close to medicine by reading medical journals every week. Then he embarked on an impassioned statement of the difficulties that psychiatrists had with their medical colleagues.

Two other psychiatrists agreed that this notion was not held exclusively by young residents, but was a difficulty experienced by most psychiatrists. He explained: "When you get away from doing physical examinations, you begin asking yourself 'Am I a real doctor?' Psychiatry is, in a sense, coming to grips with the fact that although you are a doctor, you are removed from many of the physical aspects of care. And that, to some extent, is a rethinking about one's role, letting go of skills which you've learned along the way. This has been an issue which has been around a long time."

In sum, being *a real doctor* was an issue for both psychologists and psychiatrists in different ways because of interconnected perceptions of social capacities attributed to each by virtue of the traditions and values of their separate disciplines, as well as by their positions and roles at the CMHCs. Psychologists were constantly reminded that they were *not real doctors* by patients who came to the mental health centers to see a psychiatrist, by the forms that had to have a psychiatrist's signature; by the necessity to consult a psychiatrist when they needed a prescription for medication; by their own discipline, which called itself the *second* mental health profession after psychiatry; by the fact that psychiatrists in general had higher positions in the administration of hospitals and CMHCs; and by psychiatrists themselves who were always able and willing to set the record straight.

Psychiatrists had nagging reminders that they *might not be real doctors* from patients who failed to discriminate between them and psychologists and from the general public and the press that popularized and oversimplified their specialty. It was discomforting that other health care professionals also practiced psychotherapy, even though they were not physicians, and that the American Psychological Association was trying to usurp the right to prescribe medications. Moreover, psychiatrists seemed troubled by allegations by their medical colleagues that their specialty depended on "subjective" measures and was less than scientific. But, most of all, they were troubled by their own discomfort that they were not keeping up with their hard-earned skills in the physical aspects of care.

"READING THE MIND" AND THE IMPORTANCE OF BIOLOGY

Attending to the physical and biological aspects of medical care is an extremely valued component of Western medicine. In fact, it is so important to the role of a physician that psychiatrists who think they are not using the skills of physical "doctoring" do not feel like real doctors. They are also perceived by their medical colleagues to be inexpert or out of practice in the skills that to them matter most. This has caused psychiatrists to occupy positions of lower status in the medical hierarchy. However, in CMHCs psychiatrists are the acknowledged experts in the biological and chemical aspects of physical care and in diseases and diagnoses. They are the *real doctors* and rank higher than psychologists, who although they have academic doctorates and excellent training in psychopathology and the diagnosis of mental illness, do not usually have expertise in biology or chemistry. In CMHCs psychiatrists function as administrators, consultants, and psychopharmacologists who do very little psychotherapy. These particular capacities psychiatrists in CMHCs derive from their social entitlements and responsibilities as physicians with a specialty in psychiatry. They are what one of them called the formal powers to do such things as prescribe medication and make diagnostic evaluations for psychiatric hospitalizations.

Psychiatrists are also connected traditionally and symbolically to Freud, who was a physician as well as the originator of psychoanalysis and who is credited with teaching the modern world about the "knowledge of the unconscious activities of the mind" (Freud 1965 [1900]: 647). Freud is also the founder of modern psychotherapy. So whether psychiatrists have any knowledge of psychoanalysis and even whether they actually practice psychotherapy, they become connected to Freud and acquire some of the capacities attributed to healers who have "knowledge of the activities of the mind." One psychiatrist called this capacity an informal power to analyze people's minds. In fact, all who practice psychotherapy have this capacity imputed to them even when it is not clear how they got it or what it is. This capacity to "read minds" is different from the social entitlement capacities precisely because it is neither formal nor clear; it is somewhat *mystical.*

The combination of these different capacities makes psychiatrists the kinds of *persons* they are, and are regarded to be, in the different settings in which they work and live.

Among their own medical colleagues their mystical capacities seem to somehow detract from or diminish their social entitlement capacities and responsibilities of being a doctor. Doctors are entitled and responsible to care for the human body and cure diseases. The medical community and indeed all health care institutions interpret that by placing a very high value on the biomedical components of their role. The same capacity that causes persons, therapists and non-therapists, to be in awe of them—namely, the capacity to "analyze" and "know" the workings of the mind—is regarded as subjective, amorphous, and less than scientific by their peers and by themselves.

Moreover, the mystical capacity to know the mind, spirit, soul, and other designations of what is less tangibly discernible in a person is possessed not only by psychiatrists but also by other nonmedical professionals like psychologists, social workers, and nurses, and nonprofessional practitioners like psychics and other all-purpose counselors. All professional therapists feel uncomfortable about being put in the same category as practitioners who have *only* a mystical capacity and no social entitlement to practice psychotherapy. In addition, psychiatrists are uncomfortable about being put in the same category as professional practitioners who, although they have the social entitlement bestowed on them by their course of study and degrees, licenses, and official certifications for the practice of psychotherapy are nevertheless not physicians. This is another instance when a mystical capacity exerts a negative effect or diminishes social entitlement capacities.

However, at the CMHC, psychiatrists are seen to both have the capacity to "read the mind" and expertise in the biochemical aspects of care. Their position as psychopharmacologists and consultants on medical issues actually derive from and enhance their social entitlement capacities, and even though very few of the psychiatrists at CMHCs had time to practice psychotherapy, they were nevertheless deemed to be experts in diseases of the mind, and they therefore retained their mystical capacities.

THE DREAM INTERPRETATION HIERARCHY

This became very clear when I asked who was most likely to ask about and listen to dreams. Twenty-five therapists and two staff members had things to say about this. Twenty of the twenty-five therapists and one staff member who spoke about this thought psychiatrists were most likely to ask about, listen to, and be able to interpret dreams (see Table 7). This was even though most of the therapists knew that psychiatrists were functioning almost solely as psychopharmacologists and did very little psychotherapy. Most of the

time the answer was given with an explanation of the perceived traditions of psychiatry as they were presented in the popular press and in
the perceived traditions of their original practice discipline of medicine,
as well as their relationship to psychoanalysis (see Appendix G).

Most psychiatrists thought that dream interpretation was *their*
function, and therefore, it was natural that they should do it more than
others. However, there was a range from some who said definitely that
psychologists and social workers did not know how to handle dreams
because they did not have psychodynamic training to others who said
that, although one would think that, because of the Freudian heritage,
psychiatrists would be more likely to want to interpret dreams and consider them important, this was probably a fiction.

Two of the responses were made with conditions that modified
and qualified the statements in an interesting way. These I will report
at this time. One psychiatric resident said that medical training would
tend to discourage the likelihood that psychiatrists would be interested
in dreams. This was related to the fact that psychiatrists had fewer
insight-oriented patients than therapists of other disciplines. This was
disquieting to the psychiatrist, presumably because psychiatrists *ought*
to be more interested in dreams than others.

The second psychiatrist was past his residency training. He
qualified his original answer that psychiatric training prepared
psychiatrists to have a more comprehensive approach to dreams than
other professionals in this unique way: "We see these phenomena including dreams within their biological substratum. A nurse or social
worker would have a narrower view. *But* I think psychologists, nurses,
and social workers *would make a larger effort* to explain the content of a
dream. Put more weight on it."

"I asked, "Why?" and received this answer; "If someone, let's say,
is blind, the hearing function gets hypertrophied. So let's say they may
be more prone to read things into the content of the dream since they
may not know that it might be something physiological."

He regarded the efforts other professionals put into listening to
dreams as quaint expressions of their limitations, thus affirming the
general belief that those who listened to dreams in the context of
underlying biological understandings, namely, the psychiatrists, were
best prepared to do so.

Table 7

Which of the Psychotherapy Professionals Is Most Likely to Ask about and Listen to Clients' Dreams in the Context of Psychotherapy?

ID	Site	Sex	Psychiatrists	Psychologists	Social Workers	Nurses
D1	Ri	M	X			
D4	Ri	F	q	Xq		
D5	Ri	F	Xq			
D6	Ri	M	X			
D7*	Ne	M	X	Xq	Xq	Xq
D8	Ne	M	X			
D9	Ne	M	X			
P5*	Ri	F	Xq	X		
P6	Ne	M	Xq	Xq		
P7*	Ne	M	Xq	Xq		
P8	Ne	M	Xq	Xq		
P9	Ne	F	Xq	Xq		
P10	Ne	F	Xq	Xq		
P15	Ne	F			X	X
S2	Ri	F	X			
S6	Ne	F	X			
S13	Ne	F	X			
S15	Ne	F	X			
N1	Ri	F	X			
N5	Ri	F	X			
N6	Ri	F	X			
N7	Ri	F				X
N8	Ne	F				X
N9	Ne	F				X
N10	Ne	F	X			
L6	Ne	F			X	
L9	Ne	F	X			

*Of foreign nationality, came to the United states as an adult.
Ne = Newell; Ri = Riverpool; D = Physicians; P = Psychologists; S = Social Workers; N = Nurses; L = Support staff members; q = qualified answer; M = Male; F = Female

Many of the psychologists who responded to my question also gave modified and qualified answers (see Appendix G). Most of the responses had the effect of indicating that *both* psychologists and psychiatrists would listen to dreams. Only one young psychologist, who had not completed her doctorate, said that *neither* psychologists who had their Ph.D. degree nor psychiatrists would have time to listen to dreams. She thought psychiatrists were too busy with consultations and medications to listen to patients, and psychologists were too busy doing research and testing. It was her opinion that nurses and social workers would be more receptive to talking about dreams.

The four social workers who responded to this question agreed without modification or discussion that psychiatrists were most likely to listen to dreams and interpret them.

Of the seven nurses who answered this question, four thought that psychiatrists were more likely to do it, but three said they (the nurses) were more likely to have the time and inclination to listen to patients' dreams. It will be noted that many nurses had said that they had an interest in talking about dreams even with low functioning and chronically mentally ill patients (see Table 1).

Of the two staff members who responded to this question, one thought psychiatrists would be most likely to listen to and interpret dreams, but she added that they would surely interpret them in a Freudian way, and she would not want such an interpretation. The other staff member thought psychologists would be more likely to listen to dreams because M.D.s did not spend very much time with patients at her particular part of the CMHC.

Thus, we see that although most therapists understood themselves to have capacity to "read minds" and "interpret dreams," psychiatrists, who were also seen as custodians of the physical body, were perceived to have the capacity to a higher degree. In CMHCs the mystical capacity was enhanced when it occurred in combination with social entitlement capacities.

In the remainder of this chapter I examine the perceptions of hierarchical issues about and by social workers and nurses and relate those to their capacity to ask about, listen, and interpret dreams.

WOMAN'S WORK AND WOMEN'S PROFESSIONS

The fact that social work and nursing traditionally have been women's professions and are still predominantly practiced by women was reflected unmistakably in how social workers and nurses perceived themselves and each other and in how they were perceived by others in the CMHCs. These perceptions were communicated, for the most part, as assumptions implied in what was said about roles, status, and hierarchy and in the way space and time allocations were understood and actually made in CMHCs.

These are the statements of Elizabeth, a social worker who has been a therapist for two years after completing a master's degree in social work: "He [a relative] is thinking about going into therapy, and he mentioned to me that he was considering someone who is a social worker, and I was negative about that."

I asked, "Why?" and she replied: "Well, he was considering a male social worker, and my perception is that a male social worker is going to be less bright than a female social worker, because it's a lower status profession, and smart women often do things like that [laughs loud]."

Elizabeth also said she thought psychiatrists and psychologists were better prepared to do psychotherapy and had higher status than social workers. She added that the nursing profession would be classified lower than social work because of what she called the *menial* and the *physical service aspects*, which she considered "nonintellectual."

Not all the social workers in the sample were women. Two of the male social workers, who had been clinicians for more than ten years each, mentioned the low status of the profession, the poor pay they received, and the dilemma they faced in remaining in the role. One of them said:

> Social workers don't make much money. So, I've always felt very conflicted about my profession in the sense that I enjoy it very much, and I feel that I get a lot of gratification out of doing it. On the other hand, the financial rewards are very, very poor. And, unfortunately, of course, if you're at all skilled, then you get-promoted to a supervisor's role, and from supervisor to a manager, etc. . . .! You wind up being an administrator or something, which is not at all the reason why I went into this work. However, the financial rewards are just not there, so throughout my career this has been an ongoing struggle with me, in terms of which path to take to stay with the clinical role, or to try to keep a foot in both camps.

Two of the nurses had the very same point to make about low pay and having to take on administrative roles to raise the financial rewards. Here is one statement: "I think it has to do with the nursing profession being female dominated, and being one that does not have all that much career advancement; a major way to advance is through administration, more so than clinical—that's not rewarded financially, or with any other perks in terms of time or scheduling. It's so locked into patient care in the hospital."

Elizabeth's point that the nurse's role in physical care contributed to the low status of nurses was alluded to quite explicitly by Michelle, a nurse, who had mentioned several times in passing that nurses were regarded poorly by the general public. When I asked her to elaborate more specifically, she became impatient. "You keep asking me that; do you want to hear something better? Do you want to hear better news? I think it's bad. I think people think nurses clean shit, that they take care of doctor's orders, and say 'yes, sir' and do what they are told, that they are like glorified servants."

Although social workers perceived that nurses' traditional roles contributed to lower status, nurses perceived that social workers' traditional roles were too circumscribed and narrow in their focus. Here is how one of the nurses described social workers: "I've run into a little trouble with social workers, I think sometimes they get so hung up in trying to figure out how to get the food stamp number to come out right [shrugs helplessly]; that kind of thing!"

Although the social workers and nurses functioned as therapists and administrators at both CMHCs, the traditional perceptions of their primary disciplines were that they were feminine professions. Moreover, the tasks that were regarded as traditional for each of these disciplines were customarily considered to be woman's work.

More specifically, social workers were seen as coordinators of available community resources to provide food, transportation, and help for the family. They described themselves as "do gooders" and "advice givers" for families. These tasks are considered to be tasks of homemakers in American society.

Nurses' traditional tasks are even more glaringly feminine. They take care of sick people, bathe their bodies, change their clothes, remove body secretions and excretions, feed people, wean people to different foods or treatment regimens, and at times do for people what was done to them by mothers and mother surrogates when they were infants.

Both nurses and social workers perceived that these traditional functions and perceptions of their traditions contributed to their lower status. Even though their present professions were no longer exclusively confined to these functions, they not only remained within the purview of their respective disciplines but also became symbolic of them. Thus, these traditions became part of the context even when they were doing psychotherapy. In fact, both nurses and social workers admitted that being known as a "therapist" would cause others to regard them with more respect than being known as just a nurse or a social worker.

It should be noted that both social workers and nurses valued the very functions that contributed to the low status of their professions. Social workers repeatedly spoke with pride about their tendency to have a family and community outlook, and nurses said they were "holistic" because even in doing psychotherapy they tended to *not* forget the common, everyday, physical needs of the patient.[6]

The traditional roles and functions of social workers and nurses influenced their understanding of the professional use of space and time. In fact, the way space and time allocations were understood and actually made in CMHCs reflected status, hierarchy, and the context of dream telling.

Space, Time, and Therapeutic Rules

This is a psychologist's opinion of the differences in the training of psychologists and social workers, including the way they have been taught to use space and time boundaries in their work:

> Well, I don't think social workers are as well trained in the area of diagnosis. I understand what pathology means to diagnosis—what early life events may be embedded in this diagnosis. I tend to follow a lot of the *therapeutic rules*, which I don't think social workers and psychiatric nurses follow. Therapeutic rules are some things in terms of therapeutic anonymity, clear structures with *time*: I will never go beyond fifty or below fifty minutes [for a therapy session]. I'm very careful of the *setting* and the structure of the *therapeutic field in the room*. I've talked to social workers, and they're pretty loose about all this. (Italics mine)

Therapy sessions are highly structured in terms of time and space. Every variation is methodologically significant. This psychologist considered the "therapeutic rules" a basic element of good psychotherapy. Therefore, he concluded that those who were lax with therapeutic rules must not be well trained. It will be noted that Elizabeth, the social worker, whose statement was quoted earlier, agreed with him. Other social workers said the same thing. Yet it would seem that both social workers and nurses, by virtue of the training of their primary professional disciplines, would have been taught to treat time and space in different ways in the context of their therapeutic relationships with clients. In other words, they had different "therapeutic rules" in their primary disciplines.

More specifically, social workers were expected to visit patients' homes, evaluate living conditions, make specific recommendations (give advice), speak to patients' relatives, and even report health violations to public health officials. Similarly, nurses were taught to use space and time in the context of therapeutic encounters in ways that were different from the rules of "the talking cure of psychotherapy." Nurses spent much time with patients and would be enjoined for being clock watchers. Moreover, they were expected as nurses to be involved in the activities of daily living of their patients, whether those were at the bedside or in the home. Their functions included teaching and touching their patients at appropriate times and in appropriate ways.

None of the social workers or the nurses in the sample spoke of conflicting "therapeutic rules." However, most of them made a point of telling me that their original practice discipline had been formative as well as informative, and that it had molded their thoughts and beliefs, not only about what they were doing but about *who they were*. They had different ways of expressing these aspects of their personhood: "I always think of myself as a nurse first." "I used to want to say I was a therapist and not own up to being a social worker; I don't feel that way any more." One young social worker said it eloquently:

> There's a common understanding of social workers as working in public assistance as case workers. Some people might think a social worker is that, and so there might be a tendency to identify myself as a therapist just to distinguish myself from the

case worker—although in my training that was an important part because of the holistic nature of it. *I'll never get away from thinking in those terms*, because it's an inclusive type of thinking, *even though I identify myself as a therapist.* (Italics mine)

Whereas none of the social workers or nurses admitted to breaking "therapeutic rules," sometimes they came close to advocating the very flexibility that the psychologists would call *loose*. Elaine, a very experienced nurse therapist, explained:

> As a nurse you're taught you have to look for the spiritual, the family, the financial, so these are things that always come naturally to me. I think a good therapist has to be willing to learn from clients, from other people, from wherever. I tend to want to *not* maybe accept that everything is emotional.
>
> I think a therapist also has to be willing to leave her ivory tower existence at some point if that's necessary. A good therapist in an urban setting has to be able to go to folk's homes sometimes, be able to get out of this office and meet people wherever . . . you can't always expect people to meet you where you're wanting to meet. You have to be willing to give, too, to go the extra mile for people, to get involved.

Elaine saw no reason why a good therapist should *not extend the time and place of therapy*, and she admitted coming to those conclusions because of her nursing tradition and her *nursing identity*.

To summarize, when nurses and social workers practiced psychotherapy it was customary for them to build on their earlier professional education and identity. It was impossible to take the nurse, or the social worker, out of the therapist, so to speak. It would be like trying to inactivate or totally compartmentalize a part of one's personhood. Accordingly, most therapists of all disciplines found these same issues of inclusivity in the juxtaposition of the professional and personal arenas of their life to be troublesome, because of the interconnection of their roles and the contiguity of the different aspects of their personhood (Chapter 2).

For nurses and social workers this meant that their understanding of the rules about time and space in their work was less formal and tight

than for psychologists or psychiatrists. This earned them the reputation of being "loose with the therapeutic rules," and of not having adequate training in psychotherapy.

At this point it is important to note that allocations of space and
time at both CMHCs reflected hierarchical factors. I was told at both
CMHCs by administrators, therapists, and staff members that because
psychiatrists' time was most expensive, the agency could not afford to
assign them to spend much time with clients. They were, for the most
part, assigned as consultants and psychopharmacologists, which was
less costly in terms of time. Psychologists, social workers, and nurses
did most of the primary psychotherapy. It was also true that social
workers, nurses, and psychologists who did not have doctorates were
assigned to spend *more* than the conventional fifty minutes with clients
in the day treatment and continuing treatment programs.[7] Thus, the
higher in the hierarchy, the *less* time was spent with each patient and
vice versa. This was justified economically by everyone with whom I
spoke in the matter-of-fact tones used when one is speaking the obvious.

It was not surprising that social workers and nurses were considered to be breaking therapeutic rules because they tended to extend
space and time boundaries. It was not surprising either that, for the
most part, they colluded with that opinion themselves, or that some of
them thought their training in psychotherapy had been inadequate and
others argued for more flexibility in the use of space and time in
psychotherapy.

Thus, for both nurses and social workers their identities as
psychotherapists were influenced by their primary disciplines and by
the fact that those disciplines had traditionally been professions for
women.

At the Riverpool Center allocation of space for staff lounges
reflected and became symbolic of hierarchical issues among professional groups. Some of the social workers and the nurses were irritated
by the fact that the psychiatric residents had been given a private
reading room, a room to which only they had the key. The nurses and
social workers who spoke about this said that it was not so much being
excluded from the room that was irksome but rather that their own
lounge had been used to provide the space given to the psychiatric
residents as their exclusive room.

The issue of the private doctor's lounge had upset the staff
enough to cause the director of ambulatory services, a psychiatrist, to

designate a room as a lounge for the nonmedical staff. Because psychologists had rooms on a different floor, this new lounge was now used only by social workers, nurses, and secretaries, most of whom were women. When I was becoming acquainted with the center early in my field work, one of the social workers volunteered the information that whereas the physicians' reading room was coed, the staff lounge was *for women only*; the logic of her statement became clear to me when she also said that there was only one male social worker, and he did not come to the lounge. The staff lounge was used sporadically and infrequently. Although the lounge areas for psychologists and psychiatrists were designated by professional distinctions, the lounge area for the nurses, social workers, and secretaries became, by default, recognizable by gender distinctions.

Perceptions of Hierarchical Issues about and by Social Workers

Thus, gender issues cannot be overlooked when considering the position and status of social workers in CMHCs. Two other traditional themes seemed to influence the way social workers were perceived by themselves and others. The first was the heritage of providing charitable services to the disadvantaged, and the second was systematic social organization of those services.[8] From the first, the social workers earned the description of being do gooders; that is, charitable philanthropists who were not primarily interested in personal monetary gain. Second, they had a reputation for knowing how to work with government systems. Many social workers described themselves as having been "front-line caseworkers" before they became therapists. The capacity to do psychotherapy was gained after formal completion of a master's degree in social work with an emphasis in mental health problems and psychiatric illnesses. They were, for the most part, supervised by psychologists or senior social workers. Psychiatrists acted as consultants.

Fifteen social workers were in the sample from both CMHCs. Eleven had master's degrees and two were aspiring to this achievement. Only four were men. But whether men or women, the topic of their low salaries and status on the social hierarchy at the CMHCs was frequently introduced.

The administrators at each of the three Newell sites were social workers. Some had held higher administrative positions when the agency was younger and not affiliated with hospitals. With the connection to hospitals came the need to align the agency with psychiatrists, psychologists, and nurses. Social workers' perceptions were that although *they* were the experts in community work, as well as in relationships with government agencies, they were always placed in lower positions than *the doctors*. I was told that psychiatrists were placed in the highest administrative positions to "be figureheads" (see Appendix F) even if they did not have administrative skills. As for psychologists, social workers were constantly comparing themselves to them:

> There are power issues in the infrastructure here in the sense that psychologists are paid more because people with Ph.D.s are paid more, so even though they may do the exact same thing, they get paid more because of the education. Psychiatrists have more power legally and politically and every other way.
> Because the jobs are divided up the way they are it tends to minimize the differences, but *they can pull rank on us* if they want to.

Another social worker had the same opinion: "Social workers really do therapy well. I often don't see any difference between a psychologist and a social worker—there's really no difference. It's more different according to who they are as people than how they've been trained."

Just as the name *doctor* seemed to raise the status of a psychologist, so the name *psychotherapist* seemed to raise the status of a social worker. They perceived themselves to be "the third mental health profession" after psychology. Therefore, they were constantly comparing themselves to psychologists and hoping not to be judged to be lesser. Yet they often were the strictest judges: "I found myself falling into that a lot when I was wanting to call myself a therapist instead of saying I was a social worker, or seeing myself one down to someone who was a psychologist. I can honestly say I don't feel that way anymore because I've had enough experience to see that everyone brings pluses and minuses."

Social workers perceived themselves to be in the third hierarchical position, after psychologists, in the CMHCs even though they understood themselves to be the experts in community relationships. Psychologists' perceptions of them were congruent with their own. Most psychiatrists perceived the same thing except for one experienced psychiatrist at Riverpool who thought social workers ranked fourth after nurses. Nurses at Riverpool thought they ranked higher than social workers (see Table 7), whereas nurses at Newell thought social workers ranked higher than themselves. The affiliation of the River- pool Center to the university hospital may have affected everyone's perceptions of the nurses. For just as social workers have traditional ties to the community, so nurses have traditional ties to hospitals.

Perceptions of Hierarchical Issues about and by Nurses

There were ten nurses in the sample from both CMHCs. Nine had master's degrees, and one had passed graduate courses but had not yet completed her master's degree; all were women. The nine who had master's degrees practiced primary psychotherapy. Three in the sam- ple (two from Newell and one from Riverpool) held administrative positions that provided a link between the centers and the hospitals. Seven were at the Riverpool Center and only three at Newell. This was understandable in view of Riverpool's location inside a hospital. Nurses were supervised by other nurses. Four of the nurses in the sample were supervisors to student or graduate nurses. The ex- perienced nurses at Riverpool had a system of peer supervision for their clinical work. One nurse said her clinical supervisor was a psychiatrist. Their traditional ties to the hospitals were an important aspect of their perception of their role. One of the nurse administrators expressed it well. She was talking of her work in the CMHC:

> We understand the inpatient setting. We've seen the other side of it [mental health care]. I think a lot more nurses could be represented in the community.
> My vision about what it [the CMHC] does for people is to meet their care needs in a more natural environment. Instead of the hospital, the setting is much more accessible, much more nor- malizing, especially in mental health.
> The nursing pay scale is higher in hospital systems, but it's also more demanding there. Plus nurses haven't traditionally been out here, so the work is more pioneering.

This nurse had much more to say about the low salary that nurses received; she was one of the nurses who spoke specifically about nurs- ing being a female profession.

Gender issues are more emphatically significant when considering the position and status of nurses. The very term *nurse* connotes femininity, nourishment, and the human body. Other traditional themes influence the way nurses are perceived by themselves and others. The first theme related to the heritage of being caregivers for suffering persons, and the second related to the perception that it is important to skillfully manage the environment around suffering persons for healing, for prevention of sickness, or humane dying.[9] From the first they earned the reputation of being merciful tenders and attenders of the sick; then the reputation of being bossy and intractable controllers of patients' environments, especially in hospitals. Thus, opinions and perceptions of nurses were diverse. Moreover, perceptions of hierarchical issues about and by nurses were different at the two CMHCs. At Riverpool, nurses were perceived to be powerful, but at Newell, whose sites were farther from a hospital, nurses were not very visible and therefore had lower status. This statement is true in general, with many exceptions. A few examples will illustrate.

Psychiatrists at Riverpool had the most to say about nurses. It was also noticeable that for both nurses and psychiatrists at Riverpool, it was difficult to limit their comments to the setting of the CMHC. They could lapse into comments and monologues about inpatient hospital settings for psychiatric patients. These are the comments of an experienced psychiatrist:

In a community mental health center the psychiatrist has the last word about a lot of things because he has the expertise and the best training . . . but this power is eroding somewhat.

In the inpatient units there is a struggle for power with psychiatric nurses. The whole movement toward interdisciplinary teams is because of nurses saying "we are professionals, too; we have ideas about the patient; we want to be in on the decisions including when you're going to discharge someone even; what medication you're going to use and when you're going to let somebody go out on pass; I don't think this one is safe to go out on pass." Now when nurses talk to me that way, I say, "Fine, be direct by all means." What I can't stand is when they have those feelings and when they are afraid to say it, but *cause some undermining of the treatment program* because that's what they believe. That happens all the time. It is a powerful department of nursing. (Italics mine)

This was not the only psychiatrist who was displeased with inter-disciplinary teams. These are the comments of another experienced psychiatrist:

Something about the interdisciplinary team dilutes the respon-sibility the physician feels . . . certainly if not the responsibility, the authority. Physicians, particularly in an inpatient setting, can be very constrained by the need to mobilize everybody's agree-ment. Not that if everybody doesn't agree you can't go ahead with the treatment plan. *You can go ahead, but you'll be sabotaged*; peo-ple will drag their heels. Things won't get done which you ordered or somebody also will undo it. (Italics mine)

Although this physician did not refer explicitly to nurses, his reference to physicians' orders implicates nurses rather than other members of the team because carrying out doctors' orders is a tradi-tional role of nurses.

Another psychiatrist expanded on doctor's orders: "With the nurses there is a sense of belief of the importance of doctors' orders and there is a sort of giving commands to people. You'll find that you'll get more commands out of nurses than you would out of other groups, like: 'don't do that!' 'do that!' Now I'm sure that people in any profes-sion issue instructions like that with some regularity. My experience is that nurses most often do that."

I asked a psychiatric resident who was quite vehemently upset about interdisciplinary teams, about the distinctions between the disciplines. This is what he said about nurses: "I think nurses and doc-tors think of things in the same model. Nurses don't go as deep as physicians do in finding the etiology and in the biochemical aspects. They do it superficially."

Thus, most psychiatrists perceived nurses as co-curers with limita-tions. At best they were valuable aides-de-camp in the battle against disease, faithfully following lifegiving orders and boldly instructing pa-tients to do the same. Conversely, they could be formidable op-ponents, directly challenging doctors' orders or indirectly obstructing them.

Most psychologists in the sample had very little to say about nurses. The psychologist who made the comment about nurses and social workers being lax with therapeutic rules also said that nurses did "good crisis intervention"; other psychologists thought nurses "worked long hours" and were good health educators. It should be noted that crisis intervention is a mode of therapy that can be practiced by non-professional persons in the community, and "working long hours" is occasionally perceived as the lot of persons who have low status.

I got the impression that psychologists did not know much about nurses and did not take them seriously as professional competitors. These statements of a female psychology intern will illustrate: "Well there is something like a hierarchy. Let's see psychiatrists, then psychologists, social workers next, and then nurses; nurses are at the bottom of the pole. Nurses have picked out a couple of key concepts [laughing], like 'choice' and 'responsibility', 'meaning' and 'owning'. They bandy them back and forth" [laughing]. The tone was one used to describe the quaint but harmless customs of subordinates.

One of the psychiatrists told me she perceived "open warfare" between nurses and social workers on inpatient units in the hospital. I did not observe any such open conflict at the CMHCs. Social workers who had positive comments about nurses tended to minimize the differences between them and the nurses in question: "The only thing that she brings special, I think, is in some sense, her medical experience; sometimes it is important in that I've gone to her and said, 'how do you think it affects the emotional stuff?' I don't think it makes a big difference. I really don't."

Social workers who made negative comments about nurses tended to maximize the differences between them and nurses, like the social worker who, although she recognized that both professions were female professions, nevertheless insisted that nurses were "way low down" because of the menial and physical service tasks that were not intellectual.

The social workers at Riverpool thought that nurses were powerful in that setting, and the Riverpool nurses' statements were congruent with that perception. Yet most nurses also perceived their status to be low. Both opinions would occasionally be expressed by the same nurse within the same statement. This is one of many examples:

> We're on the bottom, in terms of status. If someone has been seeing a psych resident, and he leaves because he's finished with his rotation, and that person gets referred to a nurse, they feel disap-

pointed. "Why aren't we seeing a doctor anymore?" As for social workers, we're on the faculty and they're not. I don't know if this is accurate or not, but I think they have less power in this system as a whole. I think we're viewed by other disciplines and by each other as quite competitively.

Thus, nurses' opinions of themselves were as disparate as others' opinions of them. For example, although they perceived themselves "to be regarded as less than others," they also perceived themselves to "have a lot of clout" (see Appendix F). When pressed to rank themselves in relationship to the other disciplines, all the nurses in the sample perceived psychiatrists to rank highest (see Table 7). Beyond that there was no uniform opinion. Three nurses gave qualified opinions such as the one just quoted; to paraphrase, they said that they had low status *but* they had power; or they had a lot of clout, *but* they needed to have interdisciplinary teams in the CMHC so that they would become participants in treatment decisions; or that they had low status, *but* also prestige (see Appendix F). Only one nurse's perception was congruent with the general view held by other therapists at the CMHCs; namely, that nurses ranked fourth among disciplines. None of the nurses regarded themselves as the fourth mental health profession. Four nurses thought they ranked higher than social workers, and three of those did not mention the rank of psychologists, as though psychologists were of no consequence to them in matter of rank. They did, however, have much to say about the *real doctors*, the physicians who could give orders that they had to follow or contend with and whose diagnostic pronouncements were of relevance to them and to the patients for whom they were caring. For nurses share with physicians the capacities that are ascribed to professionals who have expertise regarding the human body.

These are only two of many comments made by nurses about psychiatrists and nurses in relation to medical issues.

From my perspective psychiatrists have the knowledge of the biological, the medical concomitants of psychological problems. They are much more alert to being aware of asking the right questions like, "Is there an organic base here?" I might not think of that as readily; and then they have the ability to sign prescrip-

tions. You need the legalization of the psychiatrist's signature. I
think there's room for lots of consultation around those medication issues. Because they have the background and training that I
don't have formally other than through experience. . . . But I
think that knowledge of the body is one of the strengths of nursing in the psychotherapeutic role, that although we don't have the
level of medical background that the psychiatrist does, I think we
do have a different level of medical awareness than the social
worker or psychologist does. We are alert to some of the medical
issues that should be raised with a medical consultant, I think that
nurses tune into those things more quickly.

Here is another less favorable opinion about psychiatrists from a
nurse:

Well, I think that psychiatrists think they're the best of
everything. They think that others are not as good as they are.
They are good psychopharmacologists and follow biological
models. That does not necessarily make them better therapists.
They're becoming aware of that. I have not had good experience
with them as therapists. They don't *learn* to be therapists. They
spend a couple of years being residents. But a lot of their time is
spent doing all that other medical stuff.

Thus, perceptions of hierarchical issues about and by nurse therapists were influenced by traditional perceptions of their primary
discipline of nursing. More specifically, the fact that nursing was traditionally regarded as a profession for women contributed to the low
status of nurses. Moreover, this was accentuated by the fact that nurses
have traditionally attended to the needs of the sick, adding an appearance of servanthood to their work. However, nurses were also
perceived by others and by themselves to have privileged access to patients and to be managers of patients' environments. This seemed to
give them special capacities in a hospital. Therefore perceptions of
nurses and opinions about their status were disparate. Therapists, staff
members, and in fact nurses themselves seemed to be saying not only
that nurses had low status but also that they were powerful. There
were hints that these capacities were related to their proximity to and

their knowledge of the human body. As was established earlier the capacity to attend to the physical and biological aspects of care is an extremely valued component of Western medicine. We have also established that psychiatrists in CMHCs were seen as having the capacities both to "read the mind" and to have somatic and biochemical expertise. They were perceived to have *mystical capacities* related to psychotherapy as well as *social entitlement capacities* to take charge of the medical cure of their patients.

Although nurses were perceived to be involved in the care and cure of patients and they had knowledge of the human body and proximity to it, their capacities in relation to the human body were different from those of physicians. Psychiatrists in their capacity as physicians had *social entitlements* and responsibilities to take charge and have custody of the care of patients. They signed official documents like birth certificates, death certificates, psychiatric hospitalization forms, and prescriptions for medications. They also made official pronouncements about patient diagnoses. Nurses had a few of those capacities by virtue of their alignment to physicians. However, traditionally they had other capacities. They could wash the body, massage the body, supervise bodily functions like eating, sleeping, eliminating, and moving. This gave them access and proximity to the patients. In the hospitals, physicians order medications, but nurses stock, store, and administer them. Whereas some of these nursing functions are *professional entitlements and responsibilities*, many are traditional capacities reminiscent of early childhood caretakers. I hold that many of the capacities that nurses are perceived to possess are *mystical*; that is, powerful yet not easy to explain or comprehend in terms of other professional capacities.

It was not surprising that nurses were perceived by others and perceived themselves as of low status and yet powerful. Even though they could not take official responsibility for the biochemical aspects of care, they could take charge in the execution of both its environmental and somatic aspects.

TENDING THE BODY AND LISTENING TO THE PERSON

Although nurses in CMHCs do not often actually perform the direct body tending functions done to hospital patients, the capacity to tend the body has become a part of their personhood and it affects their relationship to their patients and influences the way they are perceived by their coworkers. Their personhood is part of the context of all their communications including dream telling. Nurses alluded to this regularly; an example will illustrate.

When it became necessary for Elaine, an experienced nurse, to refer a client to another therapist who was not a nurse, the client became concerned that he would not be able to tell the other therapist about certain religious preoccupations, sexual fantasies, and dreams. Elaine knew that such anxiety around referral to a new therapist is not uncommon, but she realized that this patient could be afraid of losing her capacities as a nurse. She explained: "I didn't think it had anything to do with my being a nurse. I think he and I had just talked a lot about his dreams as you talk about differences in people. I think here maybe he was worried that this person [the other therapist] might have a different religious background, and I think people notice these kinds of things. Also he said, *"Well, you know about the body 'cause you're a nurse."* (Italics mine) This patient was not worried about the new therapist's competence; it seemed to be more a question of not being as embarrassed at mentioning certain matters to a nurse because he thought nurses were likely to be familiar with intimate body functions; it was part of their role.

Moreover, because of nurses' traditional proximity to patients and their function of attending to the patients' physical and commonplace needs, the conversations with patients tend to have a broader range or less confinement to a particular topic: conversations could be intense or relaxed, intimate or superficial; topics ranged from the ultimate and crucial to the prosaic and banal. Nurses tried to explain this in a variety of ways. Sometimes they did so by saying they were interested in "the whole person" and sometimes by saying that they had been taught to "look at things in a broad scope," to be interested in a large range of topics regarding their patients. These topics have some relation to the body but are not strictly and exclusively related to the body.

Elaine also told how she stumbled unexpectedly on the topic of incest while talking with another patient about her family:

You're taught you have to look for the spiritual, the family, the financial; so these are things that always sort of come natural to me. An example is again because I'm a nurse I started early hearing a lot of stuff about incest and sexual abuse before it was fashionable. So that became one of the things I started to ask clients, though the physicians at first didn't want to believe me. They said that didn't happen very much, "Come on, Elaine, you're making this up." Well, I had a student who wanted to do a project—and we found there was an awful lot of incest just in that center.

Those are some of the things I question and there again, those are the holistic things that you have to see this person as a whole. I think I've taught, well I've been able to help this staff to recognize the differences in the religious and how this has played either a positive or a negative issue in some of the people's illnesses.

Elaine was not the only nurse who talked about this broad range in listening to patients. There was also a way to look at problems so that one's attention did not become too circumscribed. A young nurse considered this to be the most noteworthy difference between psychiatrists and nurses. I asked her if she listened to dreams in the same way as practitioners of other disciplines did. She said:

I've been lucky because I work with psychiatrists and psychologists who are similar [to me]. I think the only difference, and again I don't know if this has to do with dreams though, is that nurses do more managing—like the overall picture. I look at the overall picture, whereas the psychiatrist would look more at the illness. And they are just more focused; they don't see the forest for the trees. They're hung up in a tree, and I'm the one who says "well wait a minute, let's look at the forest. Let's look at the broad picture."

To summarize, nurses' communications with patients were influenced by the traditional tendency of nurses to hear specific as well as general commonplace topics from patients. In terms of contexts we can say that the personhood of nurses caused the actors, that is, both the nurses and the patients, not to confine their conversations to topics of *professional* concern, but also to include topics of incidental *personal* concern. This capacity of nurses to hear the intimate and incidental concerns was sometimes perceived to be diluting the professional role and *lowering the status* of the nurse. The capacity to hear personal (i.e., intimate and commonplace) things is a *mystical capacity* because it derives from nurses' capacity to help the patient with physical, otherwise private and ordinary, functions of the body, as well as the commonplace issues of everyday living. In the perceptions of nurses, as in perceptions of psychiatrists by their medical colleagues, the mystical capacities exerted a negative effect on their status. Thus, the nurses were perceived by others, and they perceived themselves, to have low status *and* to be powerful. They were ascribed capacities to tend the body. However, they were expected to tend the body as skilled helpers rather than official social custodians. This caused their conversations with patients to be less exclusively focused on medical issues, and more open to commonplace topics including casual, intimate, and "personal" topics.

THE DREAM-HEARING RANGE

In this chapter I examined the question of how the capacity to hear and interpret dreams is related to and sometimes even attributed to designations of role, status, and hierarchical positions in the CMHCs. I have shown that the capacities to hear and interpret dreams are embedded in the contexts of the dream telling. This involves not only the setting at each site and the reciprocal roles of the particular actors, but also perceptions of the social capacities that derive from the norms and traditions of therapists' original practice disciplines. I have found that the question, Who is most likely to ask about and listen to dreams? yielded long answers related to the complexities of *personhood*.

There was a uniform perception by all concerned that psychiatrists held the highest positions at CMHCs. There was a very strong but not uniform perception that psychologists held the second to the highest positions. Opinions about social workers' positions generally, but by no means routinely, placed them in the third hierarchical position after psychologists. Opinions about psychiatric nurses were most dissimilar, with many therapists, on the one hand, either placing them fourth or not considering them at all or, on the other hand, considering them to be powerful and in higher positions than social workers at least. These opinions were influenced by how closely each center was connected with a hospital.

Although most of the therapists and staff knew that psychiatrists were functioning as consultants and psychopharmacologists, and did not spend much time with clients, the predominant opinion was that psychiatrists were most likely to ask about and listen to dreams and be able to interpret them (see Table 7). Thus, the perception was that the higher the therapist's status, the more likely it was that dreams would be heard and interpreted.

The relationship between dream telling, dream hearing, and hierarchy is consistent with regard to psychologists, too. They were perceived to be the second professionals most likely to listen to dreams. Most social workers and nurses were not perceived, and did not perceive themselves, as very likely to ask about and listen to dreams, and they were also identified as low-status professions.

However, there were interesting exceptions: three of the nurses said that *they* were most likely to ask about and listen to dreams (Table 7). It should be noted also that more nurses said that they had an active interest in listening to dreams for any of their patients even the ones who were diagnosed as low functioning (Table 1).

When I asked therapists to describe dream telling in their experience in the context of psychotherapy, it was difficult to deduce from their comments the frequency with which the topic of dreams came up. Only one therapist told me he never listened to dreams. (When the topic was introduced, he changed the subject.) Aside from him no one said the question was not relevant to psychotherapy. A few said the topic was not frequently introduced in their work. Most gave me examples of dream telling from the context of their own work with clients. Those who could not remember examples nevertheless told me that the topic had come up. But they said much more. They told me about psychotherapy, the capacity to "read minds," the Freudian heritage, their own professional background, hierarchical positions of their disciplines, and many statements regarding the value of dreams. I was also told about psychological mindedness, which is perceived as a quality and an ideal that they liked to attribute to themselves or sought to possess. They also told me that they valued psychologically minded patients because they were expected to have good prognoses for recovery with the kind of psychotherapeutic treatment that was consistent with dream work.

Consequently, although in theory dreams were valued for their part in increasing self-awareness and considered useful for long-term,

insight-oriented therapy, practically speaking dreams were not considered as valuable resources for the kinds of therapy they were practicing at the CMHCs. Also, long-term insight-oriented therapy was
considered expensive and effectively out of the reach of all but a few
people, even those who were psychologically minded. Insight-oriented
therapy, which was most commonly related to dream work, was most
emphatically regarded *not* to be the treatment choice for "low
functioning" patients, who were most likely to come to the CMHCs.

Theoretically and ideally dreams were considered resources in
psychotherapy; but practically and actually this was not the case. For
example, a young psychiatrist (who had completed his residency)
assured me that his psychiatric training had given him a comprehensive
approach to dreams; he said he used a variety of approaches in his
work. But when I asked him for a clinical example, the one he gave me
was about a woman who had come to him with the "complaint" of having nightmares. He had prescribed medication for sleep, and the
nightmares had subsided so the patient was able to sleep better.

Although this psychiatrist was not typical of the psychiatrists with
whom I spoke, it became clear that the perception that psychiatrists
were most likely to ask about and listen to dreams was a notion based
more on perceptions of their personhood and medical psychiatric tradition than on fact. It was related to another notion; namely, that dream
telling is valuable only for gaining insight and self-knowledge, but of little use or value to those who are not psychologically minded, even
harmful to those who are mentally ill, low functioning, or otherwise
disadvantaged. The CMHCs served a large number of such patients.

It also became apparent that the professionals on the lower positions in the hierarchy actually asked about and listened to dreams more
often than those on the higher positions. The belief that dreams could
be useful only with "high functioning" patients was more prevalent
among psychologists and psychiatrists than nurses and social workers
(see Table 1). However, seven out of ten nurses said they had an active interest in listening to dreams of all patients, and five of those gave
examples of the use of dreams to comfort and support patients even
when insight could not be gained, or when gaining insight was not at
issue. Nurses spoke with patients about a broader range of topics,
some of which were intimate and others incidental and commonplace.

Nurses and social workers were perceived by psychologists as
having a tendency to break therapeutic rules with regard to time and

space. They were less likely to be scrupulous with time and space boundaries, and they spent more time with patients. It became apparent to me that nurses were not averse to "breaking therapeutic rules" regarding dream telling because they did not relate dreams *only* to the therapeutic goal of gaining insight. For nurses, communication about dreams could be prosaic, part of the talk concerning the activities of daily living. Communications about dreams could be similar to the talk about any other normal body functions. In such communication, dreams need not be interpreted. Such communication *does not count* as psychotherapy in the traditional sense of intensely investigating mental processes to treat mental and emotional disorders. For psychiatrists, the definition of what is therapeutic is related primarily to their responsibility to treat and cure mental illness. For nurses, the definition of what is therapeutic is related primarily to tending and comforting the people who are suffering because of their mental illness. The telling of dreams in each context is different because of the traditional, the ascribed, and the actual capacities of the persons involved.

CONCLUSION

The predominant opinion was that psychiatrists, who have the highest status at the CMHCs, are most likely to ask about and listen to dreams and be able to interpret them. It was also perceived that psychologists were the second most likely group to listen to dreams and interpret them. Social workers and nurses, who have low status, were not perceived to be very likely to listen to dreams. The exceptions to these perceptions were the opinions of three nurses who thought that as a professional group, the nurses were most likely to be interested in dreams and to listen to them.

Opinions about nurses were varied; they were perceived to have low status as well as to be powerful. I hold that the capacities they had were *mystical capacities* because they were difficult to define, explain, or comprehend. These mystical capacities gave them the power that others perceived them to have. However, unlike psychiatrists, they did not have strong *social entitlement capacities* to complement the negative effects of the mystical capacities. So although they were perceived to be powerful they were also perceived to have low status.

In fact, psychiatrists at the CMHCs were psychopharmacologists and consultants and did little psychotherapy; therefore, they had little time to listen to dreams. Psychologists at the CMHCs listened to dreams more often than psychiatrists. Nurses who were ranked the lowest by many psychotherapists seemed to ask about and listen to dreams more than the others. However, nurses did not listen to dreams exclusively to help the patient gain insight. They heard a broader range of topics introduced by patients and were less concerned with treating through dream telling than with listening to dreams as commonplace human experiences.

VI

Showing the Person and Knowing the Person

INTRODUCTION

There are numerous psychological studies about dreams in Western societies. There is also much information in ethnographic studies about dreams and dream telling in non-Western societies. This is an ethnographic study of dreams and dream telling in American society, a topic and setting not frequently brought together by researchers. In this chapter I summarize some of the key findings, conclusions, implications, and shortcomings of this study.

It was an assumption of this study that dreams are not only phenomena experienced by individuals, but also social communication that conveys a constellation of ideas and beliefs of local and larger communities. The literature review supports the argument by Tedlock (1987) that, *in general*, psychological researchers have ignored that their subjects' communication of dreams were socially and contextually determined, and that, *in general*, anthropological researchers have ignored the fact that dream communication in non-Western societies is partially dependent on native theories about dream experiences. In this study although the focus has been on dreams as social communication, that is, contextually determined, it was important to explore "native" theories and concepts about dream experience. To accomplish these purposes, a distinction between the concepts of *person* and *self* (Harris 1989) was maintained and the focus was placed on the concept of *person*.

The disadvantage of this approach lies in the fact that, although dreams are an experienced phenomenon of the *self*, as well as a social communication, the study focused only on the latter function of dreams. This study did not allow a thorough exploration of dreams as an expression of the *self*. For example, studies on the manifest content of the dreams as expressions of how notions of self are construed might have yielded instructive results. Dreams can represent expressions of negotiations over selfhood in dream telling as well as in the therapeutic process. These are valid topics of inquiry that merit attention in future studies.

From the emic point of view of the dreamer and dream teller, the *self* and the *person* are not separate. For most Americans dreams are considered primarily and predominantly a psychological phenomenon. In fact, several therapists in my study as well as persons who were not in my sample assumed that I was doing a psychological study. I was even told that my study of dreams ought to have used a psychological model. Among my informants, issues of personhood and experiences of the self are fused together and generally understood in terms of, and subsumed within theories of, the individualistic psychological ego. It is because of this native tendency and conceptualization that the analytic distinction between *self* and *person*, and the focus on the construct of *person* have proved particularly useful in this study. The concept of person provided a methodological tool by which every action including dream talk was seen primarily and explicitly in the context of the setting and the social relations in which it occurred. This perspective assumes that in every dream telling interaction actors communicate and, indeed, acquire the customs, attitudes, and values of their society, albeit through their own personal thoughts, feelings, and idiosyncrasies. This, in contradistinction to the native perspective that understands the former implicitly and covertly, while predominantly acknowledging only the latter.

It is important to say that these two constructs of *self* and *person* cannot be totally isolated from one another even for the purposes of analysis. They always bear a basic relationship to one another. When one is in the foreground, the other is usually in the background and vice versa. The understanding of one's own personhood in part is a function of the self, and the actions of the person always include expressions of the self. The subtle relationship between issues of *person* and issues of *self* in the contexts of dream telling have yielded the most intriguing findings. These will be briefly elucidated.

NOT SHOWING THE PERSON

Fortes understood the notion of *person* to be universal. He perceived the ideas and beliefs about personhood to be channeled into daily activities. More specifically, he asserted that the person shows him- or herself to be what he or she is supposed to be by acting with and through distinctive qualities, capacities, and roles. Looked at subjectively, it is a question of how an actor knows him- or herself to be. He posed the question: "in order to know my I-ness, do I need to show it to some or all of the world outside me?" He discovered and concluded in analyzing homogeneous traditional societies, that the only way to know one's identity is to show it all the time in objective ways (Fortes 1983: 389–401).

Fortes did not make a formal distinction between the concepts of *person* and *self*. In this way he avoided the pitfalls of, on the one hand, ignoring subjectivity and, on the other hand, taking the focus away from social relations to psychological experiences. His clarification of the dynamic relationship between the agentive and reflexive functions of the person have been helpful in analyzing the ethnographic data in this study particularly because, for the therapists interviewed, having dreams was understood to be a way to know oneself and telling dreams was a way to show oneself. Beliefs about dream telling reflected beliefs about personhood and about the ways people were accustomed to show themselves.

Therapists' identity as professionals took precedence over their identity in the personal arenas of their lives. They perceived with disgruntlement, or with good-humored acknowledgment, that it was not acceptable to show themselves "simply as persons." They were expected to *not show* aspects of their personhood in certain designated activities. This expectation went beyond the role differentiation issues that occur in the customary enactment of different roles. It was not enough to symbolically remove one's hat and wear another in different settings; psychotherapists perceived that they ought not to even show their other hats in any setting where clients might be present, such as restaurants or other recreation areas. Nor could they completely shed the psychotherapy identity in nonwork settings, as with neighbors or at social gatherings. They were uncomfortable when they were told dreams in nonconfidential contexts, and some even described discomfort when they had dreams about these situations.

By contrast there is a general expectation in America that persons will have access to certain facts about the personal lives of public and professional figures. Furthermore, there is a general atmosphere of great interest in the private lives of celebrities. This general inquisitiveness ranges from the mild interest to the intense preoccupation with exposing private and hidden facts, which is typical of numerous popular tabloid publications and revelatory biographies.

These two situations demonstrate complementary characteristics of the same phenomenon; namely, the complex relationship between knowing and showing one's personhood. It is not merely the proliferation or differentiation of roles that contribute to the complexity of the phenomenon, but rather the way in which the roles are construed by persons in relation to others and to themselves. Stepping in and out of roles is more easily shown to others when roles are multiplex than when aspects of one's personhood are not showable in numerous contexts. Thus, even when one's personhood is firmly delineated in clear contexts, the self is experienced as fragmented.

SHOWING THAT ONE KNOWS ONESELF

The data from this study demonstrated a "mythology" of dream telling and dream interpretation in the conceptualization of the psychotherapeutic role derived from psychoanalysis. In psychotherapeutic contexts, dreams were perceived to be valuable and useful for gaining insight. However, this ideal was believed to be achieved only by those who were psychologically minded. Reflection on one's dreams could make persons aware of their feelings and motivations even when they were tempted to deceive themselves, or when they felt divided within themselves. The value placed on self-awareness was so high that the more prosaic, less intense, less analytic communications about dreams were devalued and trivialized. It was also perceived that for those who were not psychologically minded and had little capacity or inclination for introspection, dreams were deemed to be neither useful nor therapeutic. Therapists were expected to be psychologically minded and to engage in self-searching and self-inspection. They were expected to "read" their own minds as well as the minds of others. They often judged themselves to be less aware than they ought to be. Reflexivity is not only a capacity but also an expectation.

This belief in the value of psychological analysis is associated with an anxious and lonely self-preoccupation and self-scrutiny, which Mauss portrays as characteristic of the Western *person*. His description of this concept is evolutionary, postulating a more highly developed sense of self in the modern Western person than in those of earlier or more traditional societies. I have demonstrated that each aspect of the category of person Mauss considers diachronically as historically discrete was part of the contemporary concurrent understanding and experience of the therapists and staff of the two community mental health centers. However, the evolutionary perspective was evident in the values of my informants. They believed that self-scrutinizing and other activities of the mind were more valuable (more highly evolved?) than other activities of their experience. In terms of dream telling, this became manifested in statements that indicated that, when dreams were told by psychologically minded, high functioning clients, the outcome could be more therapeutic than dreams told by low functioning clients who were not psychologically minded and who therefore would not have the capacity for introspection. It is not surprising to discover this value analogously reflected in the hierarchical structure among the therapists in the community mental health centers. Those who held the highest positions were perceived to be better able to interpret dreams.

The language used by therapists and staff to describe themselves and others with regard to their dreams was mechanistic. Dreams were considered to be like the red and yellow lights in the instrument panel of an automobile. They could signal faulty "functioning." Moreover, low functioning clients were described as "loosely wrapped," "broken down," "not intact." The capacity to "read the mind" was essential to the understanding of oneself because it was believed that the mind controlled other aspects of one's experience.

When images portraying the person are described as those of a functioning or nonfunctioning machine, the "reader" of the mind is seen as one who repairs it, who takes the machine apart, locates the malfunction, and puts it back together again in the correct way, unless the parts are faulty or absent. Expressions like *having a screw loose, having one's head examined*, or *not being all there* convey this mechanistic imagery. Dreams are considered to be products of the mind that might make evident this "faulty wiring." That is why telling dreams produces anxiety in most settings, especially in the presence of psychotherapists. The metaphor conveys a picture of a nonparticipatory experience. The mechanic does not participate in the machine nor does the machine participate at all. Therefore, a distance is created between the observer and the observed. When this method is applied to one's own mind, the scrutiny creates a distance and detachment from oneself. Thus, even though the self-inspecting *person* is highly valued, considered to be individualized, rational, and self-possessed, the scrutinizing person's experience of the *self* is one of isolation from others and alienation from oneself.

THE INCONGRUITIES BETWEEN PERSON AND SELF

The fact that what persons show themselves to be is not always congruent with their subjective experience of themselves is not in itself unexpected or surprising. The understanding of oneself is a unique and idiosyncratic experience. What was noteworthy about the persons who spoke with me (therapists and staff) was a perception of themselves as having inner and outer parts. The inner part gazed at one's actions and experience, and the outer part was expected to search for one's inner self through self-observation. Introspection was a quality they looked for in others and in themselves, and self-knowledge was an achievement most of them did not attain to their own satisfaction. The other remarkable thing was that all of this concern for self-inspection became activated and talked about when they were asked about dreams. Dreams were regarded as products of the mind, and because the self was described mechanistically, dreams were viewed as commodities: some were considered useful and some were not. In fact, many of the people who spoke with me did *not* experience their dreams in this way. Yet in the face of their own experience, they wondered if they ought to have better (less "crazy") dreams or whether they ought to make better use of them. Dreams were regarded as gauges that psychotherapists or other psychologically minded persons could "read" when they inspected the mind. Thus, dreams were connected to psychotherapy.

I discovered that this conceptualization of the psychotherapeutic role was incongruous with the therapists' experience of it. To many of them, psychotherapy was experienced as a dialogue of person in reciprocal roles and a specialized relationship. Most of the therapists did not, in fact, perceive themselves as inspectors of mental gauges. None of them professed to be able to "read" anyone's mind. Yet all of them perceived psychotherapists, including themselves, to have those capacities ascribed to them. I am reminded, at this point, of the nurse who confessed to me that although she believed the notion to be ridiculous, she nevertheless caught herself wondering whether her colleagues, especially the psychiatrist with whom she worked, could, at times, "read" her mind. She was not exceptional. Most persons, whether psychotherapists themselves or not, were very reluctant to tell their dreams to anyone except intimate others, and they were especially reluctant to tell their dreams in the presence of experts of the mind. Dreams were regarded as products of the inner parts of themselves that could be or ought to be used for inspection by oneself or others. Dreams were revealed very cautiously in appropriate contexts.

According to Mauss, since the Reformation, the typical Western person in modern times has an anxious need for self-scrutiny. Every individual has the right to communicate with God without the mediation of a confessor or priest. Examination of one's consciousness becomes every person's responsibility; each person is now his or her own priest. It is notable that the practice of psychotherapy as the "talking cure" for dis-ease of mind has originated in its present form in Western societies. It could be, on the one hand, a manifestation of the values placed on the individual self-searching and self-knowing *person* and, on the other hand, an expression of the needs experienced by the fragmented and isolated *self* who needs a confessor after all.

THE DISJUNCTION OF MIND AND BODY

One of the important findings that emerges from this study is the perceived relationship between mind and body as it relates to dreams and dream telling. Dreams were related more to the mind than to the body. Yet practitioners who also had special knowledge of the body, like physicians and nurses, were perceived to have special capacities in relation to hearing and interpreting dreams.

Psychiatrists were perceived to have capacities to read the mind as well as the expertise to "fix" the body. Their skills as psychopharmacologists and consultants on medical and biochemical problems represented their social entitlements and responsibilities as experts on the human body. The combination of these capacities placed psychiatrists in the highest positions in the hierarchies at both CMHCs. They were also alleged by all to be able to interpret dreams better than other therapists.

Nurse therapists were perceived like all therapists to have capacities to read the mind. They were expected to have access to the human body and to have capacities to tend the body. However, they were not recognized as official social custodians of the body. They could give well-informed opinions but could not make pronouncements or official decisions with social authority. Their access to the body and their capacity to give physical care made them natural hearers of intimate, important, or incidental concerns including dreams. But this proximity to the body, in the absence of the social entitlement to control the body, although it gave them a mystical power, also caused them to be perceived as having a low status like attendants. Caring for the body is perceived less prestigious than the social power to control decisions related to the person.

These data are manifestations not only of the disjunction of mind and body, but also of the perceived superiority of mind over body. This perception of the relationship between mind and body is also manifested in the battle between psychiatrists and psychologists with regard to the power of prescription of drugs. Drugs can control the body as well as the mind. Therefore the capacity to prescribe drugs confers power and authority.

Although psychiatrists had the highest positions in the hierarchy in the CMHCs, among their own cohort of physicians they had a low status. They understood this to be because they were not able to regularly practice and keep up their skills in the physical aspects of care. Their capacity to treat the body was not exercised directly or frequently. Moreover, their capacities in the treatment of the mind were not often empirically observable; they were mystical capacities. As experts in brain anatomy and physiology, psychiatrists enjoyed high prestige, but because their expertise in psychopathology was not always patently noticeable or measurable, a mystifying element was introduced in the role that rendered their status ambiguous. It was evident that, for psychiatrists as for nurses, the possession of a mystical capacity diminished their social entitlements. Thus although hearing and telling dreams was connected to "reading minds," that capacity had ambiguous meanings, gave rise to mixed attributions, and generated ambivalent feelings in those involved. Similarly, theoretically and ideally dreams were considered as resources for gaining insight in psychotherapy, but practically and actually they were regarded as disturbing or inconsequential.

The findings of this research about dream telling among psychotherapists and staff, at two CMHCs, which are both located in, or related to an academic environment, are curiously set in a larger social climate of growing popularity of dreams and dream telling in the country. In fact, dream telling can be regarded as a part of an inspirational social movement emphasizing spiritual values. Domhoff (1988) maintains that the mystique of dreams presents an American allegory of the perennial search for authenticity and self-improvement. It would be interesting to study dream telling in contexts related to this popular movement, or in contexts in which the main actors are not health professionals and among persons who would not identify themselves as professional persons. Quite often activities that are not fully accepted and acceptable in traditional environments will enjoy public popularity and become swept along in the tide of popular social movements. However, this study was necessary as a first step.

APPENDIX A

How Contexts Are Described

CASUAL CONTEXTS

"Dreams are social openers—casual." P2

"Funny dreams are told in passing, as ice-breakers." "If someone said, 'I had a funny dream last night,' I might say, 'I had one like that.'" P13

"Dream telling is to illustrate a clinical point; to get a good laugh." D5

"If the dreams are funny they become somewhat of a joke." L6

"Some people think dreams are silly and laugh at your interpretations." L5

"I sometimes tell dreams in a social setting like at a party—it depends on the dream. If I dream something really **personal**,' I don't want to broadcast it to everybody. Sometimes a bizarre dream that's funny, and I'll tell people I work with and we'll all say what it means." L9

"Dreams are told to fellow workers in a jocular sense to make a point, like, well I dreamt about Dr. So and So the other night, and he was wearing these awful clothes and this and that. How much is an authentic dream and how much is an indirect way of poking fun at an authority figure, I don't know." D1

The bold print in the appendix serves to highlight the frequency of the use of a word or expression by persons. In ethnographic research, it is significant when many informants use the same word. The purpose of the appendix is to give a record of these narratives. In quantitative research these would be in number tables with asterisks to highlight them.

"I've been at parties where dreams are discussed; they usually seem light, like, 'Gee! I had this silly dream last night. Wait'll you hear this one.' But I don't think people will tell a 'personal' dream at a party." L8

"You can tell funny and amusing dreams in public but not intimate or deep ones." L4

"It's not OK to talk about dreams with some folks where it would not be OK to talk about anything 'personal'." S13

"I would not tell casual acquaintances my dream unless it was a silly dream, entertaining but not 'personal.' It is not appropriate to tell a 'personal' dream to a casual acquaintance, especially a dream that is troubling you." S14

"It's OK to tell a nonsensical, silly, funny, interesting dream as a conversation piece. I would not tell sexual dreams in mixed company." P14

"I've had this funny dream I've shared with my boss. But I've had dreams I wouldn't share with him. It depends on the dream. I wouldn't share a 'personal' dream with a message type thing." L7

"Humorous dreams would be appropriate to tell; sad and scary dreams are inappropriate to tell [at a social gathering]." S9

"It's OK to tell dreams as a joke; it's a mixer. Unless—anything that goes off on the social taboo scale in terms of sex or religion." L1

"If casual acquaintances are told, you tell them only certain dreams. *Not* dreams with sexual overtones." L2

INTIMATE CONTEXTS

"I tell my dream right away to my sister or to my close friend." S9

"You're not responsible for what you dream; but some people might think you're responsible for what you dream; that's why people don't tell all their dreams in public." L9

"People tell their dreams first to spouses—then to therapists." D2

"I tell my dreams only to a couple of intimate friends." N4

"People would share their dreams only with a close person or a therapist." S6

"People share their dreams only with close allies; people they live with; confidants." N8

"I had a friend once—a man—we were not very close. He would tell me certain dreams in order to become more intimate; I thought it was seductive." S2

"In my experience people are rather cautious about sharing dreams. Maybe they are not comfortable by the level of disclosure, maybe they think they're exposing themselves too much. They tell their dreams to good friends and relatives." S11

"So I think that you might not tell a dream to a neighbor or someone you didn't have a **personal** relationship with. You might not tell just an acquaintance or your work coworkers, with whom you didn't have a **personal** relationship. The thing would be that if you had some **personal** relationship that was developed, that those would be OK, and other people would not be, those you didn't know to some further degree than just kind of an acquaintance." P11

"People tell their dreams to significant ones. People they can trust, not to strangers. People tell therapists; I've even heard of people telling chaplains." P14

"It is inappropriate to tell your dream to someone you're the boss of. They come and tell you their dream, and you think, 'What am I supposed to do with that?' *I* don't discuss my dreams with my boss." N10

"I would not talk about my dreams with my supervisor even though I respect her very much. That's a very intimate idea; I can't imagine doing that." S15

"I find that even with people I know well, it's a little risky sometimes because I wonder if other people see things in that, that I'm not aware of. But, I think, just generally that I'm going to end up talking about how I'm feeling, in some sense, and I think women that I know do that more often than men." S8

"People would not share certain categories of dreams. People know about Freud so they don't want to share certain dreams because they are very revealing." P6

CONFIDENTIAL CONTEXTS

"A client is with a therapist, and a client is talking about his dream. It is a private thing you keep your door closed and you tell it to him." P14

"They tell therapists their dreams because they expect to have their dreams analyzed." S9

"They wanted an interpretation; also reassurance that the dream was not some prophecy, that it was not going to come true. This happens when the dream is nightmarish and dreadful—a morbid thing; if they are feeling out of control and very fearful. This dream made her fear she was going insane." P14

"When people come to a therapist with a bad dream, say, of being ill, they want reassurance, specially if they're superstitious." L8

"They tell me their dream and expect because I work in mental health, that I can give them a dream interpretation. They want a dream interpretation." P15

"They expect me to give them an interpretation. I don't do that. Their wish is that someone will fix them—take care of them." P9

"Dreams are frightening to clients. That's why they tell them. Dreams cause apprehension—people think they should not dream too much. They say, 'doctor, I'm dreaming too much,' as though that were abnormal." D7

"People are apt to dream when they're under stress or have a problem; then they remember their dream." L7

"People tell a therapist a dream when it's a nightmare. Then it's a problem enough to talk about." N4

"People believe that telling a dream is part of an analytic type of therapy. I think so. Based on *New Yorker* cartoons and things like that. In a similar way that they think about being on the couch." N3

"I would not tell this dream (about a spiritual guide) to a therapist, or to my coworkers because they would think it was magical thinking." P15

"I think people tell their dreams to therapists because they are supposed to help you be more self-disclosing. You're not going to tell a dream to someone that would cut you off at the meeting." N6

"A therapist that I'd just met—I'd be hesitant to tell him a recurrent dream. I'd tell my own therapist." L6

"Therapists want to hear your dreams. They ask a lot of questions about dreams" [this was not corroborated by experience when explored]. L2

"Telling a dream is an intimate thing. To share dreams uncensored requires a level of trust which these people find difficult to do, because of their disturbance in general, and because of their problem with object relations in particular. I'll take a stab and say that probably it works best with well put together people of the sort who are going through a training analysis, or something akin thereto." D9

"I would tell my dream to a therapist if I had a therapist, but I would not tell certain dreams to a psychiatrist! [laughs] I wouldn't want them to interpret it in a Freudian way, because **personally** I don't believe in that—that's just my opinion." L9

"People think—they associate the bizarreness of the dream with their state of mind, which I don't think it does, but some people think so; if I have this crazy bizarre dream then something is wrong with my mind and people will think I'm nuts." L9

FORMAL CONTEXTS

[When looking at the text of a dream which I gave him:] "I would hate it to be your dream, for example. I would feel kind of awkward, because we don't have that kind of a contract. A **person** should be entitled by a special relationship to decide to bring a dream." P7

"A dream would never be used in a supervision group like we have; it would never be used as a self-insight, like, 'what's the client triggering in you?' They never do that kind of work. They always treat it like it's **personal**." P15

APPENDIX B

The Meaning of Crazy

IRRATIONAL, NONSENSICAL, OR MENTALLY ILL

"When people say **crazy** they don't mean mentally ill; they just mean **irrational**. I think they mean that it doesn't make any sense to them." S10

"When they say that dreams are **crazy**, I think they mean that they're silly, don't make sense, are bizarre, strange . . . but if people behave **crazy** in an unusual, strange, or bizarre manner then they think they are **mentally ill**." P14

"I don't think people connect dreams with actual **craziness**, they mean silly." L6, L7

"When an average person tells you this is a **crazy** dream, they just mean it's far out, they can't make any sense of it. It's of a bizarre nature . . . but I think people who are mentally ill when they share their dream clearly relate it to **mental illness**." N10

"It's **crazy** because they don't understand it and whatever they don't understand is **crazy**. But if people have a lot of disturbing dreams, then they fear they're becoming **mentally ill**." P15

"Certain kinds of dreams they would connect with being **crazy**. These people are frightened of powerful dreams." P9

"I don't think people tell psychiatrists their dreams at a party. If they do, you would be very suspicious of them of being some kind of **borderline** type of individual, unless, in certain circles where everybody is in analysis. But some people in analysis get pretty loose for awhile and telling, 'I had this dream about this. . . .'" D8

"The interpretation of dreams is associated with psychology, and psychology is associated with **mental illness**." L3

"There's a joking quality about psychiatrists and psychologists: that they are, you know, cuckoo, **crazy**." S12

"I think most people think of what goes on in dreams as **temporary insanity**, you know, as **crazy**." D6

"I wouldn't want to tell my dream to a stranger, because they'll think I'm **nuts**. They might associate the bizarreness of the dream with my state of mind (which I don't think it does, but I think some people think that). I think some people think that if I have this **crazy**, bizarre dream then something must be **wrong with my mind**." L9

PROBLEMS, EMOTIONAL DISTURBANCE

"Dreams are not so much an indication of **craziness** as of problems, turmoil, conflicts; but I think that people connect that more with **mental illness**." S13

"I think that if people hear someone else talk about their dreams they may kiddingly mock them about being **crazy**, but they also recognize that they probably have dreams very much like that. They don't really believe someone's really **crazy** unless someone has real bad nightmares or problems like that." S11

"I think people think of dreams as neutral, unless in extreme cases—in frequency or content—if the person wakes up in cold sweats . . . if people reported nightmares, continual nightmares, people might say those people were **mentally disturbed**." P11

RIGHT BRAINED, INTUITIVE, ESTHETIC, ECCENTRIC

"So I learned that, if I'm going to be helpful with the patient, I don't need to be quite so left hemispheric and so linear in my thinking and be kind of **crazy**, too. I need to be more **crazy** and more right hemispheric and join them in their dream state." P12

"When I think of all the **crazy** people I've met doing therapy. I don't mean **crazy**, I mean interesting eccentric people." S8

"People tend to **pathologize** dreams; we've become so cognitively oriented that the conscious mind—our analytical reductive left brain kinds of skills and functions are highly prized. There's a message that right brain kinds of things are to be **distrusted**. There's a sexist thing going on, too. It's OK for women to be more intuitive, esthetic, emotional; men should be more instrumental and logical." S10

APPENDIX C

Psychological Mindedness

"I went to a school system that was not **psychologically minded.** There was no social science talk there. . . . I think the lay public is no where as near involved with dreams as I am, because thinking about dreams, valuing them is correlated with **psychological mindedness** . . . and as awareness of an intrapsychic life; the general mass of the lay population are not as a group **psychologically minded.** . . . My brother also was **psychologically minded.**" D5

"**Higher functioning** patients will tell me their dreams . . . patients who are able to utilize insight types of therapy. Patients who are bright enough and who are **psychologically minded** enough to want to look at that kind of thing. Persons who are interested in their own thoughts and feelings and on reflecting on them as opposed to people who are not really that way." P4

"Those who can remember their dreams have better treatment prognoses than those who can't. They have a greater capacity for **psychological mindedness** or for looking inside and are not so highly defended." D8

"I think the more educated, more **psychologically minded,** more sophisticated people have the conception that hearing dreams is the number one thing that the psychiatrist will want to do. I guess what I mean by that is that they are people who are used to thinking in terms of introspection reflecting on their own experience, not just living in the world but thinking, self-conscious, and self-aware, and say how is my living in my world affecting me—a heightened level of self-awareness. That's what I would call **psychologically minded.**" D6

"My interest in dreams started with discussions with people who had an interest in the area—people who were **psychologically** minded—people who did a lot of thinking about life, about experiences, about perceptions, and dreams, and could talk about them in a particular way. Those are the people I would kind of group as **psychologically minded.**" D11

"We get very few of what therapists call **YAVISEs**: *Y*oung, *A*ttractive, *V*erbal, *I*ntrospective, *S*ocial, *E*ducated. Basically people who are educated, insightful, and motivated. If the patient is not able to use abstract thought I wouldn't try to work with symbols—if they are very psychotic I probably wouldn't touch the dream because it would promote lots of looseness of thoughts and associations and that would be harmful." P8

APPENDIX D

Higher Functioning-Lower Functioning

"I use dreams with **higher functioning** people. I think you can get in big trouble—well not necessarily big trouble, but you can create more distress for a **low functioning** person when you focus on a dream. For instance, I had a **low functioning** person who had been abused all her life and was abusing herself and her kids. She told me a very vivid, primary process dream. . . .For **higher functioning** people, I would encourage it [dream telling]. I think it's important. It's a good way of understanding the person, and of helping the person. But I would be less likely to use it with people who are more emotionally disturbed and have characterological problems. [Talking about a client:] on first flush she looks fairly **high functioning**, but really she has serious deficits." P4

"**Higher functioning** patients will tell me their dreams—patients who are able to utilize insight types of therapy; patients who are bright enough and sort of psychologically minded enough to want to look at that kind of thing. If a **low functioning** person brought it in I wouldn't think I would discourage it, but I don't have too many high hopes for, for being able to utilize it very much with **low functioning** patients—patients who are more disturbed and, I guess that's what I mean by **lower functioning**; maybe that patient's already been hospitalized; they're not the kind of patient you want to really get, have them probe too deeply inside. They're the kind of patient you want to help them keep up their defenses. Their defenses are what's been *faulty* for them so *you don't want to break them down*, you want to shore them up." P9

"I don't especially encourage talk about dreams with less healthy patients. By healthy I mean patients who have a higher level of functioning and more intact egos. Their lives are more successful in terms of object relationships, in terms of being able to work. . . . If patients have a *less good ego functioning*, then I don't want them delving into primitive material which is likely to further diffuse their ego boundaries and be regressive for them. If someone is not going to be able to pull back [from being regressed], I don't want to encourage hearing dreams from them." S3

"People who come from *more disadvantaged backgrounds* with *limited educational background* do indeed, I think, find a dynamic model foreign and hard to embrace. . . . I think there have been, in fact, reports that people who are psychotic or prepsychotic are just as apt to dream as anyone else, I think, in my experience they are less likely to spontaneously bring in dream material. When you do therapy with this sort of patient, it is not as valuable or helpful or tactically correct, you might say, to focus on dreams as it is to focus on daily events and relationships. I'll take a stab and say that it [talking about dreams] works best with **well put together people** of the sort who are going through a training analysis or something akin thereto, where they would find it easiest to talk about dreams and fantasies." D9

"She seemed to be fairly **high functioning** without any great deal of crisis. So since she was like that, I prefer to take a less active role. I think that if she had wanted to pursue kind of a meaningful thing with her dream, then we would have pursued that." P14

"I have a group that I do alone on Tuesday. It's a group of **low functioning** individuals that . . . the majority of them are not working. They've been chronic patients in the hospital. They come here because their **functioning is impaired** in some way. . . . By **higher functioning** I mean that essentially they work, and they essentially maintain some stability in their life, but there is something not right and they need to talk to someone about it. In private practice you would expect to find a group of **higher functioning** people [than in a CMHC], because *therapy is more expensive*." S14

[Talking of one of her own dreams:] "I dreamed of this elderly client who has been disorganized, depressed, and decompensating. I dreamed that I met him in the street, and he was very **high function-**

ing, you know, very conversational and very happy. It was a wish dream. [Talking of the interpretation of the watching the small boy in the water] If the client was **high functioning** enough, I'd probably press on with the dream, and that way they'd get down to telling me what they thought. I usually don't . . . I work with the chronically mentally ill." P15

APPENDIX E

Who Is a Real Doctor? (What Psychiatrists Said)

"I've come to terms with it, you know—that **I'm not a real doctor!** Because in medical school psychiatry is less prestigious. Period. So since I excelled in anatomy, patholgy, and surgery, I went into surgery. But later I got disillusioned and changed to psychiatry. You know it was accepted that you should go into a specialty that will keep you in the **real world**: medicine, surgery, and so on. I just tagged along until I thought it wasn't what I wanted to do. Well, you know, people say you're **not a real doctor** if you're a psychiatrist. The real medicine is surgery, medicine, gastroenterology, urology, endocrinology, and psychiatry is not real medicine; it's a socioanthropological thing." D3

[Asked, "do you see yourself more as a doctor or as a psychiatrist?"] [laughs wearily] "There's a kind of joke that psychiatrists are **not real doctors.** We lay on that all the time ourselves. We joke about it a lot because we get those vibes from others. . . . A **real doctor** is a nonpsychiatrist. I guess the real hard core doctor would be the family pracititioners, internists, pediatricians, obstetricians. Maybe if you get into radiologists, they aren't as real either. I can't quite define it but within the medical culture, there's a certain amount of respect accorded to these other specialties, and the rest of us kind of feel inferior about these specialties and have to defend ourselves.

"A big part of becoming a psychiatrist is coming to grips with the fact that you are no longer competent in your internal medicine skills or your pediatric skills. Part of your training relieves you of all that. So you leave all of that and take up your identity as a psychiatrist. It feels like a loss for us even if we agree that that's what we want to do for the rest of our lives. Also there's a respect for that knowledge in the community." D4

"I would say that more people now think of me as a specialized *psychiatrist rather than as a doctor*—well, you know. It certainly surprised one patient the other day when the outpatient lab was closed and I said, 'Well, let's draw the blood here.' Well, she was terrified, 'Oh, you can do that?' I said, 'Yea' (I didn't want to tell her I don't do it well). I said, 'Yea, I can do that!'" D1

"Psychiatry is very subjective. It's not like surgery where you can see an appendix that's bad. I can cut it out and it's over with. It's all so amorphous. You're not quite sure what it's all about. It's certainly different than if you were doing organic chemistry research. Too, psychiatrists in the perception of other doctors, I think, tend to have low status. Well, some are and some aren't. Psychiatrists see bizarre patients; certainly the guy sitting in the waiting room who is playing with himself is probably there to see the psychiatrist. Third, psychiatrists make less, along with pediatricians he is down there." D1

"We have a tendency to downplay the medical aspects of it. However, I think I'm going to have to change course a little bit because what a psychiatrist has to offer specially is the medical background." D2

"There is a status assigned to psychiatrists by many other physicians as 'not real doctors': It's a feeling that we don't use our physical diagnostic skills; we don't—we're not medical, surgical, pediatric or OB/GYN so we're not physical doctors—so some people regard us therefore as **not real doctors.** Usually what I think it comes from is a couple of things: one, our patients scare a lot of nonpsychiatric physicians. They think the patient's problem is all psychological, and secondly, they see that there are many nonmedical therapists and they wonder, well, gee, do you really need to be a doctor or not to do that? Anybody who thinks it through realizes, 'of course you do!'

"Another source of this notion that we're **not real doctors,** I think, comes from psychiatrists' own perception of losing their medical skills through disuse. I was just at a meeting today on a clinical instruction committee on the clerkships of medical school. We're talking about the first general clerkship for physicians; third year students take it; they learn physical diagnosis. I could see there were jokes being made about could a psychiatrist teach in the general clerkships because most of us, once we have finished with residence, we may never do another physical exam again—we certainly don't do many! Other physicians (i.e., even say an ophthalmologist) are accorded more respect as a physical type physician.

"Also, what happens often—to reinforce that, is new medications will be marketed, and so we get a patient and the patient will tell us the medications they are on saying, 'that's my heart medication, doc?' and we've never heard of it, and we ask someone and look it up. A resident might say to himself, 'it's only been six months since I was a medical intern. Oh my God! Look how fast things are changing!'

"It's been ten years since I was an intern. There's whole new categories of drugs that I've never used. So, you see, there are things in the **real world** that reinforce that we are getting further from the mainstream of physical medicine. At the same time there are many people who do not know the difference between a psychologist and a psychiatrist. The lay public remains confused about that. They do not know and they have been told again and again that psychiatrists have M.D. degrees. There always remains confusion about that." D5

"I didn't have that conflict until the third year of medical school. And I began to feel I should be a **real doctor**. I should be an internist or pediatrician. But I didn't go into medical school to be a pediatrician. I knew that I wanted to be a psychiatrist. And I have felt very comfortable continuing as a psychiatrist—there is a fear that almost every psychiatric resident has in his heart that going into psychiatry will cost them, not only their *identity as a real physician*, but also the respect of other physicians because they're **not real doctors** anymore. They over compensate for that a certain amount by focusing on the biological, drugs, the diseases, the diagnoses. They want to reassure themselves that they haven't tuned their back on their professions. They haven't lost face, status, they—they're conflicted, they want to be a psychiatrist, they want to listen to people, they want to believe in psychotherapy, they want to interpret dreams." D6

"A psychiatrist is a specialist physician. I went into medicine because I wanted to become a psychiatrist. I think a majority of *people think psychiatry is not a specialty of medicine*. They think it's a lot of mumbo jumbo. Some people would never go to a psychiatrist. They might think that only crazy people go see a psychiatrist while some people might see a psychic to foretell the future." D7

"I stay close to medicine. I read *Lancet* and medical journals like the *New England Journal* every week. But psychiatrists have such a hard time with our medical colleagues, because if you can't measure something or prove it they say it isn't there. See, the internists and so forth think we're all weird because we even look into people's feelings and all that; you're not supposed to do that, you're supposed to just stiff upper lip and do it, all these dark motives or unconscious drives, that's all subjective, and you can't measure it so to hell with it (raising his voice)—if you can't treat it with a drug, it doesn't exist. You find this split here. It's worse in England and Germany." D8

"When you get away from doing physical examinations, you begin asking yourself, 'am I a real doctor?' Psychiatry is, in a sense, coming to grips with the fact that although you are a doctor, you are removed from many of the physical aspects of care. And that, to some extent, is a rethinking about one's role, letting go of skills which you've learned along the way. This has been an issue which has been around a long time." D9

APPENDIX F

Hierarchical Issues

WHAT PHYSICIANS SAID

"For some people, psychiatrists have an aroma of being able to see inside of you—it's like in ancient Rome when they used to read the entrails of the animals and say, 'Aha, there is something there.' That, in a sense is a positive mystique to the lay public, but if I may generalize, the **status** of the psychiatrist in the profession **is low**, psychiatrists in the perception of other doctors tend to have low status. It tends to be less scientific, less well paid. You have funny patients, odd people come to see you and, I think, a psychiatrist is an odd bird as far as some people are concerned, though when they hear you're a psychiatrist, it's prestigious. Doctors would be **at the top of the prestige list** of professions.

"Psychologists are a sensitive subject because there is a feeling that psychology is overreaching and grabbing turf, and I'm sure psychologists think the psychiatrists are a bunch of pompous fuddy-duddies who really don't know what they are doing. I think the psychologists are jealous of the ability to prescribe almost to the point of being obstructionist to psychiatry.

"I'd say that in the individual, the social worker, the nurse can be an excellent therapist. I'd say collectively they probably do not get as much formal education as a psychiatrist or a psychologist." D1

"Within medicine psychiatry has **low status**, about the **lowest!** Because of a lot of things, well the whole way of thinking is different. The research is much more ambiguous, vague and less conclusive. Within a lot of settings a psychologist is dependent on the psychiatrist for prescribing medications which would make them somewhat **below** the psychiatrist. Nurses and social workers would be **beneath** those two. I don't make a lot of distinction between the two as therapists. We have to provide the medical backup. We have to sign care plans for patients we haven't seen. It's very uncomfortable for us. Yet it makes them dependent on us." D2

"Nurses and doctors think of things in the same model; but nurses don't go as deep as physicians in finding the etiology of all the biochemical aspects. They do it superficially. [Talking of team meetings:] We all meet together, even the activities therapists gives his opinion, and the secretary says, the patient is doing this, that, and the other; so everybody has an input and the patient is the one who suffers [he sounds quite impassioned]. In America it's medicine by democracy. It's like having six captains on a ship. I don't think it's a good way. Sometimes it deteriorates into a turf battle: 'Who are you to tell me?' In general medicine, that would not be the same." D3

"I was going to medical school because I recognized it was the position of **power**, and whether I knew it then, or not then, I was into **power**. I worked in a community mental health center. The psychiatrist has the last word about a lot of things. He also has the ultimate responsibility, and I appreciated that, too. In a formal way psychiatrists have enormous **power** in the society. I can throw someone in the hospital in the absence of criminal and civil charges.

"The psychiatrist has the most complex education and has the highest price tag on his or her hour. There are some states where psychologists are allowed to prescribe medication. There's a push to get that passed into law in this state. I don't know where the legislation is at this point. But if psychologists prescribe medications that feels dangerous to me.

"In the inpatient units there is a struggle for **power** with psychiatric nurses. The whole movement toward interdisciplinary teams is because of nurses saying, 'we are professionals, too! We have ideas about the patient. We want to be in the decisions including when you're going to discharge someone, even what medication you're going to use, when you're going to let somebody go out on pass; I don't think this one is safe to go out on pass.' Now, when nurses talk to me that way, I say, 'Fine!, be direct by all means.' What I can't stand is when they have those feelings and they are afraid to say it, but cause some undermining of the treatment program because that's what they believe.

"Social workers have some things mandated by the joint commissions of accreditation of hospitals. They are probably the **lowest** on the totem pole of all the disciplines." D5

"Something about the interdisciplinary team dilutes the responsibility the physician feels . . . certainly if not the responsibility, the **authority**. Physicians, particularly in an inpatient setting, can be very constrained by the need to mobilize everybody's agreement. Not that if everybody doesn't agree you can't go ahead with the treatment plan. You can go ahead but you'll be sabotaged: people will drag their heels. Things won't get done that you've ordered, and somebody else will undo it." D6

"Having a psychiatrist as director is a tradition which is very strong in some areas like this one, and is also ongoing in other areas. The psychiatrist is also the senior professional, the medical director who is charged with the chief clinical responsibilities. The psychiatrist is also the leader of a clinical team. Often the care is provided by a cadre of master's trained people who are the main staff at the health center and for specialized tasks a psychiatrist comes in on a consulting basis . . . as a psychopharmacologist for prescribing medication.

"I think if you go around the country, you will find very few places where psychiatrists are paid to do psychotherapy. The psychiatrist who gets paid more doesn't bring in any more money when he goes for an hour of psychotherapy than the bachelor's trained person or even a person with no education.

"Historically and even in the present, community mental health centers have been **one of the least prestigious** places to practice psychiatry and therefore they have attracted those psychiatrists with the least choices open to them." D9

WHAT PSYCHOLOGISTS SAID

"There is a traditional split in our society between physicians and the entire rest of the world! Anyone who is a doctor is a different sort of human being, and anyone who is not isn't. So because a psychiatrist is an M.D., **there's a lot of status** that goes along with that. Psychiatrists I have talked to in training feel that other M.D.s think that a psychiatrist is a **little less** than another M.D. A psychiatrist **feels superior** to a psychologist. I suppose most psychologists **feel superior** in general to people in those other categories, but everything is negotiable on a personal level." P2

"There's a **pecking order**. It goes, psychiatrists, psychologists, social workers, and then psychiatric nurses. I think the **highest** though would be physicians. Regular physicians." P4

"Well, there is something like a hierarchy. Let's see, psychiatrists, then psychologists, social workers next, and then nurses; nurses are at the bottom of the pool. Nurses have picked out a couple of key concepts [laughing] like 'choice' and 'responsibility', 'meaning' and 'owning'! They bandy them back and forth [laughing]." P5

"I think doctors and lawyers are **more highly regarded** than psychologists." P6

"Within the profession psychiatrists have the **higher status**. Clearly the salaries they command reflect that. And the regulatory bodies make them an indispensable part of the treatment; as a result you have to have their signature on treatments; things like that; they seem to have **the highest status**. I think next would be psychologists. *You can pretty much figure the status by salary.* Then the **lowest status** would be the master's level people, like social workers." P6

"I have noticed some people **denigrating** the skills of social workers. You certainly come across people who seem to want to exacerbate the differences to **keep territorially strong**—to keep teamwork at bay. But there are always those who have the more healthy approach to tap into the strength of one another." P7

"Psychiatrists are usually seen as **on top of the totem pole**. And that's largely because of third party payments. Almost all insurance companies want things cosigned by a psychiatrist—it comes down to money." P13

WHAT SOCIAL WORKERS SAID

"The social workers are **at the bottom of the totem pole**. It seems it's like this: psychiatry, nursing, psychology—those two. Sometimes psychology is higher but nursing seems to have a lot of power here." S2

"There are power issues in the infrastructure here in the sense that psychologists are paid more because people with Ph.D.s are paid more, so even though they may do the exact same thing, they get paid more because of the education. Psychiatrists have more power legally and politically and every other way; because the jobs are divided the way they are, it tends to minimize the difference **but they can pull rank on us,** if they want to although they very rarely choose to do that." S5

"I found myself falling into that a lot when I was wanting to call myself a therapist instead of saying I'm a social worker, or seeing myself as **one-down to somebody who is a psychologist.** I honestly can say I don't feel that way anymore." S8

"Psychiatrists are needed as figureheads even if they can't do the job [of administration]. I'm a **social worker** by training, and social workers do not make any money. The financial rewards are very very poor. Unfortunately, if you're at all skilled, you get promoted to a supervisor, and from supervisor to manager, and from manager to program director. You could wind up after many years being an agency administrator which is not at all the reason why you went into this work." S10

"The general public has the physician **up there,** and they see nurses, social workers, and everybody else **down here.**" S13

"We had a supervision group. There wasn't an actual designated leader; but she—Dr. R—*being a psychiatrist, she became the leader.* The hierarchy would be psychiatrist, psychologist, social worker. Nurses would be **below that.**" S14

"My perception is that a male social worker is going to be less bright than a female social worker, because it's a **lower status profession.** It's my perception that a social worker is clearly not a therapist of choice for an upper-middle-class education population; I know I would prefer a psychiatrist or a psychologist. My twenty-three-year-old son is thinking about going into therapy; he mentioned to me that he was considering someone who was a social worker, and I was very negative about that. Nursing is way, **way low down.** I think because of the menial aspects. The service aspect. The nonintellectual but the service aspect." S15

WHAT NURSES SAID

"We're **on the bottom, in terms of status;** if someone has been seeing a psych resident [physician], and he leaves because he's finished his rotation, and that person gets referred to a nurse, they feel disappointed. 'Why aren't we seeing a doctor anymore?' As for social workers, we're faculty and they're not. I don't know if this is accurate or not, but I think they have **less power** in this system as a whole. I think we're viewed by other disciplines and by each other as quite competitively." N3

"The **status of nurses** in general is **not too terrific.** I think it's bad. I think people think nurses clean shit, that they take care of doctors and say, 'yes, sir,' and do what they are told, that they are like glorified servants. The mystique of being a psychiatric nurse helps raise the status a bit. Then it's a little harder to think of nurses in this traditional handmaid servant role. You add to it a piece that is not quite clear. I had a woman call me a psychologist for two years. I explained the difference between a psychotherapist and a psychologist. I did all the educational things. Yet this very bright woman insisted on calling me that.

"I think that *psychiatrists think they're the best of everything*, but that is changing a little bit. I have not had good experience with them as therapists. They don't learn to be therapists.

"Around here we have a little more **prestige** than social workers. We've been around here a long time, and we're not hired by the department of psychiatry, we're hired by nursing. We have our own school, and we have faculty titles." N4

"I think that the public thinks the only person qualified and knowledgeable is the physician. People are not sure they want to see a nurse. Around here they [the resident psychiatrists] may have **more clout** in getting a room for themselves, they may have more clout in getting some of the more desirable cases, although I'm sure they would dispute that, too. I think nurses and social workers are regarded fairly equally. I think probably, if anything, nurses are regarded **a little higher in the pecking order** if there is such a thing—because there is more of an alliance between medicine and nursing." N5

"Everybody is very *territorial* and *political*. In the hospital we're big on interdisciplinary teams. I think we need to continue to work on them down here [in the CMHC].

"I like to think that nursing has a **lot of clout.** I think that nurses are the cement that tries to hold the pieces together. Nurses look at the overall picture, whereas the psychiatrist would look more at the illness.

They are just more focused, they don't see the forest for the trees. They're hung up in the tree, and I'm the one that says, 'well, wait a minute; let's look at the forest. Let's look at the broad picture'." N6

"[In CMHC] I think nurses probably don't fare as well as some. I think there are usually physicians in residence who have **more control or clout.** I think it's just because they're physicians. With regard to the others, we're maybe equal or **a little more** than social workers and equal or **a little less** than psychologists. This system is set up with a lot of administrators who are psychologists." N7

"**A nurse is regarded as less than the others.** For example, in what I do it is more acceptable for social workers to do it, and people would rather see a psychologist. The skills that we have are either not known or not used. My supervisor is Dr. A. [a psychiatrist]. I need supervision for my certification." N8

"I'm in an administrative role, so I guess at this point I don't see myself so much as a nurse. People don't understand what I do. If you were to ask my siblings or my parents what I do, they'd tell you that I'm a nurse. And that comes from people's classic impressions of a nurse.

"**Status is somewhat increased** when you say you are a therapist. **There's a mystique** to it: a mystique that you would have more of an understanding of human behavior and that you can read them better as a person.

"The nursing profession being female dominated and being one that does not have much career advancement, a major way to advance is through administration. Nurses make less than social workers and also the nursing pay scale in the hospital system **is higher.** I took a pay cut to come here." N9

WHAT SUPPORT STAFF MEMBERS SAID

"It's funny to watch how the different educational . . . if you want to put them on a straight list, psychiatrist, psychologist, social workers: The social worker will come in here and say, 'Mr. Jones is in crisis, where's the form?' and they'll start filling out the papers. The next one will come in, the psychologist, a little bit more agitated, wants to know where the forms are [raises her voice]. The third one will come in, the doctors, and they normally, although there are exceptions to the rule, they normally [peals of laughter] are *very* agitated. Where's this? We have to get this done!! Very agitated! A psychiatrist only sees people in crisis." L2

"People come and say, 'I want to see a psychiatrist,' flat out, and you say, 'Well, in our agency, you are assigned a primary therapist first and then we have psychiatrists available on a consultancy basis,' but they don't understand. Well to some extent, when they send the insurance referral over, it always has a psychiatrist's name on it, even though they may never see the medical director and have no idea who it is. But everybody here is still covered by the insurance **because they work under the doctor.**" L3

APPENDIX G

Which of the Psychotherapy Professionals are More Likely to Ask About and Listen to Dreams?

WHAT PSYCHIATRISTS SAID

"The conventional wisdom would be that a *psychiatrist* would be more likely to be versed in Freud and would be more likely to want to interpret a dream and consider it important, but that might be a fiction." D1

"I would tend to see that, if anything, the medically trained, would tend to not do it; people who would seek medical training would even be *less likely* to consider dreams as a real important part of therapy than nonmedical people. It's disquieting to know that it's so. We don't have many insight-oriented cases." D4

"I think many people when they come to see a head-shrinker or a *psychiatrist* they have certain expectations. Some of them think they are going to lie on a couch. Some of them have very negative perceptions like they are going to be fed a lot of tranquilizers. They expect to be asked about their sex life and their dreams. But it depends on your orientation and training program. If you are trained in a devoted behavioral psychology program or a neuropsychology program, you are not going to pay much attention or give credence to dreams. That could be anybody. That could be the *psychiatrist*, too." D5

"I've had patients who tell me that, 'I thought you would be more concerned about my dreams.' I've heard them say that. They think that's the number one thing that a *psychiatrist* will want to hear. And if you're not producing dreams, then you're not really doing what you ought to do. I believe that the more highly trained, that would be someone at the doctoral training level, be it *psychology* or *psychiatry*, that the more highly trained are more able to deal with the severely impaired. That's a generalization with many exceptions. So you see the question about who is more likely to listen to dreams is not easily answered." D6

"Someone with *psychiatric* training would be able to have a more comprehensive approach to dreams than, say, a nurse or a social worker, because we see these phenomena including dreams with their biological substratum. A *nurse* or *social worker* would have a narrower view. But I think *psychologists*, *nurses*, and *social workers* would make a larger effort to explain the content of a dream! Put more weight on it. If someone, let's say, is blind, the hearing function gets hypertrophied. So let's say they may be more prone to read things into the content of the dream since they may not know that it might be something physiological." D7

"Most *psychologists and social workers don't know* how to handle a dream. That requires analytic training, and a lot of them don't have that. *Psychiatric residents should learn about it* in their courses in dynamic psychiatry." D8

"I think the people in private practice would be the ones spending a good portion of time doing uncovering psychotherapy, and would be more apt to listen to dreams than someone who is working in a CMHC. It depends on the kinds of patients you see and the kind of therapy you do. *Psychiatrists* who do that kind of work will listen to more dreams than I do. I'm sure there are some *psychologists* in this town who do, by and large, insight-oriented, one-to-one therapy. I think it happens that some people in *social work* would do that kind of work—but it's a little bit less common." D9

WHAT PSYCHOLOGISTS SAID

"My perception is that *psychologists* are probably the most likely to deal with dreams. I may be biased because I am one. *Psychiatrists* would listen, too. It depends on their orientation. How well trained they are and how well rounded their education is. *Social workers?* No! Not at all I don't think. *Nurses?* Hm, I don't know! I don't think so. They would probably put it off on the patient. They would have the patient interpret their own dream." P5

"*Psychiatrists* look at people medically. *Psychiatrists* are becoming more biological and less and less analytic. *Social workers* have more training in how the environment and the social system impacts the individual. *Psychiatric nurses* are trained in medical school and their training is closely allied to the physician's training. *Psychologists* are more behavioral and introspective. Their training comes from a tradition of introspection and careful analysis. [Asked, "Are you saying that psychologists and psychoanalysts are more likely to listen to dreams?"] I think so." P6

"I guess if you did a frequency analysis, I think you would find *psychologists* are more likely to listen to dreams. Because they are more likely to be exposed to this kind of training. Whereas *psychiatrists* might be more exposed to organic psychiatry. But particular *psychiatrists* are exposed to Freud and to the exploration of dreams." P7

"I don't know! It depends on the person. I could not tell from a therapy tape if it was a *psychiatrist* or a *psychologist*, unless a prescription is being handed out." P8

"Psychologists understand the complexity of human pathology, whereas *psychiatrists* traditionally have drugs as a big part of the approach. However, the field of *psychology* is loaded with behavioral *psychologists*. So it could be that a person ends up in a *psychologist's* office and is discouraged from talking about dreams. Also there are the premiers: psychiatrists who do psychoanalysis; they've been analyzed themselves." P9

"I think there is probably a greater tendency to want to tell dreams to a psychiatrist because psychiatrists are connected in the public mind with an analyst, and everyone knows from the public press that *analysts* are people who want to hear dreams. It's not necessarily an accurate perception, but the public is quite confused about psychologists—don't know what it is they do. The first thing people want to know is if I'm a doctor. They mean a physician. That's a frequent question. 'Are you like a *psychiatrist*? What's the difference?' So you see their perceptions shade over into their views of that. So although we labor in the shadow of physicians, we are accorded great authority. We ride on their coattails." P10

"I would say that most of the *psychiatrists* I know would never discuss dreams. They see their patients for fifteen minutes and ask about the side effects of medication. *Nurses* and *social workers* are probably more receptive to talking about dreams. When psychologists go on for a *Ph.D.* then they end up doing more testing and research and less of the other things [dreams]." P15.

WHAT SOCIAL WORKERS SAID

"I guess *psychiatrists*; you see the lay public would probably say that psychiatrists are more likely to listen to dreams. But it's more according to their theoretical background." S2

"Probably *psychiatrists* because—they got the most training in psychoanalysis, and all of that interpretation of dreams. But I don't agree with their interpretations, specially if it was strictly Freudian. I don't know if *psychology students* are taught to interpret dreams. I don't know what the different schools teach." S6

"I think that *psychiatrist* going through an analytically oriented program would be most likely to be interested in dreams; *psychologists, social workers* less so; *nurses* I don't know. S13

"I would find it hard to believe that someone trained in psychoanalysis would not ask about dreams. Although I'm sure there are plenty of *psychiatrists* who would give clues by earperking during descriptions of physiological symptoms rather than dreams" [she did not consider the other disciplines]. S15

WHAT NURSES SAID

"I guess I feel very unsophisticated in the area of dreams, although I find the subject fascinating. [Talking of a patient:] When she told me a lot of these dreams, I was scared because I didn't know what to do with it. I ended up referring her to a *physician*, but I don't know if he ever did anything with her. He was not psychoanalytic either, but he was willing to take her. [To me:] You should maybe interview some *analysts*. I guess it's my fantasy that they would tell you something different." N1

"*Psychiatrists* have more formal training in psychodynamics and psychoanalysis; for those that do have this kind of background, my guess is that they would be more likely to elicit and to listen and to focus on dream material if it came." N5

"*Psychiatrists* have more education about dream telling and psychoanalysis. a *psychiatrist* would have more training in analyzing dreams so he would be more comfortable interpreting." N6

"I think that *nurses*, in general, stop and listen and do what is important to people, rather than do things that are on a list of things to do for the patient. Much more willing to try and help a person to figure out what's best for them. *Physicians* have little ability to compromise, and to see what is desirable from the patient's point of view. I think most *nurses* would listen to dreams." N7

"I think *nurses* would be most likely to listen to dreams because they're interested in being holistic. They have a strong need to care about people. I'm not so positive I would say this about some *psychiatrists* I have worked with. I don't know what *psychologists* would do. *Social workers* would not look at the physical issues. They would not look at the whole individual." N8

"A *nurse* is used to doing things that other therapists won't do. A good therapist has to be able to go to folks' homes sometimes, be able to get out of this office and meet people wherever. Sometimes just walking in the door can tell you so much that you would have missed sitting in the office. I had a patient who told me his sexual preoccupations, and he was doing a lot of dreaming about that stuff. He said to me, 'You know, about the body 'cause you're a *nurse*.' I think that makes a difference in terms of whether people will listen to dreams or not." N9

"I think that possibly *psychiatrists* as a profession may pursue asking somebody to talk about their dreams more so than other professions, unless it's an individual interest that somebody brings that into therapy sessions, if that's their style." N10

WHAT SUPPORT STAFF MEMBERS SAID

"I think *psychologists* would listen to dreams. I've heard more people say *psychologists*, the Ph.D.s. Yeah! It's in their clinical training. To help people understand what's in the unconscious. *M.D.s*, I don't know. We don't work with too many *psychiatrists* here." L6

"I think *psychiatrists* would listen more to dreams, but I wouldn't like the way that they'd interpret it. I wouldn't want them to interpret it in a Freudian way. *Psychologists* don't intimidate me as much as *psychiatrists* do." L9

NOTES

Chapter 1. Introduction: Background and Foreground

1. Community mental health centers (CMHCs) were created throughout the country in the 1960s as a result of the conclusions compiled by the Joint Commission on Mental Illness and Health in 1960. They are federally funded institutions that are intended to make available mental health services to all, including poor and middle-income families from different sectors of the community (Veroff, Kulka, and Douvan 1981: 75–76).

2. I use the word *therapist* as a generic term indicating a *psychotherapist*, or one who is engaged in the psychological treatment of emotional, mental disturbances, or illnesses. Most people I spoke with used the term interchangeably. Sometimes the word *therapist* is used in a broader sense to include any treatment including medical treatment, occupational therapy, and physical therapy. Only two social workers in the sample indicated that I needed to be aware of this distinction.

3. I was introduced to the word *shrink* very shortly after I arrived in this country, many years ago. When I asked what it meant, I was told "you know, a headshrinker, a psychiatrist, a crazy doctor." This is a frequent colloquial expression, yet only one person in the sample used it. It was a psychiatrist. The use of the word *headshrinker* is common enough to be found in a dictionary as a slang word for psychiatrist. It is also defined as a "headhunter who shrinks the heads of his victims" (Webster's Third New International Dictionary of the English Language).

4. Fiss's opinions of the limitations of psychophysiological research are strongly expressed: "The fact that sleep researchers have . . . emphasized the biological substratum of dreaming and by and large neglected the psychological experience of dreaming has given rise to a curious paradox: Despite the monumental achievements in sleep research in recent years, our prevalent notions of dreaming continue to be derived principally from clinical practice and psychoanalysis . . . as if REMs had never been discovered. In brief, the technological breakthrough of the fifties and sixties has had relatively little impact on our understanding of dreaming" (Fiss 1979: 41).

5. Weiss (1986) has done an excellent review of research on the use of dreams in psychotherapy. Some of the studies that she reviews were designed to test propositions in Freud's theory.

6. Crick and Mitchison's (1983) theory of dreaming is an example of a study derived from the study of "brains." It is based on neural net theory. They state that dreaming eliminates mental activity that might interfere with rational thought and waking activity. Because the brain makes more connections between brain cells than are needed for efficient thinking, it is the function of the dream to clear the brain of these meaningless and unnecessary connections. This has been called the *garbage disposal theory*. It received many different responses in the professional literature and the public press. Several therapists who spoke with me had heard this theory.

7. Kilborne discusses this distinction in his excellent review article in *Ethos* 9: 165–185, "Pattern, Structure, and Style in Anthropological Studies of Dreams."

8. In "Hopi Dreams in Cultural Perspectives" Eggan (1966) examined dreams of Hopi in the context of their societal values. She says: "We suggest that dreams may be thought of as a triangular production involving (1) the latent content that is said to appear in universal symbols, and represent material not accessible to consciousness; (2) the dreamer's personality organization and his personal situation at the time of the dream, and (3) the relation of the dreams to cultural provision" (pp. 238, 260).

9. *Djinn* is a demon; it refers to the belief in Islam that beneficient or malevolent spirits who inhabit the earth are capable of assuming various forms and exercising supernatural powers.

10. These articles seem to have increased since the publication of the theory on the meaninglessness of dreams proposed by Crick and Mitchison (1983), which their opponents call the *garbage disposal theory*.

11. There is an annotated bibliography of popular books on dreams in *Dream Work: Techniques for Discovering the Creative Power in Dreams* by Jeremy Taylor. Several titles in that list were mentioned to me by a few of the therapists at the two community mental health centers.

Chapter 2. The Psychotherapist: "Simply as a Person"

1. In anthropological analyses, it is important to keep the emic and etic perspectives as distinct as possible. An emic statement is like an autobiographical perception. It is a native term, whereas an etic term is one isolated from a theory to analyze the data. In this research, the word "person" is marked with quotation marks to indicate the native terms and the emic perspective, whereas the same word *person* is italicized when it is used analytically as a concept representing the etic perspective. It is neither possible nor advisable to be inflexible with these distinctions. But it helps to avoid confusion.

Chapter 3. The Contexts of Dream Telling

1. A similar synthesis of etic and emic perspectives was used to elucidate the concept of health by Toni Tripp-Reimer in "Reconceptualizing the Construct of Health: Integrating Emic and Etic Perspectives," *Research in Nursing and Health* 7 (1984): 101–109.

2. Taking off one's shoes is a sign that one is in a relaxed environment analogous to one's home. There were many references to the self-disclosure involved in telling a personal dream. "When you tell a **personal** dream you feel exposed." It follows then that personal dreams can be told to people with whom one *can* be exposed.

3. Although most Americans know that President Lincoln had a dream about his own death before he died, this comes from tradition and national mythology. It is doubtful that a living president's dream would be told or known in public.

4. The Mental Status Examination is a standard test administered to all patients in a medical interview (especially a mental health interview).

One of the categories for determining the mental condition of the patient is social judgment, which is designed to determine whether the adult patient is aware of the social consequence of his or her actions. The test for children is different; it is expected that social judgment will be developmentally determined.

5. Five different levels of functioning (1) superior, (2) very good, (3) good, (4) fair, and (5) poor—appear in *The Diagnostic and Statistical Manual of Mental Disorders* published by the American Psychiatric Association. The rationale for the classification is as follows: "As conceptualized here, adaptive functioning is a composite of three major areas: social relations, occupational functioning, and use of leisure time. These areas are to be considered together, although there is evidence that social relations should be given greater weight because of their particularly great prognostic significance. An assessment of the use of leisure time will affect the overall judgment only when there is no significant impairment in social relations and occupational functioning or when occupational opportunities are limited or absent (e.g., the individual is retired or handicapped)."

6. This psychiatrist's perceptions of American ideas related to dreams was that Americans must consider dreams and dream telling childish and unimportant, because mature adults did not speak about them.

7. A social worker who was comparing private practice to practice in a community mental health center said to me that private practice was preferable to a practice in a community mental health center because a private practice serviced a type of patient who was higher functioning as it was more expensive. Dream work was alleged to occur more frequently in private practice for that reason.

Chapter 4. Dream Interpretation: Freudian Mythology and the American Mystique of Dreams

1. Kilborne used the same dream with the Moroccan interpreters. None of them identified any sexual symbolism. Themes of authority and of reward and punishment to the dreamer for being "good" or "bad" emerged. Three of the nine Moroccans who were given this dream interpreted the palaces as being learned teachers, saints, or wise men and the house as the dreamer. Thus, they saw themselves taking a parental role in the dreams and encouraging the dreamers to take the role of "good" children, to rectify relationships, and to uphold the values of obedience, filial piety, and high regard for authority. The word *paradise* appeared in four of the nine interpretations. The interpreters seemed to

understand *paradise* as a place of future reward. The image is widely used in Islamic literature and Koranic literature (Kilborne 1981a).

Kilborne found that Moroccans do not analyze the symbols of dreams as Freud does in a self-conscious way, but take the dream as a structured whole to be interpreted as a message of social import. For example, the dreamer is supposed to do something in response to the directive from the dream, usually about a social relationship. Moreover, he analyzes shared fantasies of dreamers and dream interpreters and applies Freudian interpretations to them. He lets the emic dream interpretations stand, but he also applies Freudian analytic categories to the interpreter's fantasies and interpretations. He explains that these interpretations reinforce defensive projective mechanisms by which bad dreams are dealt with. He finds these projections widely prevalent in Moroccan life.

2. The following appears in a footnote related to this dream in Freud's *Interpretation of Dreams* (1965 [1900]): "It was not for a long time that I learned to appreciate the importance of phantasies and unconscious thoughts about life in the womb. They contain an explanation of the remarkable dread that many people have of being buried alive; and they also afford the deepest unconscious basis for the belief in survival after death, which represents a projection into the future of this uncanny life before birth. Moreover, the act of birth is the first experience of anxiety."

3. In comparing the interpretations of the therapists at the Riverpool site with the interpretations at the Newell sites, few findings appeared significant or relevant to this study. The percentage of therapists who did *not* choose to interpret the dream of the house between two palaces was much higher at the Newell sites than at the Riverpool site. A higher percentage of therapists at Riverpool said they had read Freud. It is likely (as happened in one case explicitly) that therapists who did not choose it *did* recognize it as a typical dream with sexual themes and were reluctant to talk to me about it. This could explain why more people chose the other two dreams. But it could also explain why the therapists at Riverpool were less reluctant to talk about this dream than the therapists at Newell. The Freudian ethos seemed to be stronger and clearer at the Riverpool site.

Chapter 5. Psychotherapy, Dream Telling, and Hierarchy

1. The CMHCs were also responsible for community-based partial hospitalization programs.

2. The Newell Center was also affiliated with the teaching hospital. Some of the psychologists at the Newell Center also had academic or clinical appointments at Riverpool.

3. At the time of the study the associate director of ambulatory services at Riverpool was a psychologist, and the director for clinical programs at Newell was a psychologist. The medical director, a psychiatrist, coordinated medical services for the entire Newell Center; however, the coordinator for child and adolescent cases was a psychologist.

4. Four years of psychiatric residency follow two years of general internship *after* medical school. A psychiatrist who had completed residency training would have had at least ten years of education *after* an undergraduate premedical college program. The psychiatrists in this sample who were in residency were in their third year of residency.

5. They perceived the nurses to be most guilty of this in hospital settings and psychologists to be applying political pressure to acquire certain capacities that they did not have, like prescribing medication.

6. Just as the disciplines of social work and nursing were regarded as feminine professions, psychiatry was regarded as a masculine profession. This was an implicit assumption in much of what was said, but occasionally when I pressed for more specific answers this was verbalized explicitly. A female social worker was concerned about the medical orientation of psychiatrists and the capacities it gave them to control; when I asked her to elaborate she did: "I don't think the medical modality is the best. I also think medication is overly prescribed. Although with certain clients it's necessary, and I'm glad they're there to do that, but I wouldn't go to a psychiatrist myself. You see I think a lot of psychiatrists are *men* and their patients are women, and I think *they overmedicate these women to be helpless*." [Her voice became louder and high pitched]

7. These programs consisted of group psychotherapy, community meetings, social outings, and other experiences for improving social skills of clients. Each of these took longer than fifty minutes. It was not unusual for a social worker or nurse in the day treatment program to spend much of the day interacting with the clients.

8. In the United States, Mary Richmond is credited for successfully proposing establishment of a training school for applied philanthropy, in 1897. This rapidly expanded the basic methods of case work to include work in community organization.

9. Traditionally in Western societies, nurses were women in religious orders who had a vocation for succorance and caring of the sick, injured, and incurable. The majority of nursing practitioners are no longer connected with religion. The founder of modern professional nursing, Florence Nightingale, who lived in England in the middle of the nineteenth century, is credited with seeing the ailing person as continually affected by the environment. Nature could not cure if sanitation, diet, and living conditions were poor. This expanded the focus of nursing to include assessment and management of the environment around persons.

BIBLIOGRAPHY

Adler, A. 1931. *What Life Should Mean to You*. Boston: Little, Brown and Co.

————. 1954. *Understanding Human Nature*. Greenwich, CT: Fawcett.

Allen, N. J. 1985. "The Category of the Person: A Reading of Mauss's Last Essay." In *The Category of the Person*, ed. M. Carrithers, S. Collins, and S. Lukes. Cambridge: Cambridge University Press.

Arey, L. B. 1971. "Dream in Reactive and Process Schizophrenics." Paper presented at American Psychological Association, Symposium on Process and Reactive Schizophrenia, Washington, DC.

Armstrong, R. H., D. Burnap, A. Jacobson, A. Kales, S. Ward, and J. Golden. 1965. "Dreams and Gastric Secretions in Duodenal Ulcer Patients." *The New Physician* 9: 241–243.

Aserinsky, E., and N. Kleitman. 1953. "Regularly Occurring Periods of Eye Motility and Concomitant Phenomenon during Sleep." *Science* 74 (118): 273–274.

Banton, M. 1965. *Roles: An Introduction to the Study of Social Relations*. New York: Basic Books.

Barnouw, V. 1985 [1963]. *Culture and Personality*. Homewood, IL: The Dorsey Press.

Bastide, R. 1966. "The Sociology of the Dream." In *The Dream and Human Society*, ed. G. E. von Grunebaum and R. Caillois. Berkeley and Los Angeles: University of California Press.

———. 1968. "A La Divination chez les Afro-Americains." in *La Divination*, ed. J. Caquot and M. Leibovici, vol 2. Paris: Presses Universaires de France.

Beck, A. T., and C. H. Ward. 1961. "Dreams of Depressed Patients." *Archives of General Psychiatry* 5: 462–467.

Beck. L. W. 1965. "Agent, Actor, Spectator and Critic." *The Monist* 14: 167–182.

Belicki, D. A. 1987. "Relationship of Nightmares to Psychopathology, Stress and Reactivity to Stress." *Association for the Study of Dreams Newsletter* 4, no. 1: 10.

Belicki, K. 1985. "The Assessment and Prevalence of Nightmare Distress." *Sleep Research* 14: 145.

———. 1987. "Recalling Dreams: An Examination of Daily Variation and Individual Differences." In *Sleep and Dreams: A Sourcebook*, ed. J. Gackenbach. New York: Garland Publishing.

Belicki, K., and D. A. Belicki. 1986. "A Cognitive-Behavioral Strategy for Reducing Distress Associated with Nightmares." *Association for the Study of Dreams Newsletter* 3, no. 1: 3.

Belicki, K., and P. Bowers. 1982. "Consistency in the Ability to Recall Dreams as a Moderator in Predicting Dream Recall." Paper presented at the 22nd annual meeting of the Association for the Psychophysiological Study of Sleep.

Bertelson, A. D., and J. Walsh. 1987. "Insomnia." In *Sleep and Dreams: A Sourcebook*, ed. J. Gackenbach. New York: Garland Publishing.

Boas, Franz. 1930. *The Religion of the Kwakiutl Indians*. Columbia University Contributions to Anthropology (Vol. 10). New York: Columbia University.

Bokert, E. 1967. "The Effect of Thirst and a Related Auditory Stimulus on Dream Reports." Ph.D. dissertation, New York University.

Boss, M. 1958. *The Analysis of Dreams*. New York: Philosophical Library.

———. 1977. *"I Dreamt Last Night . . ."* New York: Gardner Press.

Bourgignon, E. 1954. "Dreams and Dream Interpretation in Haiti." *American Anthropologist* 56: 262–268.

———. 1965. "The Self, the Behavioral Environment and the Theory of Spirit Possession." In *Context and Meaning in Cultural Anthropology*, ed. M. E. Spiro. New York: The Free Press.

———. 1972. "Dreams and Altered States of Consciousness in Anthropology and Research." In *Psychological Anthropology*, ed. F. L. K. Hsu. Cambridge, MA: Schenkman Publishing Company, Inc.

Brennies, C. B. 1970. "Male and Female Modalities in Manifest Dream Content." *Journal of Abnormal Psychology* 76: 434–442.

Carrithers, M., S. Collins, and S. Lukes, eds. 1985. *The Category of the Person: Anthropology, Philosophy, History*. Cambridge: Cambridge University Press.

Carroll, D., S. A. Lewis, and I. Oswald. 1969. "Effect of Barbiturates on Dream Content." *Nature* 223: 865–866.

Carter, A. 1982. "Hierarchy and the Concept of Person in Western India." In *Concepts of Person: Kinship Caste and Marriage in India*, eds. A. Oster, L. Fruzzetti and S. Barnell. Cambridge, MA: Harvard University Press.

Cartwright, R. D., L. W. Tipton, and J. Wicklund. 1980. "Focusing on Dreams: A Preparation Program for Psychotherapy." *Archives of General Psychiatry* 37, no. 3: 275–277.

Charsley, S. R. 1973. "Dreams in an Independent African Church." *Africa* 43, no. 3: 244–257.

Cohen, D. B. 1974. "Toward a Theory of Dream Recall." *Psychological Bulletin* 81: 138–154.

Cohen, D. B., and G. Wolfe. 1973. "Dream Recall and Repression: Evidence for an Alternative Hypothesis." *Journal of Consulting and Clinical Psychology* 47: 349–358.

Collins, K. 1984. "Anthropology of Dreaming in America." *Association for the Study of Dreams* 1, no. 4: 1, 3.

Cooley, C. H. 1964 [1902]. *Human Nature and the Social Order*. New York: Schocken Books.

Coulson, M. 1972. "Role: A Redundant Concept in Sociology? Some Education Considerations in Role." In *Sociological Studies 4*, ed. J. E. Jackson. Cambridge: Cambridge University Press.

Crick, F., and G. Mitchison. 1983. "The Function of Dream Sleep." *Nature* 30: 111–114.

Dahrendorf, R. 1968. "Homo Sociologicus." In *Essays in the Theory of Society*. Stanford, CA: Stanford University Press.

D'Andrade, R. G. 1961. "Anthropological Studies of Dreams." In *Psychological Anthropology*, ed. L. K. Hsu, pp. 308–332. Homewood IL: Dorsey Press.

Davidson, D. 1981 [1958]. "The Material Mind." In *Mind Design: Philosophy, Psychology, Artificial Intelligence*, ed. J. Haugeland. Cambridge: MIT Press.

Delaney, G. 1979. *Living Your Dreams*. San Francisco: Harper and Row.

Dement, W. C., and C. Fisher. 1963. "Experimental Interference With the Sleep Cycle." *Canadian Psychiatric Association Journal* 8: 395–400.

Dement, W. C., E. Kahn, and H. P. Roffwarg. 1965. "The Influence of the Laboratory Situation on the Dreams of Experimental Subjects." *Journal of Nervous Mental Disorders* 140: 119–131.

Dement, W. C., and N. Kleitman. 1957. "The Relation of Eye Movements During Sleep to Dream Activity: An Objective Method for the Study of Dreaming." *Journal of Experimental Psychology* 53: 339–346.

Dement, W. C., and E. A. Wolpert. 1958. "The Relation of Eye Movements, Body Motility and External Stimuli to Dream Content." *Journal of Experimental Psychology* 55: 543–553.

Dennett, D. 1981. *Brainstorms*. Cambridge, MA: MIT Press.

...ield, P. 1974. *Creative Dreaming*. New York: Ballantine.

——. 1984. *Your Child's Dreams*. New York: Ballantine.

...dlin, E. T. 1986. *Let Your Body Interpret Your Dreams*. Wilmett, IL: Chiron.

...man, E. 1959. *The Presentation of Self in Everyday Life*. New York: Doubleday Anchor Books.

...denough, D. R. 1967. "Some Recent Studies of Dream Recall." In *Experimental Studies of Dreaming*, ed. H. A. Witkin and H. B. Lewis. New York: Random House.

——. 1978. "Dream Recall: History and Status of the Field." In *The Mind in Sleep: Psychology and Psychophysiology*, ed. A. M. Arkin, J. S. Antrobus, and S. J. Ellman. Hillsdale, NJ: Lawrence Erlbaum Publishing.

...denough, D. R., H. B. Lewis, A. Shapiro, L. Jaret, and I. Sleser. 1965. "Dream Reporting Following Abrupt and Gradual Awakenings from Different Types of Sleep." *Journal of Personality and Social Psychology* 2: 170–179.

...en, C. 1968. *Lucid Dreams*. Oxford: Institute of Psychophysical Research.

...enberg, R., C. A. Pearlman, and D. Gampel. 1972. "War Neuroses and the Adaptive Function of REM Sleep." *British Journal of Medical Psychology* 45: 27–33.

...gor, T. 1981. "A Content Analysis of Mehinaku Dreams." *Ethos* 9, no. 4: 353–390.

..., C. S. 1953. *The Meaning of Dreams*. New York: Harper and Row.

——. 1967. "Representation of the Laboratory Setting in Dreams." *Journal of Nervous Mental Disorders* 144: 198–206.

..., C. S., and B. Domhoff. 1963. "A Ubiquitous Sex Difference in Dreams." *Journal of Abnormal Social Psychology* 66: 278–280.

..., C. S., and R. E. Lind. 1970. *Dreams, Life and Literature. A Study of Franz Kafka*. Chapel Hill: University of North Carolina Press.

..., C. S., and R. L. Van de Castle. 1966. *The Content Analysis of Dreams*. New York: Appleton-Century-Crofts.

Dentan, R. K. 1968. *The Semai: A Nonviolent People of Malaya*. New York: Holt, Rinehart and Winston.

——. 1987a. "Ethnographic Considerations of the Cross-Cultural Study of Dreams." In *Sleep and Dreams: A Sourcebook*, ed. J. Gackenbach. New York: Garland Publishing.

——. 1987b. "Senoi Authority (Interview)." *Association for the Study of Dreams Newsletter* 4, no 5: 10–12.

——.1987c. "What's in a Dream? Some Epistemological Issues." *Association for the Study of Dreams Newsletter* 4, no. 3: 9.

——. 1983. A Dream of Senoi. Special Studies Series Council on International Studies. State University of New York at Buffalo. Amherst: New York.

Devereux, G. 1951. *Reality and Dreams: The Psychotherapy of a Plains Indian*. New York: New York University Press.

——. 1957. "Dream Learning and Individual Ritual Differences in Mohave Shamanism." *American Anthropologist* 59: 177–198.

Dodds, E. R. 1951. *The Greeks and the Irrational*. Berkeley: University of California Press.

Domhoff, B. 1969. "Home Dreams Versus Laboratory Dreams." In *Dream Psychology and the New Biology of Dreaming*, ed. M. Kramer. Springfield, IL: Charles C. Thomas.

Domhoff, B., and J. Kamiya. 1964. "Problems in Dream Content Study With Objective Indicators, I, II, III." *Archives of General Psychiatry* 11: 519–532.

Domhoff, G. W. 1985. *The Mystique of Dreams: A Search for Utopia through Senoi Dream Theory*. Berkeley: University of California Press.

——. 1988. "Senoi Dream Theory and The Mystique of Dreams. Further Thoughts on an Allegory about an Allegory." *Association for the Study of Dreams Newsletter* 5, no. 2: 1–2, 16.

Eggan, D. 1952. "The Manifest Content of Dreams: A Challenge to Social Science." *American Anthropologist* 54: 469–485.

———. 1961. "Dream Analysis." In *Studying Personality Cross-Culturally*, ed. B. Kaplan, pp. 551–557. Evanston, IL: Row, Peterson.

———. 1966. "Hopi Dreams in Cultural Perspective." In *The Dream and Human Societies*, ed. G. E. von Grunebaum and R. Caillois pp. 237–265. Berkeley and Los Angeles: University of California Press.

Elkan, B. 1969. "Developmental Differences in the Manifest Content of Children's Reported Dreams." Ph.D. dissertation, Columbia University.

Emmet, D. 1966. *Rules, Roles and Relations*. London: Macmillan.

Erikson, E. 1954. "The Dream Specimen of Psychoanalysis." In *Psychoanalytic Psychiatry and Psychology*, ed. R. Knight and C. Friedman. New York: International Universities Press.

Faraday, A. 1972. *Dream Power*. New York: Coward, McCann and Geoghegan.

———. 1974. *The Dream Game*. New York: Harper and Row.

———. 1981. Book Review of *The Mystique of Dreams* by G. William Domhoff. *Associaiton for the Study of Dreams* 3, no. 4: 12–13.

Faraday A., and J. Wren-Lewis. 1984. "The Selling of the Senoi." *Dream Network Bulletin* 3, no. 4: 1–3.

Firth, R. 1934. "The Meaning of Dreams in Tikopia." In *Essays Presented to C. G. Seligman*, ed. E. Evans-Pritchard, R. Firth, B. Malinowski, and I. Schapera, pp. 63–74. London: Kegan Paul, Trench, Trubnea and Co.

Fiss, H. 1979. "Current Dream Research: A Psychobiological Perspective." In *Handbook of Dreams*, ed. B. Wolman, pp. 20–75. New York: Van Nostrand Reinhold.

———. 1983. "Toward a Clinically Relevant Psychology of Dreaming." *Hillside Journal of Clinical Psychiatry* 5: 147–159.

Fiss, H., and J. Litchman. 1976. "Dream Enhancement: An Experimental Approach to the Adaptive Function of Dreams." Paper presented at the Association for the Psychophysiological Study of Sleep, Cincinnati, OH.

Fogelson, R. D. 1982. "Person, Self and Ident pological Retrospects, Circumspects and Pro *of the Self*, ed. B. Lee. New York: Plenum Pre

Forde, C. D. 1931. *Ethnography of the Yuma Indi* versity of California Press.

Fortes, M. 1962. "Ritual and Office in Tribal *on the Ritual of Social Relations*, ed. M. Gluc chester: Manchester University Press.

———. 1969. *Kinship and the Social Order*. Chica; ing.

———. 1973. "On the Concept of Person amon *La Notion de Personne en Afrique Noire*, ed. G Editions de La Recherche Scientifique.

———. 1983. "Problems of Identity and Person *sonal and Psychocultural: A Symposium*. Atlan Humanities Press, Inc.

Foulkes, D. 1966. *The Psychology of Sleep*. New Y ner's Sons.

———. 1978. *A Grammar of Dreams*. New York:

———. 1982. *Children's Dreams: Longitudinal S* Wiley.

———. 1985. *Dreaming: A Cognitive-Psychological* NJ: Lawrence Erlbaum Association.

Freedman, N., S. Grand, and I. Karacan. 1966. the Study of Dreaming and Changes in States." *Journal of Nervous Mental Diseases* 143:

French, T. M. and E. Fromm. 1964. *Dream I* York: Basic Books.

Freud, S., and D. E. Oppenheim. 1965 [1900]. *of Dreams*, trans. James Strachey. London: Ho

Freud, S., and D. E. Oppenheim. 1958 [1911]. New York: International Universities Press.

Gackenbach, J. 1987. *Sleep and Dreams: A Sour* and London: Garland Publishing.

Hallowell, I. A. 1942. *The Role of Conjuring in Saulteaux Society*. Publications of the Philadelphia Anthropological Society, Vol. II. Philadelphia: University of Philadelphia Press.

———. 1965. "The Self and Its Behavior Environment." In *Culture and Experience*. Philadelphia: University of Pennsylvania Press.

———. 1966. "The Role of Dreams in Ojibwa Culture." In *The Dream and Human Societies*, ed. G. E. Grunebaum and R. Caillois. Berkeley: University of California Press.

Harris, G. G. 1989. "Concepts of Individual, Self and Person in Description and Analysis." *American Anthropologist* 91, no. 3: 599–612.

Hartman, E., ed. 1967. *The Biology of Dreaming*. Springfield, IL: Charles C Thomas.

———. 1984. *The Nightmare: The Psychology and Biology of Terrifying Dreams*. New York: Basic Books.

Herdt, G.H. 1987. "Selfhood and Discourse in Sambia Dream Sharing." In *Dreaming: The Anthropology and Psychology of the Imaginal*, ed. B. Tedlock. Cambridge: Cambridge University Press.

Honnigmann, J. J. 1961. "The Interpretation of Dreams in Anthropological Field Work: A Case Study." In *Studying Personality Cross-Culturally*, ed. B. Kaplan. Evanston, IL: Row, Peterson.

Hunt, H. T. 1987. "Toward a Cognitive Psychology of Dreams." In *Sleep and Dreams: A Sourcebook*, ed. J. Gackenbach. New York: Garland Publishing.

Jackson, J. A., ed. 1972. "Role." In *Sociological Studies 4*. Cambridge: Cambridge University Press.

Johnson, F. 1985. "The Western Concept of Self." In *Culture and Self Asian and Western Perspectives*, ed. A. J. Marsella, G. DeVos, and F. L. K. Hsu. New York and London: Tavistock Publications.

Jones, R. 1974. *The New Psychology of Dreaming*. New York: Penguin Press.

Jung, C. G. 1965 [1961]. *Memories, Dreams, Reflections. Recorded and Edited by Aniela Jaffe*, trans. from German by Richard and Clara Winston. New York: Pantheon Books.

————. 1964. *Man and His Symbols.* New York: Doubleday & Co.

————. 1966. *Two Essays on Analytical Psychology.* Collected Works of Carl G. Jung, Volume 7, Bollingen Series. Princeton, NJ: Princeton University Press.

————. 1974. *Dreams,* trans. R. F. C. Hull. Princeton, NJ: Princeton University Press.

Kales, J., C. Allen, T. Preston, T.-L. Tan. and A. Kales. 1970. "Changes in REM Sleep and Dreaming with Cigarette Smoking and Following Withdrawal." *Psychophysiology* 7: 347–348.

Kelsey, M. 1968. *Dreams: The Dark Speech of the Spirit.* New York. Doubleday & Co., Inc.

Kennedy, J. G., and L. L. Langness. 1981. "Introduction." Issue Devoted to Dreams. *Ethos* 9, no. 4: 249–258.

Kilborne, B. 1978. *Interpretations du Reve au Maroc.* Paris: La pensee Sauvage.

————. 1981a. "Moroccan Dream Interpretation and Culturally Constituted Defense Mechanisms." *Ethos* 9, no. 4: 294–311.

————. 1981b. "Pattern, Structure and Style in Anthropological Studies of Dreams." *Ethos* 9: 165–185.

Kleitman, N. 1923. "Effects of Prolonged Sleeplessness." *American Journal of Physiology* 66.

Kracke, W. H. 1981. "Kagwahiv Mourning: Dreams of a Bereaved Father." *Ethos* 9: 258–275.

Kramer, M. 1966. "More on Depression and Dreams." *American Journal of Psychiatry* 123: 232–233.

————. ed. 1969. *Dream Psychology and the New Biology of Dreaming.* Springfield, IL: Charles C Thomas.

————. 1986. Personal Interview. *Association for the Study of Dreams Newsletter* 3, no. 2: 8.

Kramer, M., B. J. Baldridge, R. M. Whitman, P. H. Ornstein, and P. C. Smith. 1969. "An Exploration of the Manifest Dream in Schizophrenic and Depressed Patients." *Diseases of the Nervous System* 30: 126–130.

Kramer, M., R. M. Whitman, B. J. Baldridge, and L. Lansky. 1966. "Dreaming in the Depressed." *Canadian Psychiatric Association Journal* 11: 178–192.

Kramer, M., R. M. Whitman, B. J. Baldridge, and P. H. Ornstein. 1968. "Drugs and Dreams: The Effects of Imipramine on the Dreams of the Depressed." *American Journal of Psychiatry* 124: 1385–1392.

LaBerge, S. 1985. *Lucid Dreaming*. Los Angeles: J. P. Tarcher, Inc.

LaBerge, S., L. Nagel, W. Taylor, W. Dement, and V. Zarcone. 1981a. "Evidence for Lucid Dreaming during REM Sleep." *Sleep Research* 10: 148.

LaBerge, S., J. Owens, L. Nagel, and W. Dement 1981b. "This Is a Dream: Induction of Lucid Dreams by Verbal Suggestion during REM Sleep." *Sleep Research* 10: 150.

LaFontaine, J. S. 1985. "Person and Individual: Some Anthropological Reflections." In *The Category of the Person*, ed. M. Carrithers, S. Collins, and S. Lukes. Cambridge: Cambridge University Press.

Lee, B., ed. 1982. *Psychosocial Theories of the Self*. New York: Plenum Press.

Lee, S. G. 1970. "Social Influences in Zulu Dreaming." In *Cross-Cultural Studies*, ed. D. Prince-Williams, pp. 307–328. Baltimore: Penguin Books.

LeVine, R. A. 1966. *Dreams and Deeds: Achievement Motivation in Nigeria*. Chicago: University of Chicago Press.

Levy-Bruhl, L. 1923. *Primitive Mentality*. London: Macmillan.

Lincoln, J. S. 1935. *The Dream in Primitive Cultures*. Baltimore: The Williams and Wilkins Company.

Lind, R. 1987. "Objective Content Analysis." *Dream Network Bulletin* 5, no. 6: 12–14.

Lott, I. T. 1963. "Identity Formation in the Manifest Dreams of Late Adolescents: An Exploratory Study." Honors thesis, Brandeis University.

Lowy, S. 1942. *Psychological and Biological Foundations of Dream Interpretation*. London: Kegan Paul.

Lukes, S. 1985. "Conclusions." In *The Category of the Person*, ed. M. Carrithers, S. Collins, and S. Lukes. Cambridge: Cambridge University Press.

Madow, L., and L. Snow. 1970. *The Psychodynamic Implications of the Psychophysiological Studies on Dreams*. New York: Charles C Thomas.

Malinowski, B. 1927. *Sex and Repression in Savage Societies*. London: Routledge and Kegan Paul.

Mauss, M. U. 1938. "Une Categorie de L'Esprit Humaine: La Notion de Personne Celle de Moi." *Journal of the Anthropological Institute* 68: 262–281.

McCarley, R. 1981. "Mind-Body Isomorphism and the Study of Dreams." In *Advances in Sleep Research*, ed. W. Fisbein, vol. 4, pp. 205–238. New York: Spectrum Publications.

Mead, G. 1934 [1913]. "Mind, Self and Society." In *The Social Psychology of George Herbert Mead*, 3d ed., ed. A. Strauss. Chicago: University of Chicago Press.

Meggitt, M. J. 1962. "Dream Interpretations among the Mae Enga of New Guinea." *Southwestern Journal of Anthropology* 18: 216–229.

———. 1965. *Desert People*. Chicago and London: University of Chicago Press.

Mindrell, A. 1982. *Dreambody*. Boston: Sigo.

Moffitt, A., and R. Hoffman. 1987. "On the Single-Mindedness and Isolation of Dream Psychophysiology." In *Sleep and Dreams: A Sourcebook*, ed. J. Gackenbach. New York and London: Garland Publishing.

Natterson, J. 1980. *The Dream in Clinical Practice*. New York: J. Aronson.

O'Nell, C. W. 1976. *Dreams, Culture and the Individual*. San Francisco: Chandler and Sharp Publishers.

Dentan, R. K. 1968. *The Semai: A Nonviolent People of Malaya.* New York: Holt, Rinehart and Winston.

———. 1987a. "Ethnographic Considerations of the Cross-Cultural Study of Dreams." In *Sleep and Dreams: A Sourcebook*, ed. J. Gackenbach. New York: Garland Publishing.

———. 1987b. "Senoi Authority (Interview)." *Association for the Study of Dreams Newsletter* 4, no 5: 10–12.

———.1987c. "What's in a Dream? Some Epistemological Issues." *Association for the Study of Dreams Newsletter* 4, no. 3: 9.

———. 1983. A Dream of Senoi. Special Studies Series Council on International Studies. State University of New York at Buffalo. Amherst: New York.

Devereux, G. 1951. *Reality and Dreams: The Psychotherapy of a Plains Indian.* New York: New York University Press.

———. 1957. "Dream Learning and Individual Ritual Differences in Mohave Shamanism." *American Anthropologist* 59: 177–198.

Dodds, E. R. 1951. *The Greeks and the Irrational.* Berkeley: University of California Press.

Domhoff, B. 1969. "Home Dreams Versus Laboratory Dreams." In *Dream Psychology and the New Biology of Dreaming*, ed. M. Kramer. Springfield, IL: Charles C. Thomas.

Domhoff, B., and J. Kamiya. 1964. "Problems in Dream Content Study With Objective Indicators, I, II, III." *Archives of General Psychiatry* 11: 519–532.

Domhoff, G. W. 1985. *The Mystique of Dreams: A Search for Utopia through Senoi Dream Theory.* Berkeley: University of California Press.

———. 1988. "Senoi Dream Theory and The Mystique of Dreams. Further Thoughts on an Allegory about an Allegory." *Association for the Study of Dreams Newsletter* 5, no. 2: 1–2, 16.

Eggan, D. 1952. "The Manifest Content of Dreams: A Challenge to Social Science." *American Anthropologist* 54: 469–485.

————. 1961. "Dream Analysis." In *Studying Personality Cross-Culturally*, ed. B. Kaplan, pp. 551–557. Evanston, IL: Row, Peterson.

————. 1966. "Hopi Dreams in Cultural Perspective." In *The Dream and Human Societies*, ed. G. E. von Grunebaum and R. Caillois pp. 237–265. Berkeley and Los Angeles: University of California Press.

Elkan, B. 1969. "Developmental Differences in the Manifest Content of Children's Reported Dreams." Ph.D. dissertation, Columbia University.

Emmet, D. 1966. *Rules, Roles and Relations*. London: Macmillan.

Erikson, E. 1954. "The Dream Specimen of Psychoanalysis." In *Psychoanalytic Psychiatry and Psychology*, ed. R. Knight and C. Friedman. New York: International Universities Press.

Faraday, A. 1972. *Dream Power*. New York: Coward, McCann and Geoghegan.

————. 1974. *The Dream Game*. New York: Harper and Row.

————. 1981. Book Review of *The Mystique of Dreams* by G. William Domhoff. *Associaiton for the Study of Dreams* 3, no. 4: 12–13.

Faraday A., and J. Wren-Lewis. 1984. "The Selling of the Senoi." *Dream Network Bulletin* 3, no. 4: 1–3.

Firth, R. 1934. "The Meaning of Dreams in Tikopia." In *Essays Presented to C. G. Seligman*, ed. E. Evans-Pritchard, R. Firth, B. Malinowski, and I. Schapera, pp. 63–74. London: Kegan Paul, Trench, Trubnea and Co.

Fiss, H. 1979. "Current Dream Research: A Psychobiological Perspective." In *Handbook of Dreams*, ed. B. Wolman, pp. 20–75. New York: Van Nostrand Reinhold.

————. 1983. "Toward a Clinically Relevant Psychology of Dreaming." *Hillside Journal of Clinical Psychiatry* 5: 147–159.

Fiss, H., and J. Litchman. 1976. "Dream Enhancement: An Experimental Approach to the Adaptive Function of Dreams." Paper presented at the Association for the Psychophysiological Study of Sleep, Cincinnati, OH.

Fogelson, R. D. 1982. "Person, Self and Identity: Some Anthropological Retrospects, Circumspects and Prospects." In *Theories of the Self*, ed. B. Lee. New York: Plenum Press.

Forde, C. D. 1931. *Ethnography of the Yuma Indians*. Berkeley: University of California Press.

Fortes, M. 1962. "Ritual and Office in Tribal Society." In *Essays on the Ritual of Social Relations*, ed. M. Gluckman et al. Manchester: Manchester University Press.

————. 1969. *Kinship and the Social Order*. Chicago: Aldine Publishing.

————. 1973. "On the Concept of Person among the Tallensi." In *La Notion de Personne en Afrique Noire*, ed. G. Dieterlan. Paris: Editions de La Recherche Scientifique.

————. 1983. "Problems of Identity and Person." In *Identity: Personal and Psychocultural: A Symposium*. Atlantic Highlands, NJ: Humanities Press, Inc.

Foulkes, D. 1966. *The Psychology of Sleep*. New York: Charles Scribner's Sons.

————. 1978. *A Grammar of Dreams*. New York: Basic Books.

————. 1982. *Children's Dreams: Longitudinal Studies*. New York: Wiley.

————. 1985. *Dreaming: A Cognitive-Psychological Analysis*. Hillsdale, NJ: Lawrence Erlbaum Association.

Freedman, N., S. Grand, and I. Karacan. 1966. "An Approach to the Study of Dreaming and Changes in Psychopathological States." *Journal of Nervous Mental Diseases* 143: 399–405.

French, T. M. and E. Fromm. 1964. *Dream Interpretation*. New York: Basic Books.

Freud, S., and D. E. Oppenheim. 1965 [1900]. *The Interpretation of Dreams*, trans. James Strachey. London: Hogarth Press.

Freud, S., and D. E. Oppenheim. 1958 [1911]. *Dreams in Folklore*. New York: International Universities Press.

Gackenbach, J. 1987. *Sleep and Dreams: A Sourcebook*. New York and London: Garland Publishing.

Garfield, P. 1974. *Creative Dreaming.* New York: Ballantine.

———. 1984. *Your Child's Dreams.* New York: Ballantine.

Gendlin, E. T. 1986. *Let Your Body Interpret Your Dreams.* Wilmett, IL: Chiron.

Goffman, E. 1959. *The Presentation of Self in Everyday Life.* New York: Doubleday Anchor Books.

Goodenough, D. R. 1967. "Some Recent Studies of Dream Recall." In *Experimental Studies of Dreaming,* ed. H. A. Witkin and H. B. Lewis. New York: Random House.

———. 1978. "Dream Recall: History and Status of the Field." In *The Mind in Sleep: Psychology and Psychophysiology,* ed. A. M. Arkin, J. S. Antrobus, and S. J. Ellman. Hillsdale, NJ: Lawrence Erlbaum Publishing.

Goodenough, D. R., H. B. Lewis, A. Shapiro, L. Jaret, and I. Sleser. 1965. "Dream Reporting Following Abrupt and Gradual Awakenings from Different Types of Sleep." *Journal of Personality and Social Psychology* 2: 170–179.

Green, C. 1968. *Lucid Dreams.* Oxford: Institute of Psychophysical Research.

Greenberg, R., C. A. Pearlman, and D. Gampel. 1972. "War Neuroses and the Adaptive Function of REM Sleep." *British Journal of Medical Psychology* 45: 27–33.

Gregor, T. 1981. "A Content Analysis of Mehinaku Dreams." *Ethos* 9, no. 4: 353–390.

Hall, C. S. 1953. *The Meaning of Dreams.* New York: Harper and Row.

———. 1967. "Representation of the Laboratory Setting in Dreams." *Journal of Nervous Mental Disorders* 144: 198–206.

Hall, C. S., and B. Domhoff. 1963. "A Ubiquitous Sex Difference in Dreams." *Journal of Abnormal Social Psychology* 66: 278–280.

Hall, C. S., and R. E. Lind. 1970. *Dreams, Life and Literature. A Study of Franz Kafka.* Chapel Hill: University of North Carolina Press.

Hall, C. S., and R. L. Van de Castle. 1966. *The Content Analysis of Dreams.* New York: Appleton-Century-Crofts.

Hallowell, I. A. 1942. *The Role of Conjuring in Saulteaux Society*. Publications of the Philadelphia Anthropological Society, Vol. II. Philadelphia: University of Philadelphia Press.

————. 1965. "The Self and Its Behavior Environment." In *Culture and Experience*. Philadelphia: University of Pennsylvania Press.

————. 1966. "The Role of Dreams in Ojibwa Culture." In *The Dream and Human Societies*, ed. G. E. Grunebaum and R. Caillois. Berkeley: University of California Press.

Harris, G. G. 1989. "Concepts of Individual, Self and Person in Description and Analysis." *American Anthropologist* 91, no. 3: 599–612.

Hartman, E., ed. 1967. *The Biology of Dreaming*. Springfield, IL: Charles C Thomas.

————. 1984. *The Nightmare: The Psychology and Biology of Terrifying Dreams*. New York: Basic Books.

Herdt, G.H. 1987. "Selfhood and Discourse in Sambia Dream Sharing." In *Dreaming: The Anthropology and Psychology of the Imaginal*, ed. B. Tedlock. Cambridge: Cambridge University Press.

Honnigmann, J. J. 1961. "The Interpretation of Dreams in Anthropological Field Work: A Case Study." In *Studying Personality Cross-Culturally*, ed. B. Kaplan. Evanston, IL: Row, Peterson.

Hunt, H. T. 1987. "Toward a Cognitive Psychology of Dreams." In *Sleep and Dreams: A Sourcebook*, ed. J. Gackenbach. New York: Garland Publishing.

Jackson, J. A., ed. 1972. "Role." In *Sociological Studies 4*. Cambridge: Cambridge University Press.

Johnson, F. 1985. "The Western Concept of Self." In *Culture and Self Asian and Western Perspectives*, ed. A. J. Marsella, G. DeVos, and F. L. K. Hsu. New York and London: Tavistock Publications.

Jones, R. 1974. *The New Psychology of Dreaming*. New York: Penguin Press.

Jung, C. G. 1965 [1961]. *Memories, Dreams, Reflections. Recorded and Edited by Aniela Jaffe*, trans. from German by Richard and Clara Winston. New York: Pantheon Books.

250 Dreams and Professional Personhood

———. 1964. *Man and His Symbols*. New York: Doubleday & Co.

———. 1966. *Two Essays on Analytical Psychology*. Collected Works of Carl G. Jung, Volume 7, Bollingen Series. Princeton, NJ: Princeton University Press.

———. 1974. *Dreams*, trans. R. F. C. Hull. Princeton, NJ: Princeton University Press.

Kales, J., C. Allen, T. Preston, T.-L. Tan. and A. Kales. 1970. "Changes in REM Sleep and Dreaming with Cigarette Smoking and Following Withdrawal." *Psychophysiology* 7: 347–348.

Kelsey, M. 1968. *Dreams: The Dark Speech of the Spirit*. New York. Doubleday & Co., Inc.

Kennedy, J. G., and L. L. Langness. 1981. "Introduction." Issue Devoted to Dreams. *Ethos* 9, no. 4: 249–258.

Kilborne, B. 1978. *Interpretations du Reve au Maroc*. Paris: La pensee Sauvage.

———. 1981a. "Moroccan Dream Interpretation and Culturally Constituted Defense Mechanisms." *Ethos* 9, no. 4: 294–311.

———. 1981b. "Pattern, Structure and Style in Anthropological Studies of Dreams." *Ethos* 9: 165–185.

Kleitman, N. 1923. "Effects of Prolonged Sleeplessness." *American Journal of Physiology* 66.

Kracke, W. H. 1981. "Kagwahiv Mourning: Dreams of a Bereaved Father." *Ethos* 9: 258–275.

Kramer, M. 1966. "More on Depression and Dreams." *American Journal of Psychiatry* 123: 232–233.

———. ed. 1969. *Dream Psychology and the New Biology of Dreaming*. Springfield, IL: Charles C Thomas.

———. 1986. Personal Interview. *Association for the Study of Dreams Newsletter* 3, no. 2: 8.

Kramer, M., B. J. Baldridge, R. M. Whitman, P. H. Ornstein, and P. C. Smith. 1969. "An Exploration of the Manifest Dream in Schizophrenic and Depressed Patients." *Diseases of the Nervous System* 30: 126–130.

Kramer, M., R. M. Whitman, B. J. Baldridge, and L. Lansky. 1966. "Dreaming in the Depressed." *Canadian Psychiatric Association Journal* 11: 178–192.

Kramer, M., R. M. Whitman, B. J. Baldridge, and P. H. Ornstein. 1968. "Drugs and Dreams: The Effects of Imipramine on the Dreams of the Depressed." *American Journal of Psychiatry* 124: 1385–1392.

LaBerge, S. 1985. *Lucid Dreaming*. Los Angeles: J. P. Tarcher, Inc.

LaBerge, S., L. Nagel, W. Taylor, W. Dement, and V. Zarcone. 1981a. "Evidence for Lucid Dreaming during REM Sleep." *Sleep Research* 10: 148.

LaBerge, S., J. Owens, L. Nagel, and W. Dement 1981b. "This Is a Dream: Induction of Lucid Dreams by Verbal Suggestion during REM Sleep." *Sleep Research* 10: 150.

LaFontaine, J. S. 1985. "Person and Individual: Some Anthropological Reflections." In *The Category of the Person*, ed. M. Carrithers, S. Collins, and S. Lukes. Cambridge: Cambridge University Press.

Lee, B., ed. 1982. *Psychosocial Theories of the Self*. New York: Plenum Press.

Lee, S. G. 1970. "Social Influences in Zulu Dreaming." In *Cross-Cultural Studies*, ed. D. Prince-Williams, pp. 307–328. Baltimore: Penguin Books.

LeVine, R. A. 1966. *Dreams and Deeds: Achievement Motivation in Nigeria*. Chicago: University of Chicago Press.

Levy-Bruhl, L. 1923. *Primitive Mentality*. London: Macmillan.

Lincoln, J. S. 1935. *The Dream in Primitive Cultures*. Baltimore: The Williams and Wilkins Company.

Lind, R. 1987. "Objective Content Analysis." *Dream Network Bulletin* 5, no. 6: 12–14.

Lott, I. T. 1963. "Identity Formation in the Manifest Dreams of Late Adolescents: An Exploratory Study." Honors thesis, Brandeis University.

Lowy, S. 1942. *Psychological and Biological Foundations of Dream Interpretation*. London: Kegan Paul.

Lukes, S. 1985. "Conclusions." In *The Category of the Person*, ed. M. Carrithers, S. Collins, and S. Lukes. Cambridge: Cambridge University Press.

Madow, L., and L. Snow. 1970. *The Psychodynamic Implications of the Psychophysiological Studies on Dreams*. New York: Charles C Thomas.

Malinowski, B. 1927. *Sex and Repression in Savage Societies*. London: Routledge and Kegan Paul.

Mauss, M. U. 1938. "Une Categorie de L'Esprit Humaine: La Notion de Personne Celle de Moi." *Journal of the Anthropological Institute* 68: 262–281.

McCarley, R. 1981. "Mind-Body Isomorphism and the Study of Dreams." In *Advances in Sleep Research*, ed. W. Fisbein, vol. 4, pp. 205–238. New York: Spectrum Publications.

Mead, G. 1934 [1913]. "Mind, Self and Society." In *The Social Psychology of George Herbert Mead*, 3d ed., ed. A. Strauss. Chicago: University of Chicago Press.

Meggitt, M. J. 1962. "Dream Interpretations among the Mae Enga of New Guinea." *Southwestern Journal of Anthropology* 18: 216–229.

———. 1965. *Desert People*. Chicago and London: University of Chicago Press.

Mindrell, A. 1982. *Dreambody*. Boston: Sigo.

Moffitt, A., and R. Hoffman. 1987. "On the Single-Mindedness and Isolation of Dream Psychophysiology." In *Sleep and Dreams: A Sourcebook*, ed. J. Gackenbach. New York and London: Garland Publishing.

Natterson, J. 1980. *The Dream in Clinical Practice*. New York: J. Aronson.

O'Nell, C. W. 1976. *Dreams, Culture and the Individual*. San Francisco: Chandler and Sharp Publishers.

O'Nell, C. W., and O'Nell, N. 1963. "Aggression in Dreams." *International Journal of Social Psychiatry* 9: 259–267.

Oppenheim, A. L. 1966. "Mantic Dreams in the Ancient Near East." In *The Dream and Human Societies*, ed. G. E. Von Grunebaum and R. Caillois. Berkeley: University of California Press.

Oswald, I. 1966. *Sleep*. New York: Charles Scribner and Sons.

Parsifal-Charles, N. 1986. *The Dream: 4,000 Years of Theory and Practice, A Critical, Descriptive, and Encyclopedic Bibliography*. West Cornwall, CT: Locust Hill Press.

Perls, F. S. 1969. *Gestalt Therapy Verbatim*. Lafayette, CA: Real People Press.

Piaget, J. 1962. *Play, Dreams, and Imitation in Childhood*. London: Routledge and Kegan Paul.

Pierce, C. M. 1963. "Dream Studies in Enuresis Research." *Canadian Psychiatric Association Journal* 8: 415–419.

Pitt-Rivers, J. 1970. "Spiritual Power in Central America: The Naguals of Chiapas." In *Witchcraft, Confessions, and Accusation*, ed. M. Douglas, pp. 186–206. London: Tavistock.

Rattray, R. S. 1927. *Religion and Art in Ashanti*. Oxford: Oxford Press.

Rechtschaffen, A. 1983. "Dream Psychophysiology." In *Advances in Sleep Research*, ed. M. Chase and E. Weitzman, vol. 8, pp. 401–414. New York: Spectrum Publications.

Rechtschaffen, A., E. A. Wolpert, W. C. Dement, S. A. Mitchell, and C. Fisher. 1963. "Nocturnal Sleep in Narcoleptics." *Clinical Neurophysiology* 15: 599.

Rivers, W. H. R. 1918. *Dreams and Primitive Culture*. London: Manchester University Press.

———. 1923. *Conflict and Dreams*. New York: Harcourt, Brace and Company.

Roheim, G. 1945. *The Eternal Ones of the Dream, a Psychoanalytic Interpretation of Australian Myth and Ritual*. New York: International Universities Press.

————. 1947. "The Technique of Dream Analysis and Field Work in Anthropology." *Psychoanalytic Quarterly* 18: 471–479.

Sampson, H. 1965. "Deprivation of Dreaming Sleep by Two Methods. Compensatory REM Time." *Archives of General Psychiatry* 13: 79–86.

Savary, L., P. Berne, and S. K. Williams. 1985. *Dreams and Spiritual Growth: A Christian Approach to Dreamwork.* Ramsey, NJ: Paulist Press.

Schneider, D., and L. Lauriston. 1969. *The Dream Life of a Primitive People.* Ann Arbor: University Microfilm.

Siegel, B. S. 1986. *Love, Medicine and Miracles.* New York: Harper and Row.

Snyder, F. 1963. "The New Biology of Dreaming." *Archives of General Psychiatry* 8: 381–391.

————. 1970. "The Phenomenology of Dreaming." In *The Psychodynamic Implications of the Psychophysiological Studies on Dreams*, ed. L. Madow and L. Snow, pp. 124–151. New York: Charles C Thomas.

Speck, F. G. 1935. *Naskapi. The Savage Hunters of the Labrador Penninsula.* Norman: University of Oklahoma Press.

Spier, L. 1933. *Yuman Tribes of the Gila River.* Chicago. University of Chicago Press.

Stewart, K. R. 1954. *Pygmies and Dream Giants.* New York: W. W. Norton and Company.

————. 1946. Magico-Religious Beliefs and Practices in Primitive Society—A Sociological Interpretation of their Therapeutic Aspects. Unpublished dissertation. London School of Economics.

————. 1969. Dream Theory in Malaya. In *Altered States of Consciousness*, ed. C. T. Tart. New York: John Wiley and Sons.

Taylor, J. 1983. *Dream Work: Techniques for Discovering the Creative Power in Dreams.* Ramsey, NJ: Paulist Press.

Tedlock, B. 1978. "Quiche Maya Divination: A Theory of Practice." Ph.D. dissertation, State University of New York at Albany.

———. ed. 1987. *Dreaming: The Anthropology and Psychology of the Imaginal*. Cambridge: Cambridge University Press.

Textor, R. B. 1967. *A Cross-Cultural Summary*. New Haven, CT: HRAF Press.

Tylor, E. B. 1958 [1871]. *Religion in Primitive Culture*. New York: Harper's Torchbooks.

Ullman, M. 1960. "The Social Roots of the Dream." *American Journal of Psychoanalysis* 20: 180–196.

———. 1973. *Dream Telepathy*. New York: Macmillan.

———. 1987a. Interview. *Association for the Study of Dreams Newsletter* 4, no. 1: 1–5.

———. 1987b. "On Raising the Social Priority of Dreams." *Dream Network Bulletin* 5, no. 6: 1, 4.

Ullman, M., and S. Krippner. 1970. *Dream Studies and Telepathy. An Experimental Approach*. New York: Parapsychology Foundation.

Ullman, M., and N. Zimmerman. 1979. *Working with Dreams*. New York: Delacorte.

Van Bork, J. J. 1982. "An Attempt to Clarify a Dream-Mechanism: Why Do People Wake Up Out of an Anxiety Dream?" *International Review of Psychoanalysis* 9, no. 8: 233–277.

Van de Castle, R. L. 1969. "Problems in Applying the Methodology of Content Analysis to Dreams." In *Dream Psychology and the New Biology of Dreaming*, ed. M. Kramer. Springfield, IL: Charles C Thomas.

Van de Castle, R. L., and J. Holloway. 1971. "Dreams of Depressed Patients, Nondepressed Patients, and Normals." *Psychophysiology* 7: 326.

Veroff, J., R. A. Kulka, and E. Douvan. 1981. *Mental Health in America: Patterns of Help-Seeking from 1957 to 1976*. New York: Basic Books.

Vogel, C. 1960. "Studies in Psychophysiology of Dreams: The Dream of Narcolepsy." *Archives of General Psychiatry* 3: 421–428.

Vogel, V. J. 1982. *American Indian Medicine*. Norman: University of Oklahoma Press.

Von Grunebaum, G. E., and R. Caillois, eds. 1966. *The Dream and Human Society*. Berkeley and Los Angeles: University of California Press.

Wallace, A. F. C. 1958. "Dreams and Wishes of the Soul, a Type of Psychoanalytic Theory among the Seventeenth Century Iroquois." *American Anthropologist* 60: 234–248.

Weiss, H. B. 1944. *Oneirocritica Americana. The Story of American Dream Books*. New York: New York Public Library.

Weiss, J. V. 1969. "Dreaming and Night Asthma in Children." Ph.D. dissertation, University of Denver.

Weiss L. 1986. *Dream Analysis in Psychotherapy*. New York: Pergamon Press.

Weisz, R., and D. Foulkes. 1970. "A Comparison of Home and Laboratory Dreams under Uniform Sampling Conditions." *Psychophysiology* 6: 588–596.

Whitman, R. M., C. M. Pierce, and J. Maas. 1960. "Drugs and Dreams." In *Drugs and Behavior*, ed. L. Uhr and J. Miller. New York: John Wiley and Sons.

Whitman, R., M. Kramer, and B. Baldridge. 1963. "Which Dream Does the Patient Tell?" *Archives of General Psychiatry* 8: 277–282.

Whitman, R. M., M. Kramer, P. H. Ornstein, and B. Baldridge. 1969. "Drugs and Dream Content." *Experience in Medicine and Surgery* 27: 210–223.

Whitman, R. M., C. M. Pierce, J. W. Maas, and B. Baldridge. 1961. "Drugs and Dreams: Imipramine and Prochlorperazine." *Comprehensive Psychiatry* 2: 219–226.

Wilbur, G. B., and W. Muensterberger. 1951. *Psychoanalysis and Culture. Essays in Honor of Geza Roheim*. New York: International Universities Press.

Williams, S. K. 1980. *Jungian-Senoi Dreamwork Manual*. Berkeley: Journey Press.

Winget, C., and F. Kapp. 1972. "The Relationship of the Manifest Content of Dreams to Duration of Childbirth in Primiparae." *Psychosomatic Medicine* 34, no. 2: 313–320.

Winget, C., and M. Kramer. 1979. *Dimensions of Dreams.* Gainesville: University Presses of Florida.

Witkins, H. A., and H. Lewis. 1965. "The Relation of Experimentally Induced Presleep Experiences to Dreams: A Report on Method and Preliminary Findings." *Journal of American Psychoanalytic Association* 13: 819.

Wolman, B. B., ed. 1979. *Handbook of Dreams. Research, Theories and Applications.* New York: Van Nostrand Reinhold.

Wolpert, E. A. 1960. "Studies in Psychophysiology of Dreams: An Electromyographic Study of Dreaming." *Archives of General Psychiatry* 2: 231–241.

Zolar. 1984. *Zolar's Encyclopedia and Dictionary of Dreams.* New York: Arco.

NAME INDEX

Adler, A., 8
Arey, L. B., 11
Armstrong, R. H., 10
Artemidorus of Daldis, 129
    influence of, on Freud, 7
Aserinsky, E., 3

Baldridge, B., 11
Banton, M., 53, 55, 60
Barnouw, V., 15
Bastide, R., 15
Beck, A. T., 11
Beck, L. W., 41
Belicki, K., 4, 10
Berne, P., 7
Bertelson, A. D., 10
Boas, Franz, 15
Bokert, E., 4
Bonaparte, Marie (Princess), 16
Boss, M., 9
Bourgignon, E., 15
Bowers, P., 4
Brennies, C. B., 4

Carroll, D., 4
Cartwright, R. D., 11
Charsley, S. R., 20, 147

Cohen, D. B., 4
Collins, K., 21
Cooley, C. H., 41

Dahrendorf, R., 53
D'Andrade, R. G., 15
Davidson, D., 6
Delaney, G., 13
Dement, W. C., 3, 4
Dennett, D., 6
Dentan, R. K., 14, 15, 144
Descartes, René, 7, 82
Devereux, George, 147
    ethnopsychiatry developed by, 17
    study of dream interpreters by,
        19, 20
Domhoff, B., 4
Domhoff, G. W., 14, 144, 199
    mystique of dreams, 14, 144, 199
    critique of Senoi dream theory 14,
        144
Douvan, E., 151

Eggan, Dorothy
    dream telling as socialization, 20
    ethnographic study of dreams by,
        15, 18

SUBJECT INDEX